Listening Bibliography

Second Edition

by
Sam Duker

The Scarecrow Press, Inc.
Metuchen, N.J.   1968

Copyright 1968 by Sam Duker

L.C. Card No. 68-12630

Library
UNIVERSITY OF MIAMI

Table of Contents

iii

Introduction to the Second Edition

The primary purpose of this revision of my 1964 bibliography is to bring it up to date by adding items appearing since its publication. I have also made corrections and included items previously omitted.

In general, broad limitations remain the same. Because of the great interest shown in the last several years, many more items on rate-controlled speech have been included. The original bibliography contained no items about aural projective tests. A number are included in this revision but no claim is made of comprehensive coverage. I have also included a number of items on listening to music, as I have become convinced that there are many common elements in listening to language and listening to music.

It is my hope that users of this edition will, as users of the 1964 version so generously did, call my attention to omissions and errors.

I am grateful to the many people who have helped in the preparation of this bibliography, both now and in years past. It seems appropriate to single out the Scarecrow Press and its editor, Ralph R. Shaw, for particular mention. Their willingness to publish this bibliography at a time when it was, to say the least, an uncertain venture places in their debt all of us who are interested in the extension of knowledge about the listening process.

Introduction to the First Edition

Listening always has been and continues to be the most widely used human means of receiving information. Until the last decade or two little attention was paid to the importance of developing this skill. It was taken for granted that everyone knew how to listen. That this is not so has been established beyond a reasonable doubt. Listening can be improved by proper teaching, although there are still those who refuse to accept the evidence on this as valid. Expository writing and the printed results of research have appeared on this subject during the last twenty years. The amount of material is not diminishing. It is impractical for an investigator to make the kind of thorough search of previous literature that good research demands. Hence, the need has become acute for a bibliography with annotations rather than a mere listing of items.

The first bibliography on listening was compiled by Professor Harold Anderson of the University of Chicago in 1949. Subsequent bibliographies have been compiled by Donald Bird, John Caffrey, Ralph G. Nichols and Sam Duker. All these merely listed items; so that this bibliography is the first extensive one carrying annotations.

It is difficult to define the appropriate boundaries of a bibliography on listening. This skill involves more than hearing; yet one can only listen if one first hears. Human speech is essential to the listening process. These self-evident statements contain some of the major difficulties in compiling a bibliography about listening. Where does the compiler stop? One may rationalize that any item concerned either with speech or hearing may be included in such a bibliography, but in order to keep a bibliography within manageable proportions it is necessary to eliminate most items dealing primarily with speech or hearing. The fact that listening is the major receptive skill in the human communication process makes it possible to rationalize the inclusion of all items dealing with the nature of the communicative act. However it is impossible and impracticable to make this inclusion since items on information theory alone would almost double the size of the present bibliography, and this is only one of the many theories of communication. It will, therefore, be helpful to make some brief statements about the guidelines which were used in the decisions of inclusion or exclusion of items in this book.

    1.   Generally, items dealing with audition and hearing have been excluded. However, reference is made to the reviews on these topics in the <u>Annual Review of Psychology</u>, where adequate bibliographies on these topics may be found.

    2.   There is extensive literature on the relative merits, from a learning standpoint, of oral and written presentation. As a means of learning is listening as effective, less effective, or more effective than reading? No attempt has been made to include all the literature on this topic, but a fair sampling has been included. The reader interested in probing further can consult the bibliographies in Carver (191) in Author List and in Day and Beach (275).

    3.   Most references concerning communication and communication theory have been omitted.

    4.   References concerning listening to music have been omitted.

5. Only available items have been included and
therefore a number of useful mimeographed documents are
not listed. "Availability" I interpreted to mean the inclusion
of material which may be borrowed on inter-library loan,
even when, as is the case in most master's theses, only the
original copy exists.

6. With very few exceptions chapters on listening in
textbooks of teaching methods have been omitted. Similarly
chapters in speech textbooks on listening have been omitted.

7. Material contained in elementary and high school
textbooks, as well as that to be found in curriculum bulletins and courses of study, has been omitted.

8. With very few exceptions material dealing specifically with radio and television has not been included since
it seemed impossible to find a reasonable point of demarca-
tion.

9. No item has been included that has not been personally examined and fully read by the compiler.

A word about the annotations. They are not abstracts and should not be used as such. The hope is that
they will be useful to the reader for his own purposes. It
is not intended that the annotation eliminate the necessity of
examination of the original work by an investigator. It may
well be that some authors will feel slighted by the selection
of material in the annotations, but if they will bear in mind
the difference between annotations and abstracts, they may
be more charitably inclined toward the compiler.

Effort was made to include in each entry references
to extracts, summaries, and abstracts, but it was not possible to attain absolute completeness in this respect. No
attempt has been made to include references to abstracts
contained in the publications of the university or college

where the work was done. The original documents are usually available. Reference to them would, therefore, only add to the length of the bibliography.

I should be grateful to any user of this bibliography who might be willing to inform me of any omitted references or errors made in included references. Perfection in bibliographic work may be the aim; but, it seems to me at least, it is never attained.

The compilation of this bibliography was made possible only because of the kind cooperation and assistance of many librarians and the availability of library resources. The work was begun in the Iowa State Teachers College Library in 1952 and continued in the New York Public Library, the Academy of Medicine Library, The Engineering Societies Library, the Teachers College, Columbia University Library, and especially at the Brooklyn College Library where Librarian H. G. Bousfield and his staff showed me many considerations. For the use of these libraries and the help given me by their staffs, I express my deep gratitude.

I was encouraged in my work by those interested in the area of listening and owe much to such pioneers in the field as Ralph G. Nichols, James I. Brown, Francis Cartier and the late Donald Bird, as well as to Charles Petrie and many others.

Assisting me in various ways with the many tasks leading to the present bibliography were Miss Carmela Di-Carlo, who spent many hours helping me organize my notes and develop a system of indexing during the early stages of the project; my daughter, Catherine Moran, who typed many hundreds of pages of illegible notes for me; and my wife, Laura Thompson Duker, whose help in editing and proofreading was invaluable.

No acknowledgment is sufficient to express my deep appreciation and indebtedness to Professor Guy A. Lackey of Stillwater, Oklahoma and to Miss Ethel M. Faegley, formerly of the Teachers College Library, for their part in stirring my interest in bibliographic work.

Sam Duker

Brooklyn College
Brooklyn, New York

Citation Key for Listening: Readings

Citations in Listening: Readings gave the item number under which these citations would be found in the first edition of the Listening Bibliography. Since the item numbers have all changed in this enlarged second edition of the Listening Bibliography, those using the numbers for citations in Listening: Readings should look for the number in column A below and if they wish to find the item in this second edition, use the number given in column B, below.

A	see B		A	see B		A	see B
3	5		104	143		250	352
12	14		108	147		264	373
13	20		109	148		266	375
14	21		114	160		267	376
16	23		115	161		270	380
24	36		118	164		278	397
27	42		135	188		280	400
31	48		138	191		293	416
33	50		139	192		298	435
34	51		153	214		307	449
39	60		160	226		322	468
42	66		161	227		326	474
43	67		162	228		331	480
44	68		164	230		333	482
45	69		169	237		334	485
51	78		170	238		337	490
53	80		179	251		339	492
56	83		188	262		345	503
57	84		202	285		347	505
59	88		203	288		350	508
64	95		204	290		351	510
72	104		212	302		352	511
75	107		213	303		354	514
89	126		215	305		364	526
90	127		221	316		371	533
91	128		222	317		377	541
93	131		223	318		379	543
96	134		224	319		381	547
99	137		230	327		382	548
102	141		241	340		385	553

A	see	B		A	see	B		A	see	B
387		556		553		818		713		1069
393		567		555		819		724		1092
397		572		564		838		749		1124
400		580		570		848		750		1125
406		586		571		851		757		1136
407		587		577		861		761		1142
414		607		579		863		765		1146
428		626		585		895		767		1148
434		634		587		873		768		1149
435		636		590		894		775		1156
441		642		591		879		787		1178
445		648		600		889		789		1185
449		658		604		899		791		1188
452		661		612		916		794		1194
453		662		615		924		800		1203
458		671		616		925		804		1210
461		677		619		930		834		1263
462		678		621		934		836		1265
463		679		628		945		839		1271
464		681		632		950		840		1272
465		682		636		958		845		1278
472		692		637		959		848		1285
473		693		645		970		852		1289
489		721		648		973		859		1302
510		749		657		983		864		1308
519		771		689		1037		866		1310
523		778		690		1038		874		1319
542		803		700		1054		875		1320
								878		1327

Abrams, Arnold Gerald. The Relation Between the Ability
    to Perceive Message Structure and Comprehension in
    Reading and Listening. Master's thesis. University
    Park, Md. : University of Maryland, 1964. Summary:
    Journal of Communication 16:116-25, June 1966.   1
    The Brown-Carlsen, the Nelson-Denny Reading Test,
and the Knower-Goyer Organization Test were administered
to a group of pre-college summer session students who did
not qualify for regular admission to the University of Maryland. The correlation between the Brown-Carlsen and the
Knower-Goyer was .39. It was concluded that despite the common elements in the tests, the hypothesis that "the ability to
perceive the structure of a written message correlates significantly and positively with listening comprehension" was sup-
ported. The correlation between the Nelson-Denny and the
Knower-Goyer was .29. It was concluded that despite the common elements in the tests, the hypothesis that "the ability to
perceive the structure of a written message correlates positively and significantly with reading comprehension" was upheld.
The correlation between the Nelson-Denny and the Brown-Carlsen was .28. One explanation for this low correlation, which
differed from previous studies, was the subject population.
Another explanation was the manner of weighting sub-test scores
to attain a total score on the Nelson-Denny.

Abramson, Leonard S. "A Comparison of an Auditory and a
    Visual Projective Technique." Journal of Projective
    Techniques 27:3-11, March 1963.   2
    The Braverman-Chevigny Auditory Projective Test (APT)
consists of: 1. a series of 20 utterances by a simple voice;
2. a series of eight sound effects; 3. a series of eleven
interpersonal situations enacted by professional actors; and
4. the eleven sequences of (3) spoken in nonsense language,
employing the same intonation and rhythm used in meaningful language.
    Only part 4 and TAT pictures, which were roughly
matched to each auditory sequence, were used. The subjects
were 25 schizophrenic veterans. Scoring was based on productivity, emotional tone, outcome ratings, formal factors,
identification of hero, needs, presses, theme of story, omis-

13

sions and perceptual distortions, attitudes and interests, and
antecedents.
   There was no significant difference between the tests in
productivity, emotional tone, formal factors, outcome ratings,
and identification of the hero. The APT elicited more needs
and pressures and a significantly better degree of clarity in
the identification of the hero.

Achtenhagen, Olga: "On Following Directions." Journal of
   Education 130:259, November 1947.   3
   Units at each of four high school levels are described.
Freshmen emphasize school routines, sophomores the filling
out of various blanks, juniors discuss reasons for failures
to follow directions, and seniors emphasize correct completion of college entrance and employment forms. The author
states that these units given in the English courses have resulted in more attentive listening to oral directions.

Adams, Harlen M. "Audio-Visual Aids for the Language
   Arts." Elementary English Review 20:257-64, November
   1943.   4
   Use of radio and recordings is advocated for the teaching of listening in order to develop discrimination, to improve voice, in usage and vocabulary, and in studying literature. Specific suggestions are given and examples cited for
greater use of audio-visual aids to help in unifying the language arts program.

----. "Learning to Be Discriminating Listeners." English
   Journal 36:11-15, January 1947.   5
   Listening must be purposeful, accurate, critical, and
responsive in order to improve comprehension of college lectures, radio listening, etc. The author suggests that instruction include preparation for listening, listening experience, and evaluation of material listened to.

----. "Learning to Listen: An English and Social Studies
   Plan." Clearing House 20:401-03, March 1946.   6
   We listen to obtain information, to gain ideas which will
stimulate our thinking, for escape, to improve our communication, and to increase our appreciation of good literature.
There must be proper physical and mental preparation for
listening, which is an active process involving critical evaluation and reaction.

----. "Listening." Quarterly Journal of Speech 24:209-11,
   April 1938.   7

Speaking and listening instruction cannot be separated.
One effective method is to use a variety of note-taking procedures in a speech class, which then can be used to verify
effectiveness of both speaker and listener.

----. "Teaching the Art of Listening." Nation's Schools
    34(5):51-54, November 1944.   8
    Radio has made us aware of listening. Recordings are
better than radio as practice materials for the teaching of
listening since they can be previewed. Hearing one's own
speech on tape is helpful to good listening habits.

Adams, John. Making the Most of One's Mind. New York:
    Hodder, Stoughton, G.H. Doran, 1915. Chapter 8, "Lis-
    tening and Note-Making," p. 213-39.   9
    Intelligent listening requires active action and reaction
between lecturer and audience. Poor listening involves pretending to listen and listening only partially. Taking notes
is good practice but should never interfere with "taking
note."

Adkins, Leslie Gene. The Effect of Recorded Lateral Lisp-
    ing on Listener Comprehension. Master's thesis.
    Kalamazoo, Mich.: Western Michigan University, 1959.
                                                            10
    The speech comprehension portions of both forms of the
Brown-Carlsen Test were recorded on tape, one in normal
speech and one with a lateral lisp. Twenty-eight graduate
students showed a slightly better performance on the normal
speech recording. This difference, however, was not statistically significant.

Adler, Mortimer J. "Listening Called Most Important Fac-
    tor in Art of Communicating." National Underwriter
    Life Edition. 65(30):4-5, July 29, 1961. Abstract:
    National Underwriter 65 (35):14, September 1, 1961. 11
    Listen! Do not ask another question until you have lis-
tened to the answer to the first. The answer may affect
your second question. The important thing to listen to is
not what the fact is but what will follow if the fact be true.
A listener must keep his own emotions well controlled.

Ainslie, Douglas. "Talkers and Conversationalists." Living
    Age. 303:220-28, October 25, 1919.   12
    The art of conversation involves consideration for the
thoughts of others as evidenced by good listening.

16   Listening Bibliography

Ainsworth, Stanley. 'Studies in the Psychology of Stuttering:
    XII Emphatic Breathing of Auditors While Listening to
    Stuttered Speech.'' Journal of Speech Disorders 4:149-
    56, June 1939.   13
    An experiment is described in which stutterers and non-
stutterers listened to speech of severe stutterers. It was
found that a distinct change of rate of both inhalation and ex-
halation in breathing occurred in the case of non-stutterers.
Auditors who were also stutterers showed less change in
their rate of breathing.

----, and High, Charles. "Auditory Functions and Abilities
    in Good and Poor Listeners." Journal of Communica-
    tion 4:84-86, Fall 1954. Reprinted in Listening: Read-
    ings. (Edited by Sam Duker.) Metuchen, N.J.: Scare-
    crow Press, 1966. p. 174-86.   14
    The listening test developed by Kramar, the Seashore
Measures of Musical Talent, the Templin Speech Sound Discrimination Tests, and the digit-auditory memory span test
portion of the Wechsler-Bellevue Scale were administered to
273 subjects. Results indicate that specific and separate
auditory abilities are not related to listening ability as
measured by immediate recall.

Alcott, Myra H. A Validation of a Listening Test. Mas-
    ter's thesis. Glassboro, N.J.: Glassboro State Col-
    lege, 1965.   15
    The Vidol Listening Test was administered on tape to
1000 second to fifth grade children in six schools. At almost all levels the results were significantly different from
those obtained by Winkler, the author of the test. The text
of the test is included.

Allen, Hugh S., Jr. "The Eltro Information Rate Changer
    Mark 11: Simple Quality Speech Compression." Pro-
    ceedings of the Louisville Conference on Time Com-
    pressed Speech October 19-21, 1966. (Edited by Emer-
    son Foulke.) Louisville, Ky.: Center for Rate Con-
    trolled Recordings; University of Louisville, 1967. p.
    77-86.   16
    Detailed description of the Eltro speech compression
device.

Allison, James M. Empathy and Empathic Listening: A
    Neglected Tool in Supervisor-Subordinate Relationship.
    Graduate Thesis. Maxwell Air Force Base, Ala.: Air
    Command and Staff College, Air University, 1966. 17

Empathic listening by the supervisor is a means of understanding subordinates and improving relationships in face-to-face communication. The author concludes that: 1. empathic ability can be developed and measured; 2. empathic listening is applicable in many areas of society; and 3. this ability should be cultivated by persons aspiring to positions of supervisory responsibility. A comprehensive bibliography on empathy is included.

Alston, Fannie C. and Williams, R. Ora. "Johnny Doesn't
   Listen - Didn't Hear." Journal of Negro Education 33:
   197-200, Spring 1964.   18
Forty minutes of weekly listening instruction for twelve weeks failed to result in better performance by the experimental group of 95 college students than by a control group. The Brown-Carlsen Test was used for pre- and post-testing.

Altshuler, Morton W. Responses to Expanded Speech by
   Hard-of-Hearing Aged Subjects. Doctoral dissertation.
   Boston: Boston University, 1963. Abstract: Disserta-
   tion Abstracts 25:7069, 1965.   19
Employing 300-word passages and 36 hard-of-hearing subjects, the author found no significant differences in intelligibility when the rate was expanded 10, 20, and 30 per cent. The subjects, however, expressed a preference for the slower rates.

Anderson, Harold A. "Needed Research in Listening." Elementary English 29:215-24, April 1952. Reprinted: Areas
   of Research Interest in the Language Arts. Chicago: National Council of Teachers of English, 1952, p. 27-36.
   Listening: Readings. (Edited by Sam Duker.) Metuchen,
   N.J: Scarecrow Press, 1966. p. 174-86.   20
Suggested areas for research in listening: how much time is devoted to listening in and out of school? how important is listening in modern life? how well do pupils listen? what are the similarities and differences between listening and reading? what is the nature of listening as a language art? what factors influence the quality of listening in and out of school? 52-item bibliography.

----. "Teaching the Art of Listening." Under "Educational
   News and Editorial Comment." School Review 57:63-67,
   February 1949.   21
Since listening is the most used language art, the school has a responsibility to teach listening skills. This involves awareness by teachers of its importance; knowledge of the understandings, attitudes, appreciations, abilities and skills acquired through the spoken word; assessment of the present

listening abilities and habits of pupils; provision for a better listening climate in the classroom; and direct, systematic instruction in listening.

----. "Teaching the Art of Listening." Perspectives on
    English. (Edited by Robert C. Pooley). New York:
    Appleton-Century-Crofts, 1960. Chapter 8, p. 89-106.
                                                              22
    To teach listening skills effectively it is necessary to establish a favorable listening climate, make clear to pupils why good listening habits are important, be aware of the similarities and differences between reading and listening, and make provisions for systematic instruction.

Anderson, Irving H. and Fairbanks, Grant. "Common and
    Differential Factors in Reading Vocabulary and Hearing
    Vocabulary." Journal of Educational Research 30:317-
    24. January 1937.   23
    The Iowa Silent Reading Test and two forms of the Inglis Test of English Vocabulary were administered to 220 college freshmen. One form of Inglis was orally administered, the other in the usual written form. The authors found correlation between oral and written vocabulary to be . 80, between oral vocabulary and reading test . 61, between reading vocabulary and reading test . 80. Both types of vocabulary were found to be closely related to general intelligence. Results are similar to those reported by Young.

Anderson, Jack Charles. The Relative Effectiveness of Per-
    sonal and Recorded Presentation of Persuasive Speeches.
    Master's thesis. Norman, Okla.: University of Okla-
    homa, 1950. Abstract: Speech Monographs 18:200,
    August 1951.   24
    Using 136 speech students as subjects, the author found that there was no noticeable difference in degrees of attitude change between the effects of a recorded speech and the same speech delivered in person.

Anderson, Lorena and Frackenpohl, Helen. "Listen My Chil-
    dren and You Shall Hear . . ." Reading Newsletter 26.
    Educational Development Laboratories, Inc., Huntington,
    N.Y. November 1962, p. 1-15.   25
    The authors suggest that the most important emphases in teaching listening are on syntax and on evaluating speakers' ideas.

Anderson, Rhea, Minshall, Lucille, and Comfort, Iris Tracy.

Anderson, R., Minshall, L., and Comfort, I. T.   19

"How to Teach Better Listening." N.E.A. Elementary
Instructional Service Leaflet. Washington: National
Education Association, 1962.   26
    A compact statement of the essentials of the teaching of
listening. Suitable for distribution to a school staff as an
introduction to this topic.

Andrade, Manuel, Hayman, John L., Jr., and Johnson,
James T. Jr. "Measurement of Listening Comprehension in Elementary School Spanish Instruction." Elementary School Journal 64:84-93, November 1963.   27
    The guidelines for the development of a listening test
for comprehension of Spanish are discussed and a test is described.

Anilla, Sister Mary. "Accuracy Is the Goal: Language
Skills." National Catholic Educational Association Bulletin 60(1):402-07, August 1963.   28
    Common factors in all language arts are vocabulary, au-
ditory discrimination and organization of ideas. Physiologi-
cally and psychologically listening comes first and thus un-
dergirds the whole language arts program. Listening is a
difficult process of thinking; a process by which what is
heard is weighed, analyzed, sorted, related, classified,
evaluated and judged.
    The primary-grade child is receptive to the teaching of
listening skills when he is interested in what is being said
and when the general atmosphere is conducive to listening.

Anunson, Duane Harley. A Comparison of the Results of
Two Approaches to Listening to Music in the Elementary
Grades. Master's thesis. Des Moines, Iowa: Drake
University, 1964.   29
    An experiment with 52 fourth and fifth grade pupils.
Listening to music was taught more effectively through dra-
matizing the music, sensing the mood, and using imagina-
tion to create stories than through emphasizing the basic
elements of music such as tempo, melody, harmony, timbre,
and rhythm.

Appell, Clara and Appell, Morey. "If We Learn to Listen,
We'll Understand." Practical Home Economics 33(4):7-
8, December 1954.   30
    The teacher who truly listens to children creates an at-
mosphere which encourages pupils to develop an appreciation
for listening.

Applegate, Mauree. Everybody's Business - Our Children.
Evanston, Ill. : Row Peterson, 1952. p. 181-83.   31
It is erroneous to assume that a child will either listen
well or not. The child is entitled to be trained in this skill.
Teachers should take advantage of the many natural listening
situations in the school day. Pupils should be taught how to
listen to informative material, stories, announcements, and
directions.

----. "To Listen Imaginatively." Grade Teacher 74(4):38,
December 1956.   32
Some specific techniques for teaching listening at the
elementary school level: encourage children to have a purpose in listening; use the information listened to in some
way; play listening games; have older children learn to make
notes on speaker's remarks; urge children to see mental
picture of what they are listening to and to evaluate the speaker and the content of the speech.

"Are You a Good Listener?" Western Business and Industry
39(2):26-27, February 1965.   33
Despite a large amount of literature on the subject,
there is a failure of communication in the business world
largely due to ineffective listening. Supervisors have a
much higher opinion of their own approachability than do their
subordinates. The problem is not getting subordinates to
talk, but getting management to listen.

"Are You Listening?" 195 Magazine 36(10):14-16, November
1963. Reprinted: Supervisory Management 9(1):51-53,
January 1964.   34
Report on a speech by Dr. Ralph Nichols to the Public
Relations Society of America.

Armentrout, W. D. "Discriminate Listening Basic." Journal
of the Association for Education by Radio, 5:87-88,
February 1956.   35
Mutual understanding among peoples can be gained
through the proper use of radio. This includes clear thinking and expression, moral and ethical qualities on the part
of the speaker, and discriminate listening by the audience.

Armstrong, Hubert Coslet. The Relationship of the Auditory and Visual Vocabularies of Children. Doctoral dissertation. Stanford, Calif. : Stanford University, 1953.
Excerpts: Listening: Readings. (Edited by Sam
Duker.) Metuchen, N.J. : Scarecrow Press, 1966. p.

106-17.   36
Using as subjects 200 children in grades 1-8, the author
estimated the following vocabulary developments:

age	visual	auditory
6 1/2	648	3048
7 1/2	1184	3476
8 1/2	1900	4240
9 1/2	4040	5120
10 1/2	6040	6600
11 1/2	6080	6640
12 1/2	7240	7480

The author concludes that the size of an auditory vocabulary is direct evidence of potential improvement in ability to
read and that visual vocabulary is itself a measure of reading achievement.

Armstrong, Martin. "The Art of Listening." The English
    Association, Essays and Studies, Volume 9 of the new
    series. London: John Murray, 1956. p. 21-26.   37
It is easy to listen to speakers who are visible but difficult to sustain attention when listening to a radio set's unseen speaker.

Arndt, C.O. and Husband, John. "Listen." English Journal
    29:371-78, May 1940.   38
A detailed set of standards is presented by which listening high school students may judge the value of content and
presentation of aural reports. The development of alert,
effective listening fostered by these standards is essential in
the proper utilization of present-day mass media of communication.

Arnold, Margaret. "Teaching Critical Listening." Illinois
    English Bulletin 44(2):1-17, November 1956. Reprinted:
    Listening: Readings. (Edited by Sam Duker.) Metuchen,
    N.J: Scarecrow Press, 1966. p. 267-82.   39
To teach critical listening effectively it is necessary to
make pupils aware of qualities in their own backgrounds affecting their listening, of the effect of the speaker, the
spoken word and the speaking situation, of semantic pitfalls,
and of fallacies in reasoning and propaganda devices.

Arnold, Robert Lloyd. An Investigation of Learning from

Auditory and Visual Stimuli.   Doctoral dissertation.
Columbus, Ohio: Ohio State University, 1964. Abstract:
Dissertation Abstracts 25:2661, 1964 and Speech Monographs 32:333, August 1965.   40
A television lecture was presented with sound only, with
and without printed objectives, and with both sound and video.
Subjects were 611 college freshmen and sophomores. No
significant differences resulted from the presence or absence
of the video.

"The Art of Listening." Business Week No. 1833:76-77,
      October 17, 1964.   41
The listener is not a lamb; he may be stubborn and re-
sistant. Distractions while listening may lead to higher acceptance of what is being said because the listener cannot
marshall his arguments against what he is listening to. A
credible source is believed more readily, but good arguments
presented by a non-credible source tend to make belief last
longer, if they are accepted at all, than beliefs engendered
by the credible source.

Artley, A.S.   "Research Concerning Interrelationship Among
      the Language Arts." Elementary English 27:527-37.
      December 1950.   42
      Seventy-one item bibliography.

Asher, James John.   An Experimental Study of Listener
      Comprehension of News Commentary When Rate of De-
      livery Is Varied.   Master's thesis.   Houston, Tex. :
      University of Houston. 1955.   43
      This is a report of an experiment using 41 college
speech students as subjects. Results show that comprehension is significantly diminished when news commentaries are
delivered at either a slower or a faster rate than normal.

Asher, James J.   "The Learning Strategy of the Total Physi-
      cal Response: A Review." Modern Language Journal
      50:79-84, February 1966.   44
      Fluency in foreign language is promoted by a total bodi-
ly response to words listened to.   This is shown in controlled studies in learning of both Japanese and Russian.

Atkinson, Chester J.   "Intelligibility of Speech Heard at High
      Altitude and Sea Level." Office of Naval Research Pro-
      ject Designation No. N.R. 142-922, 1952.   45
      It is reported that while speaking becomes difficult at a

Atkinson, Chester J.   23

simulated altitude of 43,000 feet, listening is not noticeably affected.

Austin, Martha Lou. "Methods and Materials for Teaching
    Comprehension in Kindergarten Through Grade Three."
    Sequential Development of Reading Abilities. Proceed-
    ings of the Annual Conference on Reading. Chicago:
    University of Chicago Press, 1960. p. 57-59.   ·   46
Common reading skills, such as following directions,
locating main ideas, recalling sequence, making judgments
and drawing conclusions, recognizing emotional reactions,
classifying related ideas, and surveying a story, can be
taught during listening instruction.
    Instruction in listening may be essential throughout the
primary grades if all pupils are to develop adequate reading
comprehension.

Auston, John T. "Improving Everyday Speaking and Listen-
    ing Efficiency." Journal of Communication 4:49-53,
    Summer 1954.   47
The author reports that listening, as measured by the Dow
Test, was improved in remedial speech classes when stu-
dents worked in pairs.

Bakan, Paul. "Some Reflections on Listening Behavior."
    Journal of Communication 6:108-13, Autumn 1956. Re-
    printed in Listening: Readings. (Edited by Sam Duker.)
    Metuchen, N.J.: Scarecrow Press, 1966. p. 450-55.
                                                        48
    The author questions five basic assumptions upon which,
he says, listening instruction is based: listening is a unitary skill; uniform training in listening should be given to
all students; listening skill is teachable; listening skill is
relatively independent of other psychological variables; and
the effectiveness of training in listening can be evaluated by
means of a listening test administered at the end of the
training period.

Baker, Howard S. The High School English Teacher: Con-
    cepts of Professional Responsibility and Role. Toronto:
    Ryerson Press, 1949, p. 37 and 102.   49
    Data are given showing the increasing awareness on the
part of secondary school teachers of the importance of listening.

Baker, William D. "Listening - A Functional Part of Com-
    position." Journal of Communication 6:174-78, Winter

1956.   50
An awareness of acceptable forms and styles of the English language is most helpful to written and oral communication. Activities which will create this awareness include
reading aloud, criticizing speeches, and learning matters of
style by listening.

Baldauf, Robert John. A Study of a Measure of Listening
    Comprehension and Its Relation to the School Achieve-
    ment of Fifth Grade Pupils. Doctoral dissertation.
    Boulder, Col.: University of Colorado, 1960. Abstract:
    Dissertation Abstracts 21:2979-80, 1961. Summary:
    Anderson, Harold M. and Baldauf, Robert J. "A Study
    of a Measure of Listening." Journal of Educational Re-
    search 57:197-200, December 1963.   51
The author reports on correlations between listening
ability and achievement in various school subjects based on
a study using 420 fifth grade pupils as subjects. Data are
also reported on the reliability of two forms of the STEP
Listening Test.

Ball, Thomas S. and Bernardoni, Louis C. "The Applica-
    tion of an Auditory Apperception Test to Clinical Diag-
    nosis." Journal of Clinical Psychology 9:54-58, January
    1953.   52
A recorded projective test is described. Sounds used
were of mechanical devices, musical instruments, crowds,
non-verbal human sounds, and sounds from nature. Protocols
from several administrations are given and discussed.

Ballenger, Marcus Taylor. A Study of the Effectiveness of
    Teaching Listening Through a Planned Daily Program.
    Master's thesis. Lubbock, Texas: Texas Technologi-
    cal College, 1963.   53
A sixteen week course of daily instruction in listening,
accompanied by weekly testing, resulted in a substantial improvement of listening skills as measured by the STEP test.

Bang, Read. "Are You a Halfer?" Spotlight 35(19):4+.
    September 18, 1954.   54
A promotional flyer issued by Field Enterprises emphasizing the importance of the practice of good listening by
sales personnel.

Bar, Asher. Effects of Listening Instructions on Attention
    to Manner and Content of Stutterers' Speech. Master's
    thesis. Pittsburgh, Pa.: University of Pittsburgh,

1964.   55
Two groups listened to a taped speech by a severe
stutterer. One group was instructed to listen to content and
the other to the manner of speech. Both groups were more
accurate in judging the amount of stuttering than in answering questions on content. No significant differences appeared
between the two groups.

Barbara, Dominick A. The Art of Listening. Springfield,
    Ill. : Charles C. Thomas, 1958. Excerpts: Today's
    Speech 5(1):12-15, January 1957; 7(1):5-7, February
    1959; 9(1):1-3, February 1961; and Listening: Readings.
    (Edited by Sam Duker.) Metuchen, N. J. : Scarecrow
    Press, 1966. p. 95-101. Reviewed: Journal of Com-
    munication 10:218, December 1960.   56
A comprehensive treatment of the importance of listen-
ing from the psychoanalytic viewpoint: The Art of Listen-
ing; Listening with the Outer Ear; Listening with the Inner
Ear (Listening to Ourselves): Listening with a Receptive
Ear (Listening to Others); The Magic of Listening; Listening
to the Essence of Things; The Disease of Not Listening;
Listening with a Modest Ear; Listening with a Rebellious
Ear; Listening with a Deaf Ear; Listening with the Third
Ear; The Sound of Silence; When We Stop Listening.

----. "Listening to the Essence of Things." Southern
    Speech Journal 25:134-40, Winter 1959.   57
When we listen totally with purpose, we listen to the essence of things. To listen fully we must be receptive and
attentive to other people's ideas. To listen effectively we
should abandon prejudices and preconceived judgments. Active holistic listening is contrasted to vicarious listening.
There must be a mutual relationship between listener and
speaker. Listening depends upon a common definition of
terms used. Effective listening can have profound curative
value.

----. "On Listening." Today's Speech 5(1):12-15, January
    1957.   58
In many public rituals today, passive listening takes
place. The distinction between listening and hearing is as
strong as the difference between active holistic listening and
passive vicarious listening.

----. Your Speech Reveals Your Personality. Springfield,
    Ill. : Charles C. Thomas, 1958. Chapter 11 "On Lis-
    tening," p. 124-33.   59

Successful listening presupposes hearing and precedes understanding. Inner conflicts, anxieties, and inflexibilities place inhibitions and blockages in the path of real understanding by the listener.

Barbe, Walter B. and Meyers, Robert M. 'Developing Listening Ability in Children." Elementary English 31:82-84, February 1954.   60
In this plea for the inclusion of listening training in the language arts program, stress is placed on the close relationship between a child's listening ability and his emotional status.

----, and Carr, Jack A. 'Research Report - Listening Comprehension as a Measure of Potential Reading Ability." Reading in Action International Reading Association Conference Proceedings, Volume 2, 1957. New York: Scholastic Magazines, 1957, part III, Chapter 8, p. 120-22.   61
Suggests the possibility, based on an experiment with 46 elementary grade pupils, that listening ability may be a better predictor of reading potential than intelligence.

Barker, Larry L. and Wiseman, Gordon. 'Research Report No. 57: A Comparative Study of Recall and Recognition Produced Through Programmed Instruction and Lectures on Listening When Time Is Constant." (Reviewed by Frank E. X. Dance.) Central States Speech Journal 16: 140-41, May 1965.   62
When time spent was constant no significant difference was found, either on an immediate or a delayed recall test after three weeks, between those taught by lecture and those using programmed materials. Subjects were 150 college speech students.

Bateman, David, Frandsen, Kenneth and Dedmon, Donald. 'Dimensions of 'Lecture Comprehension:' A Factor Analysis of Listening Test Items." Journal of Communication 14:183-89, September 1964.   63
Section E (Lecture Comprehension Section) of the Brown-Carlsen test was administered to 100 freshman speech students. Analysis revealed two factors: (1) listening for details and (2) drawing inferences. Additional factors mentioned in the test manual were not revealed.

Beardsley, Paul W. Listening Versus Listening and Reading: A Study of the Appreciation of Poetry. Master's

thesis.   Norman, Okla.:   University of Oklahoma, 1950.
                                                              64
Report of an experiment showing that reading and listening together are more effective than listening alone in gaining appreciation of poetry.

Beattie, William Edward.   The Historical Development of
Listenability-Readability in Presidential Inaugural Addresses.   Master's thesis.   Pullman, Wash.:   Washington State University, 1965.   65
The Flesch readability formula was applied to excerpts
from addresses.   The author concludes that this formula is
a satisfactory measure of listenability.

Beery, Althea.   "Experiences in Listening."   Elementary English 28:130-32, March 1951.   66
Teachers need to analyze their own listening habits and
encourage thoughtful study of listening situations by children.
As children develop concern for their own listening competence a more effective meeting of minds in the classroom
will occur as a result.

----.   "Interrelationships Between Listening and Other Language Arts Areas."   Elementary English 31:164-72,
March 1954.   Reprinted: National Conference on Research in English.   Interrelationships Among the Language Arts.   Chicago: National Council of Teachers of
English, 1954, p. 34-42.   67
Since listening and reading are closely related, the elementary school teacher should take advantage of this fact by
developing both reading and listening simultaneously and not
attempt to thwart a relationship between the two.

----.   "Listening Activities in the Elementary School."   Elementary English Review 23:69-79, February 1946.   68
Specific suggestions for the teaching of listening at the
elementary level include: sensing the relationship between
listening and other phases of communication; understanding
the psychological process of listening; providing conditions in
the classroom that are conducive to listening; utilizing opportunities for listening; understanding the developmental levels
and goals of the listening process; and being alert to new
equipment and devices which will aid the program of teaching
listening.

Beighley, Kenneth C.   An Experimental Study of the Effect
of Four Speech Variables on Listener Comprehension.

Doctoral dissertation. Columbus, Ohio: Ohio State University, 1952. Abstract: Dissertation Abstracts 18: 1894-96, 1958. Excerpts: Speech Monographs 19:249-58, November 1952 and 21:248-53, November 1954, and Journal of Communication 2(2):58-65, November 1952.
                                                                    69
Using beginning college speech students as subjects, Beighley found that the degree of organization of a speech had little effect on comprehension. The theory is advanced that this may be a function of insufficient training in listening.

----. "An Experimental Study of the Effect of Three Speech Variables on Listener Comprehension." Speech Monographs 21:248-53, November 1954.   70
Repeating the experiment reported in his doctoral thesis, the author confirmed his findings on the comprehension of easy and difficult speeches by skilled and poor speakers. The organization of a speech had no significant effect on comprehension, either on immediate or delayed recall.

Bellamy, Martha Jean McLaughlin. An Experimental Study to Compare the Comprehension of Speeded Speech by Blind and Sighted Children. Master's thesis. Austin, Tex.: University of Texas, 1966.   71
Thirty-one blind and 26 sighted junior high school pupils listened to a scientific passage on blood circulation compressed to a rate of 275 wpm. A multiple choice test and an interview (six questions) were used to evaluate comprehension. There was no significant difference in the multiple choice test results but the blind subjects had significantly higher scores on the interview. The correlation between the two tests was .65 for the blind and .24 for the sighted subjects. This difference was statistically significant.

Bennett, Clayton L. and Dixon, Carmen. "The Art of Listening." Educational Screen and Audio-Visual Guide 41: 314, June 1962.   72
Poor listening habits may be fostered in the classroom when listening experiences are not organized, rewarding, and worthwhile.

Benoit, Robert W. Listening Versus Reading in Teaching Eighth Grade Literature. Master's thesis. Plymouth, N.H.: Plymouth Teachers College, 1963.   73
Several types of literature were presented to 16 pupils by phonographic recordings. Slightly better test results were

obtained from the recorded literature than from tests following the reading of similar materials.

Berarducci, Joanne. Original Stories for Teaching the Vocal
   Skills of Speaking and Listening. Master's thesis. Bos-
   ton: Boston University, 1956.   74
   Ten stories with exercise material are presented.

Berg, Paul C. "Reading in Relation to Listening." Reading
   Teacher's Reader, (Edited by Oscar S. Causey.) New
   York: Ronald Press, 1958. Chapter 5, p. 22-26. Also
   in: Fourth Yearbook Southwest Reading Conference,
   1955, p. 52-59.   75
   A review of previous research.

Berry, David R. and Victor, Russell F. "How Are Your
   Listening Habits?" Banking 59:48+, October 1966.   76
   The Basic System's taped course, Effective Listening,
was given to a single bank department of 23 people and to
188 supervisors. The course was "completely satisfactory"
and highly praised by those who took the tests and course.

Biggins, Mildred E. A Comparison of Listening Comprehension and Reading Comprehension in Second and Third
   Grades. Advanced thesis. Terre Haute, Ind. : Indiana
   State College, 1961. Abstract: Teachers College Journal 33:54-55, December 1961.   77
   Using California Reading Test, California Mental Maturity Test, and Evan L. Wright Listening Test, the author reports correlations in second and third grades, respectively,
as follows: listening and reading, .45 and .70; listening
and mental age, .69 and .75; listening and teachers' evaluations of listening ability, .55 in both grades.

Biggs, Bernice Prince. Construction, Validation, and Eval-
   uation of a Diagnostic Test of Listening Effectiveness.
   Doctoral dissertation. Denver, Colo. : University of
   Denver, 1954. Summary: Speech Monographs 23:9-13,
   March 1956.   78
   Test is described but text is not included.

Bird, Donald E. "Are You Listening?" Office Executive 30
   (4):18-19, April 1955.   79
   Some false assumptions about listening are: listening is
a passive function; listening is easy; hearing is listening;
listening is an automatic involuntary reflex; listening can be
commanded; speaking is more important than listening; the

speaker is 100 per cent responsible for the success of communication; listening skill develops naturally; and listening
is only a matter of understanding the speaker's words.

----. "Developing Literate Listening." Oral Aspects of
    Reading, Proceedings of the Annual Conference on Read-
    ing, Chicago: University of Chicago Press, 1955. p.
    105-10.   80
    A review of the literature on listening.

----. "Have You Tried Listening?" Journal of the Ameri-
    can Dietetic Association 30:225-30, March 1954.   81
    A survey of the nature of listening and of the importance
to dieticians of listening sympathetically, accurately, and
critically to colleagues, hospital workers, food service employees, and patients.   A 15-item quiz is included.

----. "Listening." NEA Journal 49(8):31-33, November
    1960.   82
    An excellent expository article on the nature of listening
and the need for teaching it.

----. "Teaching Listening Comprehension." Journal of Com-
    munication 3:127-30, November 1953.   83
    A description of the instructional program in listening at
Stephens College.   Five stages involved were: exploration
of the importance of listening to students; examination of
the process of hearing and listening; study of factors that
help or hinder listening; ways in which listening can be improved; and practice in listening during out-of-class experiences.

----. "This Is Your Listening Life." Journal of the Ameri-
    can Dietitic Association 32:534-36, June 1956.   84
    A report on 110 responses to a questionnaire about lis-
tening habits of dieticians.   Data showed that listening was a
skill used frequently but not with a high degree of effectiveness.

Bischoff, Robert W.   "Improvement of Listening Comprehen-
    sion in Partially Sighted Students." Sight-Saving Review
    37:161-65, Fall 1967.   85
    Sixty-three partially sighted children in grades 4-9 were
divided into two experimental groups and one control group.   The
experimental groups used Weekly Reader and SRA materials for
a sequential program of listening instruction.   There were two
sequences of 20 fifteen-minute lessons, each given at the

rate of two a week. The lessons consisted of a presentation, a comprehension check and an answer check. The lessons stressed main thoughts or ideas, specific word meanings, and general comprehension. The STEP test was used
as the pre- and post-test but the answer blank had no reading material on it. The experimental groups showed a gain
in scores while the control group showed a loss.

Bixler, Ray H. and Foulke, Emerson. "Current Status of
    Research in Rapid Speech." International Journal for the
    Education of the Blind 13:57-59, December 1963.   86
    Research on compressed speech and its comprehension
at the University of Louisville.

Black, James Menzies. "Learn to Listen." Supervisory
    Management 7(6):39-40, June 1962.   87
    A good listener anticipates what is going to be said,
mentally summarizes what has been said, encourages the
speaker by asking questions, understands the intended meaning of the words used, and hears the speaker out before responding.

Black, John W. A Relationship Between Speaking and Listen-
    ing. Joint Project Report No. NM 001 104 500.54.
    Pensacola, Fla. : The Ohio State University and Acous-
    tic Laboratory, U.S. Naval School of Aviation Medicine,
    1955.   88
    One hundred and eighty panels, each having twelve mem-
bers, responded to two forms of a multiple choice intelligibility test. Correlations between listening and speaking
scores ranged from .02 to .87. The median value was .21.
The author doubts that there is a valid relationship between
these two skills.

Blain, Beryl Bruce. Effects of Film Narration Type and of
    Listenability Level on Learning of Factual Information.
    Doctoral dissertation. Bloomington, Ind. : Indiana Uni-
    versity, 1956. Abstract: Dissertation Abstracts 16:
    2398, 1956.   89
    Six hundred fifty-eight fifth and eighth grade pupils were
shown factual films with commentary at several levels of difficulty as measured by the Dale-Chall readability formula.
No significant differences were found in comprehension or
retention.

Blair, Herbert. "The Art of Listening." Education 52:563-
    64, May 1932.   90

An amusing editorial on the evils of not listening.

Blake, Howard E. "A Code for Teachers of Listening."
  Elementary English 39:48-49, January 1962.   91
  A twenty point list of essentials for a teacher of listening is given with emphasis on the need for integrating the
teaching of listening with all other school subjects.

----, and Amato, Anthony J. 'Needed Research in Oral Language. Part II: Listening." Elementary English 44:
  259-60, March 1967.   92
  The following areas need research: 1. an accumulation
of the best that has already been established; 2. an investigation of the structure of listening, especially at the elementary school level; 3. development of better measuring
instruments; and 4. further investigation of the relationship
between listening and the other language arts.

Blake, Marie Frances. Comparisons and Relationships of
  Listening, Speaking, and Reading Abilities of Second
  Grade Pupils. Master's thesis. Atlanta, Ga. : Atlanta
  University, 1965.   93
  The Durrell-Sullivan Reading Capacity Test, the Durrell
Analysis of Reading Difficulty Test, the Gray Oral Reading
Test, and a teacher-made test of speech were administered
to 36 pupils. No differences between boys and girls were
found. The following correlations with listening were re-
ported: speaking .40; silent reading .33; and oral read-
ing .47.

Bland, Merton Lois. A Test of Oral Comprehension of
  French for Use in Elementary Schools. Doctoral dissertation. Los Angeles, Cal. : University of California,
  Los Angeles, 1966. Abstract: Dissertation Abstracts
  27:1699A-1700A, 1960.   94
  The development and validation of a 30-minute test to
measure vocabulary, form and order, and phonemic discrimination. Twelve separate administrations are described in
detail. Text of the test is included.

Blewett, Thomas T. An Experiment in the Measurement of
  Listening at the College Level. Doctoral dissertation.
  Columbia, Mo. : University of Missouri, 1949. Summary: Journal of Communication 1(1):50-57, May 1951
  and Journal of Educational Research 44:575-85, April
  1951. Abstract: Speech Monographs 18:174-75, August
  1951 and Microfilm Abstracts 9(3):87, 1950.   95

Description of the construction and validation of a taped
listening test. Text of the test is included.

Bliesmer, Emery P. A Comparison of Bright and Dull Chil-
   dren of Comparable Mental Ages with Respect to Various
   Reading Abilities. Doctoral dissertation. Iowa City,
   Iowa: State University of Iowa, 1952. Excerpts: Listening: Readings. (Edited by Sam Duker.) Metuchen,
   N. J. : Scarecrow Press, 1966. p. 131-34.   96
Bliesmer constructed a listening test by taking 44 items
from the reading test portion of the Iowa Test of Basic
Skills. He administered this test to 28 children with I. Q. 's
of 116 and over and to 28 older children of the same mental
age with I. Q.'s of 84 and less. He reports that the high
I. Q. subjects performed significantly better on the listening
test than did the low I. Q. subjects.

Bloom, Anna K. "Taught not Caught." English Journal 43:
   367-70, October 1954.   97
A description of the teaching of listening at the high school
level.   Pupils should learn to follow oral directions given
once, observe good audience manners, get sense of power
of words from recordings, etc. A detailed unit is given in
which pupils learned criteria for the evaluation of news-
casters on television and radio.

Blount, Sam and Crawford, Sallilu H. "Better Speaking and
   Listening." Clearing House 35:159-62, November 1960.
                                                        98
The authors present a "listening self-evaluation guide"
based on an oral communication and listening survey made
in a senior high school.

Blubaugh, Jon A. An Experimental Study of the Effects of
   Information, Instruction and Motivation on Listening Behavior. Master's thesis. Lawrence, Kan. : University
   of Kansas, 1963.   99
Three lectures about listening were prepared, one purely
informative, one instructional, and one motivational. The
last included the promise of a monetary reward for good
performance on the post-test. Part I of the STEP Test was
used as a measure of listening. In an experiment involving
six groups of beginning college speech students as subjects,
the motivational lecture was found to be the most effective,
but there were no significant differences between the pre-
and post-tests.

Bohan, Ruth. Listening and First Grade Reading Comprehen-
    sion. Master's thesis. Natchitoches, La.: Northwest-
    ern State College of Louisiana, 1963.   100
    The author gives a series of lesson plans for teaching
listening to first graders.

Bohn, Thomas W. A Study of Immediate and Delayed Recall
    as a Function of Mode of Presentation and Anticipation
    of Reward. Master's thesis. Carbondale, Ill.: South-
    ern Illinois University, 1964.   101
    One hundred and twenty college speech students served
as subjects. A twelve-minute television lecture was presented to half the group with video on and to half with video
off. Half the group was promised exemption from the course
final examination if they scored high on the tests based on
the lecture. The speech was followed immediately by a test
and by a delayed test after 3 weeks. No significant difference was found between the two modes of presentation on
either immediate or delayed recall. The group which was
promised the reward performed significantly better on both
immediate and delayed recall than the other group. Only for
the group promised a reward was the auditory channel more
effective than the auditory and visual combined. This was
explained as possibly due to anxiety produced by the promised
reward.

Bois, J.S.A. "The Art of Listening." The Clarkson Letter.
    Potsdam, N.Y.: Clarkson Institute of Technology, May-
    June 1952. Reprinted in Listening: Readings. (Edited
    by Sam Duker.) Metuchen, N.J.: Scarecrow Press,
    1966. p. 43-47.   102
    A semanticist's view of the importance of listening.

Boltwood, Robert M. "An Approach to Listening." Journal
    of the American Society of Training Directors 15(4):48-
    50, April 1961.   103
    The author describes a two-hour training session on lis-
tening given to first-level office supervisors. Since it was
felt that there was insufficient time to teach detailed techniques, emphasis was put on creating an awareness of the
problem of listening. Prepared and "on the spot" tape recordings were used.

Bonner, Myrtle Clara Stoddard. A Critical Analysis of the
    Relationship of Reading Ability to Listening Ability. Doc-
    toral dissertation. Auburn, Ala.: Auburn University,
    1960. Abstract: Dissertation Abstracts 21:2167-68,

1961.   104
Using 282 subjects in fourth, fifth and sixth grades, and
employing Stanford Achievement Test, Pintner General Ability Test, Sonotone Hearing Test, and STEP Listening Test,
the author reports a number of linear and multiple correlations:

Listening and intelligence: .38 to .59
Reading and intelligence: .50 to .67
Reading and listening: .53 to .65
Reading and listening with intel-
    ligence held constant: .30
Other correlations are also reported.

Bopp, Sister John Mary. An Experiment in the Development
    of Basic Listening Skills Through the Teaching of Poet-
    ry. Master's thesis. Milwaukee, Wisc. : Marquette
    University, 1960.   105
Two equivalent groups of second graders were taught poetry. Listening skills were emphasized in one group. The
results of a teacher-made test, modeled after the Brown-
Carlsen Listening Comprehension Test, showed that this
group increased its listening ability more than the other
group. Text of the test is not given.

Bossard, James H. S. "Family Life: Conversation is the
    Key." Presbyterian Life 11(2):7-9+, January 25, 1958.
                                                      106
A report of 200 tape recordings made of family dinner
table conversations in a variety of homes. "The steadiness
and warmth of love among parents can be gauged by how
they talk and how they listen."

Breiter, Lila R. Research in Listening and Its Importance
    to Literature. Master's thesis. Brooklyn, N. Y. :
    Brooklyn College, 1957.   107
An analysis of communication time of a group of housewives revealed that 48 per cent of their time was spent in
listening; 35 per cent in speaking, 7 per cent in writing and
10 per cent in reading. This confirms the findings of Rankin and Bird.

Brennen, Frances Robinson. A Program of Listening Ac-
    tivities to Aid in the Development of Auditory Discrimi-
    nation in the Kindergarten Child. Master's thesis.
    Providence, R. I. : Rhode Island College, 1966.   108
Thirty lessons on listening were taught to twelve kindergarten pupils over two months. On the Wepman Auditory

Discrimination Test, the California Test of Mental Maturity,
and the Harrison Stroud Profiles, the experimental group
showed significantly greater gains than a comparable control
group. The difference on an inventory of listening skills,
prepared by the author, favored the experimental group, but
not significantly. Texts of the lessons are included.

Brewster, Laurence Walter. An Exploratory Study of Some
    Aspects of Critical Listening Among College Freshmen.
    Doctoral dissertation. Iowa City, Iowa: State Univer-
    sity of Iowa, 1956. Abstract: Dissertation Abstracts
    16:1735-36, 1956 and Speech Monographs 24:86-87, June
    1957.   109
    Using 323 college students in communication courses as
subjects, the author investigated reaction to speeches containing fallacious arguments. Results show that listening was
very inefficient.

Brigance, William Norwood. "How Fast Do We Talk?"
    Quarterly Journal of Speech Education 12:337-42, Novem-
    ber 1926.   110
    A phonograph record of Bryan's "Cross of Gold" speech
was analyzed. His rate was 150 wpm, which was faster than
Bryan ordinarily spoke. Phonograph records of Shakespeari-
an plays showed rates varying from 80 to 170 wpm. Twenty
winners of intercollegiate oratorical contests spoke at rates
varying from 83 to 154 wpm.

Briggs, Thomas H. and Armacost, George H. 'Results of
    an Oral True-False Test." Journal of Educational Re-
    search 26:595-96, April 1933.   111
    An experiment using two college classes showed that the
reliability of the oral true-false test employed was .69.
The authors conclude that such a test as a measure of immediate recall compares favorably with the same test in visual form. They call attention to the fact that these findings
are consistent with those of Stump and Lehman.

Bright, Catherine May. The Development of a Test of Lis-
    tening Ability of Stutterers. Master's thesis. Ann Ar-
    bor, Mich.: University of Michigan, 1947. Abstract:
    Speech Monographs 15(2):214-15, 1948.   112
    A test was developed to test various abilities of listen-
ing, including recognition of different vowel sounds. These
items gave 28 stutterers a great deal of difficulty.

Brilhart, Barbara Lieb. Speaker-Message Perception and

Brilhart, Barbara Lieb 37

Attitude Change of Listeners as a Function of Field Independence. Doctoral dissertation. University Park, Pa.: Pennsylvania State University, 1966. Abstract: Dissertation Abstracts 27:1462A, 1966 and Speech Monographs 34:222-23, August 1967. 113

The degree of field-independence of 88 engineering students was determined by the Embedded Figures Test. These subjects then heard a speech of good quality delivered by a poor speaker and a speech of poor quality delivered by a good speaker. They were then tested on 567 message-oriented items and 241 speaker-oriented items. No consistent linear relationship between the degree of field-independence and responses was shown, but there were sufficient data to justify the belief in a relationship, which is not clearly defined.

Listeners tend to make more accurate judgments of speaker quality than of message quality. An excellent review of the literature and an extensive bibliography are included.

Broadbent, Donald E. "Attention and the Perception of Speech." Scientific American 206(4):143-51. April 1962. 114

It is difficult to understand two messages simultaneously but one message can be understood if the other is ignored. Comprehension is improved if the two messages differ, e.g. if one is spoken by a man and the other by a woman. Spatial separation also helps.

----. "...Clinical Implications of Recent Experiments on the Psychology of Hearing." Proceedings of the Royal Society of Medicine 48:961-68, May 16, 1955. 115

The author discusses the significance of every-day listening tasks in his experimental findings.

----. "Failures of Attention in Selective Listening." Journal of Experimental Psychology 44:428-33, December 1952. 116

This is a meticulously designed experiment involving reception of simultaneous messages. Reported results are:
1. Listening to one voice continuously is clearly better than shifting from voice to voice.
2. It is easier to answer two messages which occupy different periods of time than to answer two which occupy scattered portions of the same period.
3. Irrelevant speech produces a definite effect when it occurs between the sections of a relevant message.

----. "Listening Between and During Practiced Auditory
    Distractions." British Journal of Psychology 47(1):51-
    60, February 1956.   117
    From a carefully designed experiment, Broadbent reports
findings and concludes that when an extra signal occurs during listening, and when this signal may not be ignored but
is meant to produce some action from the listener, the
speech is impaired both at the instant of this extra response
and also between responses.

----. "Listening to One of Two Synchronous Messages."
    Journal of Experimental Psychology 44:51-55, July 1952.
                                                          118
    A carefully designed experiment involving the simultane-
ous reception of two messages showed that definite advance
knowledge of which voice among several was to be answered,
improved performance. The principal difficulty appeared to
be the identification of which message was to be answered
rather than the understanding of the message once the voice
had been identified.

----. Perception and Communication. New York: Perga-
    mon Press, 1958.   119
    The psychology of communication, with particular refer-
ence to listening behavior, is discussed in depth. The following chapters are included: Hearing and Behavior; Selective
Listening to Speech; Verbal and Bodily Response; The Assessment of Communications Channels for Ease of Listening;
The Effects of Noise on Behavior; The General Nature of
Vigilance; Some Data on Individual Differences; The Nature
of Extinction; Immediate Memory and the Shifting of Attention; The Selective Nature of Learning; Recent Views on
Skill.

----. "The Role of Auditory Localization in Attention and
    Memory Span." Journal of Experimental Psychology 47:
    191-96, March 1954.   120
    In a well-designed and controlled experiment subjects
were required to answer messages occasionally presented
together. When this occurred, only the message that started
with a particular call-signal was to be answered. It was
found that spatially separated sources led to more correct
answers.

----. 'Speaking and Listening Simultaneously." Journal of
    Experimental Psychology 43:267-73, April 1952.   121
    In a well-designed experiment, subjects were required

to give verbal responses to simple questions coming from a loudspeaker. Sometimes they were presented with a new question while still answering a previous one. This simultaneous speaking and listening caused a significant impairment in both the interrupted responses and the responses to the interrupting questions. The extent of the impairment was not serious, except when the interruptions occurred for each question.

Broadway, JoAnn Chamberlin. An Experimental Study in the Comprehension and Retention of Expository Prose Resulting from Silent Reading and from Listening to Oral Reading. Master's thesis. Auburn, Ala.: Auburn University, 1966. 122
An experiment with 179 tenth grade students in which no difference was found between reading and listening comprehension. The California Reading Test was used for reading ability and the California Mental Maturity Test for listening. There was a significant relationship between the skill of reading and performance on the listening test, but not between the skill of listening and performance on the reading test.

Brodie, Tom. "Can We Ignore This Problem?" Phi Delta Kappan 39:57, November 1957. 123
This is a sceptical view on the teaching of listening.

Brodinsky, B. P. Casebook on Classroom Teaching. New London, Conn.: Arthur C. Croft, 1955, p. 24-25. 124
The role and importance of listening in promoting good human relations is discussed.

Brooks, Keith and Wulftange, Sister I. Marie. "Listener Response to Oral Interpretation." Speech Monographs 31:73-79, March 1964. 125
Short stories were presented to 120 college freshmen by tape, by television, and face-to-face. The face-to-face method led to the highest aesthetic response while television elicited the greatest interest. In general, comprehension is unrelated to the method of presentation.

Brown, Charles T. "Introductory Study of Breathing as an Index to Listening." Speech Monographs 29:79-83, June 1962. 126
Using 14 students as subjects, Brown reports that his experiment failed to substantiate the hypothesis that a good listener tends to imitate the breathing characteristics of the speaker. It was found that the breathing characteristics of

listening differed from vegetative and speaking breathing in
being more rapid. This substantiates the statement that listening is an active process.

----, and Keller, Paul W. "A Modest Proposal for Listen-
    ing Training." Quarterly Journal of Speech 48:395-99,
    December 1962.   127
    The author suggests that more emphasis be put on the
listening act in speech classes. Students should listen for
the substance of communication and not only to the speaking
techniques. Training should be given in predicting what will
be said, developing flexibility, and in creating greater awareness by the listener of his own thoughts.

----. "Studies in Listening Comprehension." Speech Mono-
    graphs 26:288-94, November 1959.   128
    In a report based on work with 51 college speech stu-
dents as subjects, Brown says that there is an improvement
in performance on the STEP Listening Test when a short introductory statement about the test is made.
    Using 47 college speech students as subjects, Brown
found only a very small positive relationship between a theoretical interest in listening as measured by the Allport Vernon Lindsey Study of Values Scale, and listening.
    Using 51 college speech students as subjects, the author
reports that he found no relationship between listening ability
and the ability to make a large number of word associations
in a given time.

----. "Three Studies of the Listening of Children."
    Speech Monographs 32:129-38, June 1965.   129
    In a school population, half of which was Amish and did
not have television sets at home, those children watching
television were better listeners as measured by the STEP
test. There was no support for the hypothesis that those
who watched television for a few hours daily were better listeners than those who watched longer. No difference was
found in the listening abilities of boys and girls.
    A second study showed that children from small families
were better listeners than children from large families.
Birth order had no effect.
    Correlations are also reported between mental ability,
reading, school achievement and listening. While reading
ability appears to be more important than listening in
achievement test results, listening ability appears to be more
important in teachers' grades.

Brown, Donald Pardie. "And Having Ears They Hear Not."
   NEA Journal 39:586-87, November, 1950.   130
The greatest source of errors in listening is problems
in vocabulary. Use of the International Phonetic Alphabet is
suggested as a way to solve this problem. "Auding" is defined as the gross process of listening to, recognizing, and
interpreting spoken symbols.

----. Auding as the Primary Language Ability. Doctoral
   dissertation. Stanford, Calif. : Stanford University,
   1954. Abstract: Dissertation Abstracts 14:2281-82,
   1954.   131
The need for the term "auding" is developed in this thesis. Extensive reviews of previous studies on deafness and
on aphasia are included.

----. "Auding Problems." English Journal 43:287-88,
   September 1954.   132
A brief description of an assignment given to a high
school English class which required the class to list listening difficulties and to learn some of the International Phonetic Alphabet symbols.

----. "Concepts and Practices in Teaching Aural English."
   English Journal 45:540-46, December 1956.   133
The author pleads for the use of the term "auding" rather
than "listening." Functions of a teacher of "auding" are
listed and discussed in detail.

----. "Teaching Aural English." English Journal 39:128-
   36, March 1950.   134
The author urges the use of the term "auding" instead of
the word "listening." Brown suggests vocabulary building as
a way of improving listening at the high school level.

Brown, James I. "Can Listening Be Taught?" College English 15:290-91, February 1954.   135
Using as subjects two groups of 24 college freshmen of
equal initial listening ability, Brown found that the group
given intensive instruction in increasing listening efficiency
for one quarter showed a statistically significant greater increase in listening ability, as measured by the Brown-Carlsen Test, than the group which took the regular freshman
communication course.

----. "A Comparison of Listening and Reading Ability."
   College English 10:105-07, November 1948.   136

This is a report of an experiment in administering Part
V of the Purdue Placement Test in English in written and in
oral forms.   The author found a correlation of .35 and
concludes that skills involved in listening differ from those
involved in reading.

----.   The Construction of a Diagnostic Test of Listening
    Comprehension.   Doctoral dissertation.   Boulder, Colo. :
    University of Colorado, 1950.   Summary: Journal of
    Experimental Education 18:139-46, December 1949.   Ex-
    cerpts: Listening: Readings.   (Edited by Sam Duker.)
    Metuchen, N. J. : Scarecrow Press, 1966. p. 416-29.
                                                      137
    Describes construction and validation of the Brown-Carl-
sen Listening Comprehension Test.

----.   "Evaluating Student Performance in Listening." Edu-
    cation 75:316-21, January 1955.   138
    A report of procedures used with college freshman
classes.   Interest is associated with better listening.   Note-
taking interferes with most students' listening.   Informal appraisal of listening skills can and should be combined with
teaching.   Nine-item bibliography.

----.   "How Teachable Is Listening?" Educational Research
    Bulletin 33:85-93, April 14, 1954.   139
    Test data of a group of college sophomores showed the
correlation between honor point ratio and reading ability,
as measured by the Nelson-Denny Test, to be .37 and between honor point ratio and listening ability, as measured by
the Brown-Carlsen Test, to be .41.

----.   "Listening - The New Frontier in Reading." Reading
    and the Language Arts.   Proceedings of the Annual Con-
    ference on Reading.   Chicago: University of Chicago
    Press, 1963. p. 47-55.   140
    Research findings on the relative effectiveness of read-
ing and listening as modes of learning might be reversed if
listening were taught.   Listening is a skill often needed because of its speed in transmitting ideas in an age of crisis.

----.   "The Measurement of Listening Ability." School and
    Society 71(1):69-71, February 4, 1950.   Also in Read-
    ing Teacher's Reader (Edited by Oscar S. Causey.) New
    York: Holt, 1958.   Chapter 30, p. 122-25.   141
    In constructing a listening test three variables should be
taken into account: 1. the test should not involve reading;

2. listenability standards are needed since readability formulas are not satisfactory for this purpose; 3. equating of
the groups used to standardize the test should not be based
solely on intelligence.

----. "A New Listening-Type Examination." AAUP Bulletin 36:304-07, Summer 1950.   142
The author suggests that an objective type test administered orally is efficient, flexible, and economical. Brown
says such tests are satisfactory measures which give equal
opportunity to a student who listens well but who perhaps
does not read well.

----. "The Objective Measurement of Listening Ability."
Journal of Communication 1:44-48, May 1951.   143
A preliminary report on research involved in preparing
the Brown-Carlsen Listening Test.

----. "A Plea for Action." Newsletter, Business and Professional Speaking Group, SAA, November 1962, p. 1-2.
                                                     144
A reply to Petrie's article on the inadequacy of existing
knowledge about listening.

----. "Report of the Reading Committee." Journal of Communication 6:38-39, Spring 1956.   145
Report of an experiment in which listening and reading
were found to be about equally amenable to improvement.

----. "Teaching Listening Through Listening-Type Tests."
College English 13:224-25, January 1952.   146
This is a report of an informal experiment comparing
oral and written administration of an objective test. It was
found that college students did better on the written form,
especially on more difficult questions.

----. "Why Not Teach Listening?" School and Society 69:
113-16, February 12, 1949.   147
Critical listening in an audience situation is more difficult than critical reading, and the dangers of uncritical listening are more pronounced. Teaching of listening should
not be left only to English teachers but should concern
teachers in other curricular areas.

----, and Carlsen, G. Robert. Brown-Carlsen Listening
Comprehension Test. Yonkers, N.Y.: World Book Co.,

1955.   Excerpts: Listening: Readings.   (Edited by Sam
Duker.) Metuchen, N.J., Scarecrow Press, 1966. pp.
430-31, 432-36.   Reviewed: Educational Research Bulletin 34(2):83-84, March 9, 1955.   148
A listening test for grades nine through 13.   Two forms
are available.

Brown, Kenneth Lee.   An Analysis of the Speech and Listen-
    ing Content of Selected Pupil Textbooks in the Language
    Arts for the Elementary Schools: Grades Three Through
    Six.   Doctoral dissertation.   Evanston, Ill.:   Northwest-
    ern University, 1965.   Abstract: Dissertation Abstracts
    27:1948A-49A, 1966 and Speech Monographs 33:299-300,
    August 1966.   Excerpts: Elementary English 44:336-
    41, April 1967 and 44:461-65+, May 1967.   149
A content-analysis study of 54 basal language arts textbooks, published between 1959 and 1964.   The listening content was extremely sparse.

Brunson, F. Ward.   "Creative Teaching of the Culturally
    Disadvantaged."   Audiovisual Instruction 10:30-31, Janu-
    ary 1965.   150
Listening skills must be taught to the disadvantaged as
they do not learn as much from reading or listening as
might be desired.   A series of tapes of social studies text
material was prepared with guide sheets requiring key words
to be filled in.   These tapes were used in five high school
classes and led to better attention and listening.

Buck, Myrtress Crawford.   A Study on the Skill of Listen-
    ing.   Master's thesis.   State College, Arkansas: Ar-
    kansas State College, 1964.   151
A well-organized review of some of the literature on
the listening process and ways of teaching listening skills.

Bull, Storm.   "Listen."   American Music Teacher 15(4):19+,
    February-March 1966.   152
The selective manner of listening to music is discussed.   Before one can listen as an effeotive musician, one
must acquire a great deal of interrelated information that
should be both intuitively and purposefully learned.   Learning experiences of these kinds deserve more help than
merely the admonition to "listen."

Bureau of National Affairs, Inc.   How to Listen and Why.
    Washington, D.C.:   Author, 1951.   153
Listening to employees gives them a feeling of being

recognized and results in their doing better work.   Listening by the supervisor promotes respect for him.   Listening warns of impending trouble and is therefore a help in handling grievances.

Burns, John Walter.   An Exploratory Study of Assumed Attention Given to Audio and Visual Elements in an Elementary Science Television Series.   Doctoral dissertation.   Detroit, Mich. :   Wayne State University, 1966.
Abstract: Dissertation Abstracts 27:2268A-69A, 1966.
                                                            154
A study involving 89 fifth-grade pupils of the effect on attention of fifteen audio and seventeen visual categories.   A very low relationship was found between "attention," as defined in this study, and learning.

Burns, Paul C.   "Teaching Listening in the Elementary School."   Elementary English 38:11-14, January 1961.
                                                            155
According to the author, the best way to interest teacher-trainees in learning about teaching listening is to give them an advanced level listening test.   Eight-item bibliography.

Burton, Mary.   A Comparison of Hearing and Reading Comprehension of Vocabulary Among High School Seniors.
Master's thesis.   New York: Fordham University, 1943.   Summary: School Review 52:47-50, January 1944.   156
An experiment in which both oral and written vocabulary tests were given to 175 twelfth grade students revealed that the reading of tests was significantly superior to listening to them for both boys and girls.

Bushby, Martha J.   Improving Listening of Third Graders.
Master's thesis.   Union, N. J. :   Newark State College. 1961.   157
Teaching of listening is described.

Butler, Samuel.   "Thought and Language."   Collected Essays, Vol. II.   Shrewsbury Edition of the Works of Samuel Butler, Vol. 19.   (Edited by Henry Festing Jones and A. T. Bartholomew.)   New York: E. P. Dutton, 1925, p. 59-90.   158
Discusses the necessity of a "sayee" as well as a "sayer."

Caarewe, Glendoris and Cantrell, Clara.   "Interrelating

Reading and Listening in Kindergarten Through Grade
Three." Reading and the Language Arts. Proceedings of
the Annual Conference on Reading. Chicago: University
of Chicago Press, 1963. p. 56-59.   159
Listening is important in the early school grades because it is a transitional medium to reading, helps develop
a basic vocabulary, and helps in developing phonics.

Caffrey, John.   "Auding." Review of Educational Research
    25:121-38, April 1955.   160
A review of the research on listening for the years
1952-1954.

------. Auding Ability as a Function of Certain Psy-
    chometric Variables.   Doctoral dissertation.
    Berkeley, Calif. :   University of California, 1953. Sum-
    mary: "Auding Ability at the Secondary Level" Educa-
    tion 75:303-10, January 1955.   161
The construction and validation of the California Auding
Test is described.   The text of the test is not included.   A
correlation of .59 is reported between auding, as measured
by this test, and mental age.   Other correlations are reported.   It was found that the reliability of this test was not
affected when the test was administered by means of a recording.

------. " 'Auding' as a Research Problem." California Jour-
    nal of Educational Research 4:155-61, September 1953.
                                                          162
The author advocates the use of the term "auding" to
embrace the hearing act, the listening act and the comprehending act.   Specific suggestions for 19 possible areas for
research in listening are made.

------. "The Establishment of Auding-Age Norms." School
    and Society 70:310-12, November 2, 1949. Digest:
    Education Digest 15(5):18-20, January 1950.   163
Basic problems in establishing satisfactory means of
evaluating listening are: elimination of irrelevant factors as
items to be measured by test, such as attention; isolation of
test items from reading factors; and the standardization of
methods of presentation to nullify the variations which occur
when different speakers present the same test materials.

------. "An Introduction to the Auding Concept." Education
    70:234-39, December 1949.   164
An explanation of the term "auding" is given together

with an argument favoring its use over "listening." The relationship and parallels of reading and listening are discussed.

Calearo, C. and Lazzaroni, A. "Speech Intelligibility in Relation to the Speed of the Message." Laryngoscope 67:
410-19, May 1957.   165
Lists of short significant sentences at three speeds,
145, 250, and 350 wpm, were used. Three methods of compression were used: 1. using a speaker having exceptional
possibilities of accelerating his speaking rate; 2. transfer-
ring the recording to tape which could be rotated at different
speeds; and 3. employing a special apparatus which allows
a direct acceleration of the message without alteration of
frequency. The results showed no difference.
"In a normal subject the impairment of discrimination
due to an increase of the syllabic rate per minute is almost
completely neutralized by a simultaneous slight increase of
intensity."
Aged subjects and those having hearing defects had difficulty with speeded speech, but they also had difficulty with
normal speeds.
"We reiterate the conclusion that the study of the articu-
late scores as a function of the speed of delivery of speech
may be useful for an investigation of the superior aditory
functions, showing trouble in the elaboration and identification of the message which may escape attention with the usu-
al methods of examination. An increase in the speed of delivery of speech puts a strain on the centers and the effort
of discrimination is possible only when the superior hearing
mechanisms are unimpaired; therefore, we feel that the accelerated speech test can be adopted in audiological practices and may throw further light on hitherto unknown aspects
of hearing at a superior level."
The experiment was performed in Italy.

Callahan, Gertrude M. "Unit on Listening." Boston: Warren English Project, Boston University School of Education. (Mimeo.) n. d.   166
A comprehensive list of suggested activities suitable for
a teaching unit on listening at the elementary school level.

Calway, Marion Fladstol. The Relative Effects of Instruc-
tion with Narrative and Factual Materials on Listening
Skills. Doctoral dissertation. Minneapolis, Minn.:
University of Minnesota, 1962. Abstract: Dissertation
Abstracts 23:2748-49, 1963.   167

Using 673 fifth and sixth grade pupils as subjects, Calway devised and administered a listening test. She then caused varied types of listening instruction to be given. The results of this instruction were tested using another form of the same listening test. The only significant difference found was on that portion of the test dealing with narrative materials. Here it was found that those pupils instructed in listening to narrations did significantly better than did those who did not receive such instruction.

Campanella, S. Joseph. "Signal Analysis of Speech Time Compression Techniques." Proceedings of the Louisville Conference on Time Compressed Speech, October 19-21, (Edited by Emerson Foulke.) Louisville, Ky. : Center for Rate Controlled Recordings, University of Louisville, 1967. p. 108-14.   168
Three methods of speech compression, simple speed-up, discarding segments, and parametric representation, are clearly described. The last method will probably yield the most satisfactory results although it is the most expensive.

Campbell, Howard Josef. An Analysis of the Ability to Structure Material Auded as a Factor Contributing to Auding Effectiveness. Doctoral dissertation. Berkeley, Calif. : University of California, 1959.   169
Using as subjects 171 college speech students, the author found correlations between scores on the Brown-Carlsen Listening Test and his own test on ability to structure material to be .53. Various other correlations are reported. The text of the structuring test is given.

Campbell, Paul Newell. An Experimental Study of the Retention and Comprehension of Poetry Resulting from Silent Reading and Oral Interpretation. Doctoral dissertation. Los Angeles, Calif. : University of Southern California, 1959. Abstract: Dissertation Abstracts 20: 3426, 1960.   170
In an experiment using 72 college students as subjects, Campbell found that silent reading was significantly superior to oral interpretation for retention. Comprehension was not significantly different.

Canfield, George Robert. "Approaches to Listening Improvement." Elementary English 35:525-28, December 1958.
                                                                171
Necessary for effective instruction in listening are: adequate physical conditions; an experience adjusted to in-

terests and level of the children; understanding and acceptance of experience by the listeners; interspersal of opportunities for self-expression; minimization of auditory and
visual distractions; good rapport; and a variety of types of
listening experiences.

----. A Study of the Effects of Two Types of Instruction on
the Listening Comprehension of Fifth Grade Children.
Doctoral dissertation. Syracuse, N.Y.: Syracuse University, 1960. Abstract: Dissertation Abstracts 21:
2622, 1961. Summary: Elementary School Journal 62:
146-151, December 1961.   172
Using 149 fifth graders as subjects, Canfield reports on
an experiment in which classes taught listening directly and
indirectly made a significantly greater gain in listening, as
measured by the STEP test, than did a group which had no
instruction in listening. Correlations of .60 between listening and reading and of .74 between listening and school
grades are reported. Sample listening lessons are included
in the appendix.

"Can't Talk and Listen Both." Science Newsletter 61:373,
June 14, 1952.   173
A brief comment on the experiments reported by Broad-
bent.

Cantor, Nathaniel. Learning Through Discussion. Buffalo,
N.Y.: Human Relations for Industry, 1951.   174
The importance of active listening in discussions is em-
phasized.

Cantril, Hadley. The Invasion from Mars. Princeton,
N.J.: Princeton University Press. 1940, passim. 175
An account of how Orson Welles' famous radio program
was accepted as fact by many undiscriminating listeners.

Canute, Russell J. An Exploratory Evaluation of Certain
Aspects of the Listening Program as Part of the Study
Skills Course at the University of Wyoming. Doctoral
dissertation. Laramie, Wyo.: University of Wyoming,
1961. Summary: Journal of Educational Research 59:
51-54, October 1965.   176
Using 244 college freshmen as subjects, Canute reports
a significant gain in scores on the Brown-Carlsen listening
test after a one-semester study skills course in which three
somewhat similar but differing methods of teaching listening
were employed. There was no difference as a result of the

varying methods and Canute did not find a significant relationship between listening tests and college grades, although he
reports that the listening test scores, when used in connection with a scholastic aptitude test, served as a predictor of
grades.

"La Capacité d'Ecouter est-elle Mesurable?" Ecole Ontari-
     anne 55:187-89, May-June 1966.   177
     A review of some of the literature on listening research
in the United States. Research in this area, particularly in
evaluation of listening performance, is just beginning. The
importance of the area makes research urgent. (in French.)

Cardozo, Robert. "He Can Listen but He Won't." Elemen-
     tary English 40:165-67, February 1963.   178
     Listening will be promoted by home cooperation with
school and teacher. Efficient listening is necessary for
proper use of audio-visual aids.

Carlson, Evelyn F. "Effective Listening." Chicago Schools
     Journal 30:187-91, March 4, 1949.   179
     The skill of critical listening closely parallels critical
reading. It involves awareness of possible bias, qualifica-
tions for communication, search for color words, determination of whether or not all facts are given, looking for facts
on both sides of an issue, guarding against extravagant
claims, and avoidance of arriving at fixed opinions before
all the information is received.

Carlson, Raymond P. The Effects of Auditory Word Stimuli
     Presented During the Hours of Sleep on the Formation
     and Modification of Word Associates. Doctoral disserta-
     tion. Minneapolis, Minn.: University of Minnesota 1959.
     Abstract: Dissertation Abstracts 20:2140, 1960.   180
     Using 78 college students as subjects, this study found no
learning effect as a result of oral stimuli presented during sleep.

Carlton, Robert L. An Experimental Investigation of the Re-
     lationship Between Personal Value and Word Intelligi-
     bility. Doctoral dissertation. Columbus, Ohio: Ohio
     State University, 1958. Abstract: Dissertation Ab-
     stracts 18:1141, 1958.   181
     It was found, as the result of an experimental study,
that personal values of the listener as well as of the speaker had a significant effect on intelligibility. The Allport-
Vernon Study of Values Scale was used.

Carnegie, Dale. How To Win Friends and Influence People.
New York: Simon and Schuster, 1936, passim.   182
"Be a good listener . . ."

Carpenter, Edith Caryl. A Comparative Study of Listeners'
Reactions to Speech and Voice Disorders. Master's
thesis. Columbus, Ohio: Ohio State University, 1964.
                                                  183
Groups, untrained in speech correction, listened to
taped speech by persons with a variety of moderate to severe speech defects.   Their ratings of degree of pleasant-
ness were consistent.

Carpenter, Helen M. "Learning to Listen." Instructor 75
(4):26-27+, December 1965.   184
Advocates teaching listening in the way research has
shown reading is effectively taught.

Carroll, John B. "Problems of Measuring Speech Rate."
Proceedings of the Louisville Conference on Time Compressed Speech, October 19-21, 1966. Louisville, Ky.:
Center for Rate Controlled Recordings, University of
Louisville, 1967. p. 88-94.   185
Speech rate is a critical variable in speech compression.
Measuring is complicated. The input rate before compression is crucial. Reporting a rate as x units of speech per
unit of time is not the same as reporting y units of time
per unit of speech output, as the arithmetic mean of the latter is not comparable to the arithmetic mean of the former.
The geometric mean must be used for comparison.
Syllables per unit of time are more satisfactory than
wpm, due to the variation in length of words. Even the syllable measure varies with the text.

Carter, Burnham. "How To Use Educational Recordings Effectively." New Outlook for the Blind 56:332-34, November 1962.   186
Interviews with 366 blind, full-time college students revealed that three fourths of them received all their textbook
information aurally. Eighty-five per cent of textbook information for all these students was aural. The principal problem
encountered by the students in listening was that of concentration.   Those students taking notes while listening
achieved higher grades than those who did not do so.

Carter, Raymond E. Listening-Improvement Training Programs in Business and Industry in the United States.

Master's thesis. Lawrence, Kan.: University of Kansas. 1963. Abstract: Program in Organizational Communication. Bulletin No. 1. Lawrence, Kan.: Department of Speech and Drama, University of Kansas, February 1965. Excerpts: Listening: Readings. (Edited by
Sam Duker.) Metuchen, N.J.: Scarecrow Press, 1966.
p. 365-68.   187
A survey of 754 large industrial firms, to which 540
firms responded, revealed that 344 firms had no listening-
improvement programs in existence or in contemplation; 43
firms had no such program but reflected an interest in developing one; 153 firms had some sort of training in listening-improvement. Of the last, 32 had discrete programs of
listening-improvement training; 84 integrated such training
in "Communications" training programs; 41 integrated it with
"Human Relations" training programs; and 63 firms reported
some listening-improvement training in connection with "Conference Leadership" and/or "Executive Development" training
programs. In most cases listening-improvement training
was confined to management personnel. There was a strik-
ing lack of evaluative procedures. The extensive bibliography includes reference to ten films dealing with listening.

Cartier, Francis A. Jr. An Experimental Study of the Effect of Human Interest Factors in Listenability. Doctoral dissertation. Los Angeles, Calif.: University of
Southern California, 1951. Abstract: Speech Monographs 19:114, June 1952. Summary: "Listenability
and Human Interest." Speech Monographs 22:53-57,
March 1955.   188
This study was done to ascertain the effect on listener
comprehension of greater and lesser numbers of "personal
words," as defined by Flesch's readability formula. It was
found that there was little, if any, difference in comprehension.

----. "The Social Context of Listenability Research."
Journal of Communication 2(1):44-47, May 1952.   189
While teaching listening skills is important, it is equally necessary that research be done on listenability so that
choice of language may be made to convey the maximum
possible amount of meaning to untrained audiences.

Caruthers, Helen Post. Elementary School Teachers' Opinions About Listening Compared with Research Findings
and Professional Opinions. Master's thesis. Atlanta,
Ga.: Atlanta University, 1961.   190

Caruthers, Helen Post   53

A comparison is made between 30 teachers' opinions
about principles of listening, as revealed by a questionnaire,
and the opinions found in a number of periodical articles.
In general the teachers agreed that the principles found in
the articles in professional journals were sound.

Carver, Merton E. A Study of Conditions Influencing the
    Relative Effectiveness of Visual and Auditory Presenta-
    tion. Doctoral dissertation. Cambridge, Mass. : Har-
    vard University, 1934. Excerpts: "Listening Versus
    Reading." The Psychology of Radio. (Edited by Hadley
    Cantril and Gordon W. Allport.) New York: Harper,
    1935. Chapter 9, p. 159-80.   191
An excellent review and analysis of 31 previous research studies is included. Using 91 subjects, an elaborate
study was made of the relative merits of auditory and visual
presentations. Results were not definitive.

Casambre, Alejandro Jiminez. The Effects of Certain Vari-
    ables in Informative Speaking on Listener Comprehension.
    Doctoral dissertation. Columbus, Ohio: Ohio State Uni-
    versity, 1962. Abstract: Dissertation Abstracts 23:
    3022-23, 1963.   192
One important finding of an experimental study was that
on immediate and delayed recall tests on the content of a
speech there was no significant difference between a visible
speaker and a taped presentation. The findings also showed
that visual clues aided aural comprehension and retention of
a speech, and that there was no significant difference between auditory and visual modes of testing on immediate recall. However, a significant difference in favor of the visual on delayed recall was found.

Cashman, Mildred Berwick. "Channel L-I-S-T-E-N." Edu-
    cation 82:50-52, September 1961.   193
Mispronunciation by young children may, in some cases,
be a sign of difficulty in listening rather than speech difficulty. Cashman suggests giving listening practice in the elementary grades on three levels: specific concepts without
details; with some detail; and with many details.

Cashman, Paul H. "Techniques in Teaching Listening
    Skills." Reading in Relation to Mass Media. A Report of
    the Fourteenth Conference and Course on Reading.
    Pittsburgh, Pa. : University of Pittsburgh, 1958, p. 49-
    57.   194
Courses in listening are common in colleges and be-

coming so in secondary schools. Proper attitudes must be developed, and the listener must adjust himself to the speaker, the subject, and the occasion.

----. "What Research Tells Us About the Development of Listening Skills." Reading in Relation to Mass Media. A Report of the Fourteenth Conference and Course on Reading. Pittsburgh, Pa. : University of Pittsburgh, 1958. p. 31-42.   195
A review of previous research.

Caskey, Clark Charles. "Listen and Learn." Supervision 23(7):16-19, July 1961.   196
Efficient listening is essential to success as an industrial supervisor. To improve listening skill, read pertinent articles and books, practice listening, learn to be able to repeat what you have listened to, notice the listening habits and techniques of others, improve your own note-taking ability, and select a good location for listening.

Caughran, A. M. The Effect on Language Comprehension of Three Methods of Presentation. Doctoral dissertation. Columbia, Mo. : University of Missouri, 1953. Abstract: Dissertation Abstracts 13:1113, 1953.   197
Material was presented visually, orally, and as a combination of visual and oral to 500 elementary school pupils. Visual-oral was generally most effective. Children with mental ages above 13 did better visually than orally. The opposite was true of children with mental ages of 13 and below.

Cecile, Sister Marie. "Training in Communications: Listening." Catholic Educator 25:260-61, December 1954.
                                                            198
There are three steps in listening: 1. preparation- the removal of all distracting agencies; 2. act of listening - absorption; and 3. response. In the secondary school there should be an emphasis on a critical response to information.

Chafe, Warren J. , Solberg, Rona, and Wade, Mary Jane. A Comparison of Imagery Evoked by Silent Reading with Imagery Evoked by Listening in Grades III, VI, VI. Master's thesis. Boston: Boston University, 1958.
                                                            199
Using a checklist and personal interviews, two of the authors, using 74 third and fifth grade pupils as subjects, found no significant differences in the amount or kind of

imagery evoked by reading and listening. Solberg, using 38 sixth grade pupils as subjects, found that auditory imagery was higher in silent reading, that pictures were clearer from listening and pictures were more blurred from silent reading.

Chall, Jeanne S. and Dial, Harold E. "Predicting Listener Understanding and Interest in Newscasts." Educational Research Bulletin 27:141-53+, September 1948.   200
The difficulty level of radio newscasts may be measured validly by use of the Dale-Chall and Flesch formulae developed for the measurement of reading difficulty.

Chapman, J. Crosby. "A Group Intelligence Examination Without Prepared Blanks." Journal of Educational Research 2:277-86, December 1920.   201
An orally administered test which can be scored by having the subjects exchange papers. Correlations are: Otis and Haggerty Intelligence Tests .63; the author's test and Otis .68; and the author's test and Haggerty .61.

Chapman, W.D. 'Speech Compression by Tape Loop and by Computer." Proceedings of the Louisville Conference on Time Compressed Speech October 19-21, 1966. (Edited by Emerson Foulke.) Louisville, Ky. : Center for Rate Controlled Recordings; University of Louisville, 1967. p. 98-107.   202
A compression method described in detail. The desirability and possibility of selective compression by deleting only those portions of the speech signal that do not contribute to the apparent pace of speech are discussed.

Chase, Stuart. Power of Words. New York: Harcourt-Brace, 1953, passim. Excerpt: "Are You Listening." Readers Digest 81(488):80-82, December 1962.   203
Sympathetic and critical listening are extremely important. Listening involves literal interpretation as well as interpretation of the speaker's intentions.

Cheatham, Paul G. A Comparison of the Visual and Auditory Senses as Possible Channels for Communication. Air Force Technical Report, No. 5919, 1955.   204
Bibliography contains 139 items.

Chenette, Louis F. "Perceptive Listening - Key to Improved Performance." School Musician 37(2):58-59, October 1965.   205
The quality of choirs and instrumental performers is

raised when participants listen for resonance, intonation, timbre, and expression. Such listening must be purposeful.

Childers, Dorothy Bell. A Study of Listening with Third
    Grade Children. Master's thesis. Columbus, Ohio:
    Ohio State University, 1963.   206
    Listening lessons were given to 35 third grade children
during one school year. There was a significantly greater
gain in listening and reading ability in this group than in a
control group. California Achievement Tests were used to
measure reading and the STEP test to measure listening. No
correlation was found between listening improvement and reading improvement.

Chisholm, Francis P. "A New Kind of Comprehension
    Test." Journal of Communication 5:83-88, Fall 1955.
                                                                 207
    The relation between what the speaker says and what the
listener hears is not a one-to-one symmetrical relationship.
A test is proposed in which the subject is asked to state
how he thinks the speaker would answer a question, as well
as how he himself would answer it.

Christensen, Gordon V. A Study of Listening Intelligibility
    Skills of Honor Students Versus Probation Students at
    Brigham Young University. Master's thesis. Provo,
    Utah: Brigham Young University, 1961.   208
    Using Black's Multiple Choice Intelligibility Test, 27
word items were presented by tape at four degrees of intensity. Matched groups of honor and probationary students
showed no statistically significant difference in the listening
skills involved.

Chrobak, Jean Frew. An Investigation of Means by Which
    Accuracy in Listening Can Be Measured at the First
    Grade Level. Master's thesis. Morgantown, West Va. :
    West Virginia University, 1964.   209
    A test intended to measure comprehensive, concentra-
tive, and critical listening was administered to 156 pupils in the
ninth month of the school year. The test consisted of short
multiple choice questions which followed the reading of a
one-sentence statement. Answers were drawn by the pupils
with colored crayons on the answer sheet boxes. The results were skewed because most pupils scored rather high.
No comparison was made with any other test results or with
observations of the children.

Clark, Genevieve. It's Fun to Listen. New York: Van-
      tage, 1953.   210
   A charming account of experiences in listening to various sounds of nature.

Clark, Kathryn B. "Make Shorthand Students Better Lis-
      teners." Business Education World 38(9):15+, May
      1958.   211
   A knowledge of shorthand facilitates note-taking except
when indiscriminate note-taking interferes with selecting the
important ideas as well as the principles, facts, and appeals
being presented.
   The importance of knowing how to listen in business employment is stressed in connection with careful, attentive following of instructions.

Clymer, Theodore. "New Ventures in the Teaching of Read-
      ing." National Elementary Principal 43(4):26-30, Febru-
      ary 1964.   212
   In a national survey by the University of Minnesota, the
most important skill needed in the kindergarten reading
readiness program was reported to be listening.

Cochran, John Rodney. Validated Batteries of Speaking and
      Listening Predictors. Doctoral dissertation. Salt Lake
      City, Utah: University of Utah, 1959. Abstract: Dis-
      sertation Abstracts 20:3427, 1960.   213
   Basing his report on factor analysis procedures, the author reports that tests for auditory retention and speech
sound discrimination developed in this study were effective
predictors of listening ability. Text of these tests is given.

Cody, Mother M. Irene. An Investigation of the Relative
      Effectiveness of Four Modes of Presenting Meaningful
      Material to Twelfth-Grade Students. Doctoral disserta-
      tion. New York: Fordham University, 1962. Abstract:
      Dissertation Abstracts 23:1270-71, 1962.   214
   Using 1200-word biographical sketches of famous personalities, the author found that 132 twelfth grade students had
better comprehension when reading was employed; that the
results of simultaneous reading and listening were better
than listening alone; and that listening with note-taking was
more effective than listening without taking notes.

Coffey, Sister M. Sylvester. "The Use of Radio as a Lis-
      tening Project in the School." Projects of the Fourth
      Workshop in Basic Communications, University of Den-

ver, 1946. (Edited by Edwin L. Levy.) Denver, Colo. :
University of Denver Press, 1946, p. 81-89.   215
The use of radio and recordings is recommended as a
way to guide the improvement of listening processes of
school pupils.

Coffman, William E. and Stodola, Quentin. The Effect of
   Conditions of Administration on Listening Comprehension
   Test Scores. College Entrance Examination Board Research and Development Reports, Research Bulletin RB-
   61-4. Princeton, N. J. : Educational Testing Service,
   1961.   216
   The STEP Listening Test was administered to 252 college students divided, at random, into 12 classes. The
method of administration varied. In some classes, the
reader of the script was in the same room, some viewed the
reader on closed circuit TV, and some received only the
sound from the TV. There were significant differences in
mean test scores among classes with different readers, but
the different media of administration made no significant difference in performance.

Cohen, John. Humanistic Psychology. London: George Allen & Unwin, 1958. p. 139-55.   217
   In committee work, receptivity to novel suggestions
would be improved by training in listening. This presupposes an alertness to one's preconceptions, prejudices, and
stereotypes.

----, Hansel, C. E. M. , and Sylvester, J. D.   "Mind
   Wandering." British Journal of Psychology 47:61-62,
   February 1956.   218
   One hundred and sixty-five subjects listened to music
and to lecturing. They were directed to push a bell-button
whenever they "became aware that their attention had returned to the music or the lecture." The lecture group
averaged four bell pushes in 40 minutes. The number was
higher for music. Fourteen per cent did not press the bell-
button and four individuals pushed the button 20 or more
times. Classes of hearing and of deaf children were observed for lapses of attention through a one-way screen.
The lapse rate was one per minute and higher.

Cohen, Rose G. Listen and Learn. Master's thesis.
   Newark, N. J. : New Jersey State Teachers College at
   Newark, 1956.   219
   Teaching of listening is described.

Cole, Sister Mary Ethel. The Effect of Intensive Instruction
in Listening Comprehension with Different Intelligence
Groups in Grade One. Master's thesis. Milwaukee,
Wisc.: Cardinal Stritch College, 1961.   220
Using a group of 141 first-grade pupils in four classes
as subjects, the author found that a 15-minute daily listening lesson for some groups resulted in substantially greater
improvement for them in both reading and listening compared
to the reading and listening improvement of groups having
only conventional language arts instruction.

Coladarci, A. P. and others. "Effect of Prestige Symbols on
'Critical Listening' Behavior." California Journal of
Educational Research 5:202-08+, November 1954.   221
Using 169 high school seniors as subjects, the experi-
menter found that the students reported understanding a
speech better when the speaker was identified as a col-
lege president than when he was identified as a Parent-
Teacher Association member.

Collins, Beverly Nann. A Study of the Role of Listening in
Elementary Language Arts Education. Master's thesis.
Ithaca, N. Y.: Cornell University, 1958.   222
An excellent summary of the literature on procedures
for teaching listening at the elementary school level.

Collins, Helene I. A Program for the Improvement of Auding Skills in a Fifth Grade Classroom. Master's thesis.
New Britain, Conn.: Central Connecticut State College,
1966.   223
Listening was taught for 20 minutes daily for eight
weeks to 25 pupils. Ideas stressed were finding main concepts, identifying sequence, noting significant details, detecting author's purposes, and making inferences. STEP was
used as a pre- and post-test. With only three exceptions,
none of the pupils made significant gains on the post-test.
There was no control group.

Comfort, Iris Tracy. "How to Get Your Child to Listen."
Parents' Magazine 38(1):46-47+, January 1963. Digest:
Family Digest 18(8):63-68, May 1963.   224
Young children tend to be good listeners when speech is
tailored to their needs and to the occasion.

Commins, W. D. "A Factor in Language Ability." Journal
of Educational Research 21:77-78, January 1930.   225
From data presented the author concludes that the abil-

ity to reproduce material presented auditorially may be related to general language ability quite apart from any relationship to general intelligence.

Commission on the English Curriculum of the National Coun-
cil of Teachers of English. The English Language Arts.
New York: Appleton-Century-Crofts, 1952. Chapter 14,
"The Program in Listening," p. 328-47. Bibliography,
"Teaching of Listening," p. 457-58.   226
A thoughtful and comprehensive chapter on the importance
of the role of listening in the classroom.

----. The English Language Arts in the Secondary School.
New York: Appleton-Century-Crofts, 1956. Chapter 8,
"Developing Competence in Listening." p. 251-92.   227
This discussion of the place of listening in high school
deals with the impact of radio and television research on listening, the values of the listening ear, listening as a total
school problem, listening as a study procedure, listening as
an aesthetic experience, and the evaluation of a developmental listening program.

----. Language Arts for Today's Children. New York:
Appleton-Century-Crofts, 1954. Chapter 4, "Listening,"
p. 71-105.   228
This thought-provoking discussion of the role of listening
in the elementary classroom deals with reasons for teaching
listening, the nature of listening, conditions fostering effective listening, developmental levels in listening, classroom
activities involving listening, and ways of improving listening
ability.

Communicating in the Air Force. Air Force, Air Science,
Vol. 3. Montgomery Alabama: Air University,
AFROTC, 1953.   229
Listening consists of preparation for listening, the listen-
ing process itself, and the post-listening period, which
should emphasize immediate recall to aid retention.

Conboy, William Andrew. A Study of the Retention of Speech
Content as Measured by Immediate and Delayed Recall.
Doctoral dissertation. Evanston, Ill. : Northwestern
University, 1954. Abstract: Dissertation Abstracts 14:
2434-35, 1954; Speech Monographs 22:143, June 1955.
                                                            230
Using 354 college students as subjects, the author re-
ports that immediate recall of a taped persuasive speech,

as measured by written reproduction of the speech, showed
a loss of half the content. Metaphorical expressions, highly effective quotations, human interest features, and highly
affective materials were most often recalled. The results
of the study indicate that a process of warping or modifying of
the speech occurred during the immediate recall by reproduction. After a ten-day delay there was less recall but the
correlation between immediate and delayed recall was high.
The author concludes that the listener's bias has an important effect on recall.

Condon, Edwyna Forsyth. An Analysis of the Differences
   Between Good and Poor Listeners in Grades Nine, Elev-
   en, and Thirteen. Doctoral dissertation. Lawrence,
   Kan.: University of Kansas, 1965. Abstract: Dissertation Abstracts 26:3106, 1965.   231
The Brown-Carlsen was administered to 874 secondary
school pupils. Good readers performed significantly better
on this test, as did those who had completed speech units in
their speech courses and those who were more active in
extra-curricular activities. No significant difference was
found between the sexes. The upper quartile on the Brown-
Carlsen was superior to the lower quartile in grade point
average, English grades, and intelligence.

Conlon, Sister Therese Ellen. An Experimental Study of
   the Effects of Training in Listening Comprehension Skills
   on Reading Comprehension with Retarded Readers in the
   Third Grade. Master's thesis. Chicago: De Paul University, 1959.   232
Listening instruction given to a group of third grade, retarded readers appeared to have no effect on reading skills.

Cook, Joseph W. Improving Learning Through Teaching Listening Techniques. Master's thesis. Logan, Utah:
   Utah State Agricultural College, 1954.   233
Using 60 high school junior year English students as subjects, the author reports no difference in comprehension of
oral passages between a group given a short explanation of
listening techniques and a group not given such an explanation.

Coomaraswamy, Ananda K. "The Bugbear of Literacy."
   Asia 44:53-57, February 1944.   234
It is a false notion that a culture exists only where there
is literacy. Many cultures transmit knowledge, literature,
and heritage orally and do not see values in western "liter-

acy." 'Our blind faith in literacy. . .becomes a prime factor in the spiritual impoverishment of all the 'backward'
people whom we propose to 'civilize.' "

Cooper, J. Louis. "The Effect of Training in Listening on
    Reading Achievement." Vistas in Reading. International
    Reading Association Conference Proceedings, Vol. 11,
    Part I, 1967. (Edited by J. Allen Figurel.) Newark,
    Del.: International Reading Association, 1965. p. 431-
    35.   235
    Three   pre-taped listening exercises were taught to 74
eighth-grade pupils for nine weeks. The STEP test was
used as a pre- and post-measure. The experimental group
made significantly greater gains in both reading and listening
than did the control group. Both groups, however, made
gains in both reading and listening.

Corey, Stephen M.   "The Efficacy of Instruction in Note Tak-
    ing." Journal of Educational Psychology 26:188-94,
    March 1935.   236
    Equated groups of college freshmen, one of which was
given instruction by lecture on note-taking techniques, did
not show a significant difference in comprehension of a lecture.

----. "Learning from Lectures Versus Learning from
    Readings." Journal of Educational Psychology 25:459-70,
    September 1934.   237
    Data gathered in an experimental study showed that for
college students: 1. Immediate recall was better for material read than for material heard in a lecture, 2. On delayed recall there was little difference, 3. There is a
tendency for students scoring in the highest quartile on psychological tests to do relatively better on reading than on
lecture tests.

----. "The Teachers Out-Talk the Pupils." School Review
    48:745-52, December 1940. Reprinted in Listening:
    Readings. (Edited by Sam Duker.) Metuchen, N.J.:
    Scarecrow Press, 1966. p. 81-89.   238
    A six-day stenographic record of high school classroom
discussions projected to a one-year period revealed that
teachers asked 35,000 questions, compared to only 4,000
asked by pupils.

Corson, John J.   "Management - Tongue Tied, Deaf, and
    Blind?" Advanced Management 11:101-04, September

1946.   239
The need for two-way communication in industry.

Cortright, Rupert L.   A Technique for Measuring Perception Differences for Radio and Direct Audience Speaking.
Doctoral dissertation.   Ann Arbor, Michigan: University of Michigan, 1935.   240
In an experiment using college students as subjects, the
author found that passages delivered by radio and personally
delivered material yielded substantially equal comprehension
scores.

Cotton, Jack C.   'Syllabic Rate: A New Concept in the
Study of Speech Rate Variation." Speech Monographs
3:112-17, September 1936.   241
Words-per-minute is an unsatisfactory measure in scientific speech study.   Syllable rate is better, but there is
also a great difference in duration among syllables.

Coulter, V. C.   "Reading and Listening." Education 65:375-
82, February 1945.   242
The author advocates instruction in critical listening and
reading by teaching skills designed to facilitate the recognition of facts and rumor, authority, attributed motives, subjective words, passives, abstract words, assumptions behind
statements, predictions, analytic thinking, and what is not
said.   He states that training should be in evaluation rather
than in the development of thoughtless skeptics.

Cox, Marion Monroe.   'The Relationship of Speech and
Reading in an Elementary School Program." Speech
Teacher 8:211-18, September 1959.   243
The author advocates giving the teaching of listening the
same emphasis that is given to reading.   An excellent circle
chart illustrating the interrelationships of the various language arts is included.

Coyne, John Martin.   Prestige Suggestion Influences in Communication Analysis.   Doctoral dissertation.   Stanford,
Calif.:   Stanford University, 1956.   Abstract: Dissertation Abstracts 16:1955, 1956.   244
Using 236 high school seniors as subjects, Coyne reports that more meaning was attributed to an intrinsically
meaningless speech when it was identified as being made by
a low-prestige speaker (a restaurant cook) than when it was
identified as the product of a high-prestige speaker (a university instructor) or by an unidentified person.   The author

suggests that the subjects may find failure to understand a
high-prestige speaker more acceptable than failure to understand a low-prestige speaker.

Cramer, H. Leslie. "The Intelligibility of Time-Compressed
    Speech." Proceedings of the Louisville Conference on
    Time-Compressed Speech, October 19-21, 1966. (Edited
    by Emerson Foulke.) Louisville, Ky.: Center for Rate
    Controlled Recordings, University of Louisville, 1967.
    p. 126-48.   245
    Ninety-eight short (five to seven words) sentences from
the Harvard University Psycho-Acoustic Laboratory Test
were presented at compressed speech rates of 465, 597, 663,
730, 862, and 930 wpm. The sampling interval was more
significant in terms of intelligibility than the discard interval. The optimum sampling interval had a relationship to
the pitch period of the speaker's voice. Intelligibility at
930 wpm was between 20 per cent and 40 per cent, while at
465 wpm it was 80 per cent. The experiment differed from
previous studies in that intelligibility had previously been
tested only with compressed lists of single words, while only
overall comprehension had been tested in compressed connected speech.

Crane, Forrest F. "Does He Listen? Do You?" Life In-
    surance Courant 61(3):17+, March 1956. Reprinted in
    Listening: Readings. (Edited by Sam Duker.) Metuchen,
    N.J.: Scarecrow Press, 1966. p. 394-98.   246
    Good listening is a key to selling life insurance. If a
prospect makes objections, he proves that he is listening to
the presentation. The prospect should be listened to. We
can train ourselves to be good listeners by constant practice.

Crawford, C.C. "The Correlation Between College Lecture
    Notes and Quiz Papers." Journal of Educational Re-
    search 12:282-91, November 1925.   247
    A content-analysis of the lecture notes and quizzes of
211 students showed that with respect to specific information,
"taking notes does not guarantee its being recalled at the time
of the quiz but failure to take notes on it very greatly de-
creases its chances of being recalled."

Crawford, C. DeLisle. Critical Thinking and Personal Val-
    ues in a Listening Situation. Doctoral dissertation.
    New York: New York University, 1956. Abstract: Dis-
    sertation Abstracts 19:1845, 1959.   248
    Using 89 college students as subjects and employing the

Allport Vernon Lindsay Study of Values Test and the Watson-Glaser Critical Thinking Appraisal, the author reports that when a change was made from reading to listening there was a significant decrement in critical thinking.

"Creativity in Listening." Instructor 71:3+, October 1961.
249
    Listening is not in itself creative. It can be either dullness personified or an exciting springboard for other activities. The teacher controls the quality by setting a proper mood. Environment makes a difference; for example, an overheated room is not conducive to good listening. Listening instruction and experiences should be planned to be as important as any other part of the language arts program.

Crink, Cedric L. and Buntley, Arline. "Learn to Listen."
    Grade Teacher 72(3):51+, March, 1955.   250
Nine kinds of listening that should be taught in the elementary school are listed: casual, conversational, background, appreciative, creative, explanatory, interrogative, concentrated, and critical.

Crook, Frances E. "Interrelationships Among a Group of
    Language Arts Tests." Journal of Educational Research
    51:305-11, December 1957.   251
A battery of tests was administered to 141 tenth-grade pupils. Included were tests of mental ability, language ability, reading comprehension and study skills, as well as the Brown-Carlsen Listening Test. Correlations between all tests and sub-tests are reported. Transmittive and receptive skills in communication tend to form two separate clusters.

Crosby, Muriel. "Interrelationships of Reading and the Other Language Arts." Reading and the Language Arts.
    Proceedings of the Annual Conference on Reading. Chicago: University of Chicago Press, 1963. p. 23-30.
252
Until the relationships between oral and written forms of language are clearly comprehended by the teacher, and until the mutually supportive function of listening, speaking, reading, and writing skills is understood, it is unlikely that a child will reach his full potential in any one of them, particularly in reading.

Cross, M.A. "The Art of Listening." Textile World 109
    (5):119+, May 1959.   253

Poor listening habits include fake listening, being a dubious listener more intent on finding flaws than in listening to what is really said, and being a tired listener who is most concerned with the ending of a discussion. Undivided attention, a proper setting, and a spirit of empathy are needed for good listening.

Cullen, Stanley R. "Teamwork and Productivity." Journal of Communication 1(2):5-11, November 1951.   254
Effective two-way communication between employer and employee meets the needs of the individual worker in industry by giving him the chance to be heard.

Curtis, Alberta. "The Reliability of a Report on Listening Habits." Journal of Applied Psychology 23:127-30, February 1939.   255
It is reported that in a survey of radio listening habits only 65 per cent of those interviewed made the same statements during a second interview.

Cypreansen, Lucile. "Listening as a Skill." Childhood Education 37:268-70, February 1961.   256
Nineteen-item bibliography.

Dahle, Thomas L. "An Evaluation of Communication Skills Training." Journal of Communication 9:127-30, September 1959.   257
A survey of 435 Michigan State University graduates revealed 31 who found their training in listening to have been the most helpful part of their training while 129 found it the least helpful. Only 11 were impressed the most favorably by their training in listening while 48 found it the least favorable part of their communication skills training.

----. An Objective and Comparative Study of Five Methods of Transmitting Information to Business and Industrial Employees. Doctoral dissertation. Lafayette, Ind.: Purdue University, 1953. Summary: Speech Monographs 21(1):21-28, March 1954.   258
A survey showed that a combination of written and oral communication was the most effective means of communication in industrial situations. Oral, written, bulletin board, and the grapevine were decreasingly effective in that order.

Dale, Carol. A Study of Listening Instruction and Comprehension of Ninth Grade Students of Donnell Junior High School in Findlay, Ohio. Master's thesis. Bowling

Green, Ohio: Bowling Green State University, 1965. 259
Six 55-minute lessons on listening, which are described
in detail, were given to 43 pupils. On the Brown-Carlsen,
used as a pre- and post-test, substantial gains were made,
but they were not significantly greater than the gains made
by a control group.

Dale, Edgar. Audio Visual Methods in Education. Revised
Edition. New York: Dryden Press, 1954, p. 278-79
and 294-95.   260
To teach listening effectively it is necessary to regard
communication as sharing, to earn the right to speak by listening, to create a mood or disposition to speak, to make the
classroom a place in which listening or not listening matters
to the student, to know what others are saying, to move
from the simple to the complex, to teach evaluation of logic
of a speech, and to teach critical listening.

----. "Learning by Listening." The Newsletter, Bureau of
Educational Research, Ohio State University 16(2): 1-4,
November 1950.   261
Good taste is essential to good listening. Good listening
cannot be secured by command and is best fostered when the
teacher himself is a good listener.

----. "Why Don't We Listen?" The Newsletter, Bureau of
Educational Research, Ohio State University 22(5):1-4,
February 1957. Also in: Alabama School Journal 83:4-
5+, February 1966; Georgia Educational Journal 57:10,
December 1963.   262
A listener must become involved if he is to listen well,
but speakers can influence good listening if they use good
practices. Much poor listening is caused by speakers who
are not plainly heard.

----. "Why Don't We Listen?" The Newsletter, Bureau of
Educational Research, Ohio State University 28(6):1-3,
March 1963.   263
Sometimes people do not listen to a speaker because
they cannot hear him, due, for example, to poor seating ar-
rangements. Another reason is that they do not become involved. Several techniques for the improvement of listening
in schools and colleges are suggested.

Dance, Frank E. X.   "Review of 'The Role of Listening in
Management.' " Speech Teacher 10:321, November 1961.
                                                                  264

A review of a taped lecture about listening by Ralph G. Nichols.

Daniels, J. T. and Hinds, George L. An Introductory Study
    of Identification Reactions in Reading, Writing, Speaking,
    and Listening. Master's thesis. Denver, Col. : Uni-
    versity of Denver, 1946.   265
    This study was undertaken from a general semanticist's
viewpoint. It is based on returns from a questionnaire given
to college freshmen in which blocks to effective use of communication were investigated. Findings were inconclusive.

Darley, Frederic L. A Normative Study of Oral Reading
    Rate. Master's thesis. Iowa City, Iowa: State Univer-
    sity of Iowa, 1940.   266
    Two hundred speech students were asked to read three
passages aloud, as if they were reading to a small group.
The passages were monosyllabic, average, and polysyllabic.
Each contained 300 words, but the number of syllables were
300, 440, and 660 respectively. Mean rate in wpm was 200,
166, and 115 respectively and in syllables per minute 200,
251, and 253. There was no significant difference between
sexes, and correlations with speed of reading were: for silent reading .24, and for reading comprehension .14.

Davis, Carl J. and Nolan, Carson Y. "A Comparison of the
    Oral and Written Methods of Administering Achievement
    Tests." International Journal for the Education of the
    Blind 10:80-82, March 1961.   267
    The oral administration of the Stanford Achievement Test
to blind children in grades five to nine yielded higher scores
than the administration of the test in braille. The differences were statistically significant only at the fifth and
seventh grade levels, which were the lowest levels to which
the intermediate and advanced level tests were administered.

Davis, H. , Davis, P. A. , Loomis, A. L. , Harvey, E. N. ,
    and Hobart, G. "Electrical Reactions of the Human
    Brain to Auditory Stimulation During Sleep." Journal of
    Neuro-Physiology 2:500-14, November 1939.   268
    The brain of a sleeping person makes electrical re-
sponses to auditory stimuli even when the person does not
awaken.

Dawson, Mildred A. and Zollinger, Marian. Guiding Lan-
    guage Learning. Yonkers, N. Y. : World Book, 1957.
    Chapter 7, "Helping Children to Listen Effectively," p.

Dawson, Mildred A. and Zollinger, Marian   69

160-92.   269
    The authors suggest, as means for developing more ef-
fective listening on the part of pupils, that the classroom atmosphere be relaxed, comfortable, and quiet, and thus conducive to listening; that the teacher take advantage during
the day of opportunities for listening; that children sense a
suitable purpose for listening; that pupils be led to expect
meaning whenever they listen; that pupils be prepared for
what they are about to hear; that long periods of listening
be broken up by other activities; that the occasion for listening suit the circumstances and the maturity level of the children; that pupils be guided in evaluation of what they hear;
that opportunities be arranged for the reproduction of the material listened to; and that children set up standards for effective listening.

----. "Interrelationships between Speech and Other
    Language Arts Areas." National Conference on
    Research in English. Interrelationships Among the Lan-
    guage Arts. Chicago: National Council of Teachers of
    English, 1954, p. 23-33. Also in Elementary English
    31:223-33, April 1954.   270
    A review of previous studies. The emphasis is on the
responsibility of the speaker to speak clearly and in a well-
organized manner.

----. "Learning to Listen." Language Arts Notes Number
    3, Yonkers, N. Y. : World Book, n. d.   271
    Conversational and courteous listening can be helped by
discussing ways of recognizing signs of inattention, setting
standards of courteous listening and conversations, and by
joint teacher-pupil evaluation.

----. "Listening Is Important." Instructor 65(9):31, May
    1956.   272
    The importance of developing listening skills in learning
to read and write is emphasized. It is advocated that oral
directions be given only once.

----.   "The Role of Reading in Relation to
    Other Areas of Communication." New Frontiers in
    Reading. International Reading Association Conference
    Proceedings, Vol. 5, 1960. (Edited by J. Allen Figu-
    rel.) New York: Scholastic Magazines, 1960. p. 156-
    60.   273
    Reading serves as a check on listening as well as a sup-
plement to listening. Reading seems to improve listening.

Increasing the reading vocabulary helps the listening vocabulary. Listening is better than reading for getting main points for younger pupils and for older slow learners, while reading is better than listening for getting details for advanced pupils and for bright pupils.

Day, Phyllis Winifred. The Construction of a Workbook to Develop Specific Skills in Listening. Master's thesis. Boston: Boston University, 1955.   274
Four units with exercises are included: 1. Why do you listen? 2. How well do you listen? 3. Do you think about what you hear? 4. Do you enjoy what you hear?

Day, Willard F. and Beach, Barbara R. "A Survey of the Research Literature Comparing the Visual and Auditory Presentation of Information." A. F. Technical Report No. 5921, November 1950. Excerpts: Listening: Readings. (Edited by Sam Duker.) Metuchen, N. J.: Scarecrow Press, 1966. p. 401-05.   275
A review and analysis of 34 major studies.

De Boer, John J. "Some Sociological Factors in Language Development." National Conference on Research in English. Child Development and the Language Arts. Chicago: National Council of Teachers of English, 1953, p. 6-16.   276
At the kindergarten level, upper class children tend to listen to each other and comment on each other's speech more than lower class children do.

----, Kaulkers, Walter V. , and Miller, Helen Rand. Teaching Secondary English. New York: McGraw-Hill, 1951, p. 197-203.   277
The difficulty with typical instructional situations in schools is that most listening is compulsory, most listening takes place only when the teacher speaks, and little help is given pupils in learning to listen efficiently.

de Hoop, Wietse. Effects and Interaction Effects of Speaking Rate, Visual Limitation and Intelligence Level on Aural Acquisition and Retention of Sentences. Doctoral dissertation. Athens, Georgia: University of Georgia, 1965. Abstract: Dissertation Abstracts 26:3752-53, 1966.
                                                      278
Fourteen visually limited (10/ 70 or less) children between seven and thirteen who were mentally retarded (I. Q. 60 to 88), and fourteen who were normal (I. Q. 89+), as well as two similar groups of 24 normally-sighted children, some

of whom were mentally retarded and some normal, were
used as subjects. They listened to sentences of 20 words
containing 23 phonetic syllables. The original speed was
175 wpm. It was then compressed to 210, 245, and 280
wpm. The 280 wpm rate resulted in significantly less acquisition and retention than the other rates. The 210 wpm
rate was most favorable, though not on a two-week delayed
recall test. The visually limited were significantly better
than the normally-sighted at 210 and 245 wpm. The children
of normal intelligence were significantly better than were the
mentally retarded, except at the 280 wpm rate, where no difference was observed.

----. "Effects and Interaction Effects of Speaking Role;
   Visual Limitation and Intelligence Level on Aural Acquisition and Retention of Sentences." Proceedings of the
   Louisville Conference on Compressed Speech, October
   19-21, 1966. (Edited by Emerson Foulke.) Louisville,
   Ky.: Center for Rate Controlled Recordings, University of Louisville, 1967. p. 115-125.   279
   Two groups of 38 pupils between seven and fourteen
years old, one visually handicapped, the other normally-
sighted. Fourteen in each group were mentally retarded.
Subjects listened to four sentences of 23 phonetic syllables at
175, 210, 245, and 280 wpm respectively. There was little
acquisition at 280 wpm. Immediate and two-day retention were
better at 175 and 210 wpm but after two weeks there was no difference between rates of 175, 210, and 245 wpm. The visually
limited were better than the sighted at 210 and 245 wpm. The
performance of the mentally retarded was lower at all speeds.

----. "Listening Comprehension of Cerebral Palsied and
   Other Crippled Children as a Function of Two Speaking
   Rates." Exceptional Children 31:233-40, January 1965.
                                                    280
   In an experiment involving 63 cerebral palsied children
and 105 children crippled from other causes, the latter group
showed better comprehension of taped material at both 175
wpm and 275 wpm. This difference was significantly smaller at the more rapid rate.

Demos, George and Grant Bruce. "Sharpening Your Communication Skills." Education 87:174-76, November
   1966.   281
   Listening errors causing faulty communication include:
1. not paying attention; 2. thinking about what you want to
say while attempting to concentrate on what is being said by

another;   3. neglecting to ask questions when clarification is needed.

To eliminate listening errors: 1. If your attention wanders, ask pertinent questions to determine the speaker's frame of reference; if your concentration is distracted by other problems, excuse yourself and attempt to deal with these difficulties;   2. whenever you cannot focus on the words being spoken because of what you wish to say yourself, realize that a wise reply must be based upon comprehension of the thought to which you are responding;   3. if you are unable to ask pertinent questions, learn more about the subject; questions are inspired by interest.

Two guiding principles for improving all communication are: 1. talk less, listen more and 2. listen as if you were going to be required to repeat verbatim whatever is being said.

Denny, Terry. "In Grades Four Through Eight." Meeting Individual Differences in Reading, Proceedings of the Annual Conference on Reading. Chicago: University of Chicago Press, 1964, p. 37-40.   282
Teachers should give oral lessons in, for example, arithmetic, to good-listeners-poor-readers. Simultaneously, diagnostic and remedial steps should be underway to improve reading. Children should learn to have different purposes for both reading and listening.

De Sousa, Albert M. The Effect of Training on the Listening Ability of Seventh Grade Students. Doctoral dissertation. New Brunswick, N.J.: Rutgers University, 1967. Abstract: Dissertation Abstracts 28:1729A, 1967.   283
One group of students was given purposive listening instruction in daily lessons for four weeks; another was given lessons in literature, and a third served as a control. The total number of pupils involved was 97. The STEP test was used as a pre- and post-evaluation. No statistically significant difference was found among the three groups.

Deutschman, B. "Are Your Children Good Listeners?" Instructor 63:34, January 1953.   284
The author advocates the use of phonograph records in promoting full auditory participation by children in the classroom.

Devine, Thomas G. The Development and Evaluation of a Series of Recordings for Teaching Certain Critical Lis-

tening Abilities. Doctoral dissertation. Boston: Boston University, 1961. Abstract: Dissertation Abstracts 22:3546-47, 1962.   285
Ten 22-minute lessons were recorded to help ninth-grade pupils to grow in ability to recognize any bias of a speaker, the competence of a speaker to speak on a given topic, speakers' inferences, and to distinguish between emotive and reporting language. Using 445 junior high school pupils as subjects, it was found that groups listening to these recordings over a four-week period showed significantly greater improvement in listening than did those groups which did not hear them. A number of correlations are reported. Tests used included the Brown-Carlsen and the Watson-Glaser.

----. "Listening." Review of Educational Research 37:152-58, April 1967.   286
A review of the research on listening for the years 1964-1966.

----."Listening: The Neglected Dimension of the Reading Program." Improvement of Reading Through Classroom Practice. International Reading Association Conference Proceedings, Vol. 9, 1964. (Edited by J. Allen Figurel.) Newark, Del.: International Reading Association, 1964. p. 119-20.   287
Each of the familiar skills taught in reading has its counterpart in listening.

De Wick, Henry N. "The Relative Effectiveness of Visual and Auditory Presentation of Advertising Material." Journal of Applied Psychology 19:245-64, June 1935.
                                                          288
Aural presentation was found to be more effective than visual in advertising new products, especially on later recall.

Diamond, Rose and Kinney, Richard. "The Place of Speech Comprehension in Academic Study." Proceedings of the Louisville Conference on Time Compressed Speech, October 19-21, 1966. (Edited by Emerson Foulke.) Louisville, Ky.: Center for Rate Controlled Recordings, University of Louisville, 1967. p. 36-54.   289
A one-hour recording compressed to 250 wpm was listened to by 63 visually handicapped students. They scored higher on a comprehension test than did a control group. Another group, which used rapid playback of the compressed

speech, did not do as well. The need for a playback apparatus, which would enable the listener to determine his own
rate of listening, is stressed.

Dias, Earl J. "Three Levels of Listening." English Journal
     36:252-54, May 1947.   290
The author describes three stages of listening instruction used in a high school: listening to short reports by
pupils, listening to difficult passages read by a teacher, and
listening to a "Town Meeting" radio program at home. Assignments and means of evaluation are described.

Diehl, Charles F., White, Richard C., and Burk, Kenneth
     W. "Rate and Communication." Speech Monographs 26:
     229-32, August 1959.   291
Speeded speech, in which only pause time had been altered, was recorded at 145, 172, 160, 135, and 126 wpm.
Using 371 college freshmen as subjects, the experimenters
report that there was no significant difference in comprehension when the speeds were altered.

Dietze, Hildegard. A Study of the Understandability of De-
     fective Speech in Relation to Errors in Articulation.
     Master's thesis. Pittsburgh, Pa.: University of Pitts-
     burgh, 1952.   292
The speech of 25 third, fourth, and fifth grade pupils
with articulatory difficulties was recorded. Using 77 college
psychology students as subjects, the author reports a significant negative correlation between poor articulation and intelligibility.

Dills, Eva. L. Listening the Key to Learning, Including the
     Results of Listening Projects Carried out in the Alfred
     I. DuPont and Faulk Road Schools, Wilmington, Dela-
     ware. Master's thesis. Newark, N.J.: New Jersey
     State Teachers College at Newark, 1955.   293
This is a good review of the importance of listening in
various aspects of social living. A fourth grade program to
improve listening is described. It included reading stories
aloud, practice telephone conversations, following directions,
emphasis on listening on trips, vocabulary practice, socio-
drama to illustrate courtesy, and writing or taping contents
of oral presentations.

Dixon, Norman R. "Listening: Most Neglected of the Lan-
     guage Arts." Elementary English 41:285-88, March 1964
                                                          294

Listening instruction should not be neglected.

"Do You Hear Everything You Listen To?" Administrative
Management 23(7):45, July 1962. 295
Listening is not as much a matter of remembering as of
understanding. The important thing is to get the central
idea. Do not go out of the way to avoid difficult listening.
Do not judge a speaker's possible contribution by his appearance. Do not be distracted by words and phrases that upset
you emotionally. Do not daydream while listening. Take
notes only on main points, and learn to use abbreviated
forms for notes. Hear a person out before planning rebuttal.

Doden, Sheila M. A Listening Presentation with Audio-Visual Aids for Fourth Grade. Master's thesis. De Kalb,
Ill.: Northern Illinois University, 1965. 296
A plan for teaching listening to music with tapes and
transparencies containing a theme chart.

Dolcini, Mary Ellen. Children's Listening Comprehension of
Fictional and Factual Materials at Two Levels of Difficulty. Doctoral dissertation. Berkeley, Calif.: University of California, 1964. Abstract: Dissertation Abstracts 25:6428, 1965. 297
Two hundred eighty-eight fifth graders took the STEP
Listening Test and the California Test of Mental Maturity.
More difficult 2000-word passages resulted in lower listening comprehension than easier ones. Narrative passages
yielded better comprehension than factual passages. A correlation of .72 was found between STEP test results and
comprehension. No significant correlation between comprehension and intelligence.

Donald, Brother. "Listening! It Can Be an Important Vo-
cational Tool." Catholic School Journal 60(9):23, November 1960. 298
The author stresses the need for listening to adolescents
who may be considering a religious vocation. They should
be listened to, not only when the adult feels like listening,
but whenever the youngsters wish to speak.

Doob, Leonard W. Propaganda: Its Psychology and Technique. New York: Holt, 1935. passim. 299
While this book does not deal with listening as such, the
excellent treatment of propaganda is relevant to the student
of critical listening.

Dorval, Bertha Mae. A Descriptive Study of a Series of
    Units on Listening in a Fifth Grade. Master's thesis.
    Boston: Boston University, 1959.   300
    The use of seven units on listening in a fifth grade
classroom with 36 pupils is described. A significant improvement in listening ability as measured by the STEP
Test is reported. The units deal with recall, concentrative
listening, attentive listening, purposeful listening, appreciative listening, listening to determine sequence and listening
to dramatizations.

Dover, C. J. "Listening - The Missing Link in Communica-
    tion." General Electric Review 61(3):7-10+, May 1958.
    Reprinted in Listening: Readings (Edited by Sam Duker.)
    Metuchen, N. J.: Scarecrow Press, 1966. p. 369-81.
                                                          301
    It is reasonable to suppose that deficiencies in listening
skills cause business and industry to lose millions of dollars
annually. Dover lists the following pitfalls of listening comprehension: allowing the details of what you hear to ob-
scure the speaker's central theme; permitting one's mind to
wander to other matters while listening to someone talk;
allowing one's built-in emotional filter to disturb the listening process; allowing a listening environment to interfere
with listening efficiency; letting excessive note-taking dimin-
ish your listening efficiency; overlooking opportunities to improve one's listening through practice; and rejecting what is
heard because it appears to be trivial, completely familiar,
or completely unfamiliar.

Dow, Clyde Walton. The Development of Listening Compre-
    hension Tests for Michigan State College Freshmen.
    Doctoral dissertation. East Lansing, Mich. : Michigan
    State College, 1952. Abstract: Speech Monographs
    20:120, June 1953, and Dissertation Abstracts 13:268-
    69, 1953. Excerpts: Speech Teacher 4:239-46, Novem-
    ber 1955.   302
    Text of test is given. Correlations are reported.

----. "Integrating the Teaching of Reading and Listening
    Comprehension." Journal of Communication 8:118-26,
    Autumn 1958.   303
    Common elements, common principles of teaching and
common questions involved in reading and listening are discussed.

----. "A Listening Comprehension Test as Motivation for

Listening Instruction." Journal of Communication 4:64-
66, Summer 1954.   304
Basic communication students who were beginning a unit
on listening were given a listening test based on a talk on
listening. It was found that the test served not only as an
evaluative device but as a motivational one.

----. "Listening Instruction at Michigan State: 1954-55."
Journal of Communication 5:110-12, Fall 1955.   305
This describes the plans to include listening instruction
in the basic communications program at Michigan State College.

----. (ed.) "Papers Given at a Conference on College
Courses in Communication; Chicago Feb. 28-March 1,
1947." East Lansing, Mich.: Clyde W. Dow, Department of Written and Spoken English, Michigan State College, 1947. (mimeo.)   306
A number of reports on college level communication
courses show very little emphasis on listening.

----. "Testing Listening Comprehension of High School
Seniors and College Freshmen." Speech Teacher 4:239-
46, November 1955.   307
The Dow Listening Test is discussed.

----, and Irvin, Charles E. "How We Teach Listening."
Bulletin of the National Association of Secondary School
Principals 38:137-39, January 1954.   308
Description of the listening phase of the freshman com-
munications program at Michigan State College.

Doyle, Loretta. "Methods for Improving Oral Expression in
Kindergarten Through Grade Three." Oral Aspects of
Reading, Proceedings at the Annual Conference on Reading. Chicago: University of Chicago Press, 1955, p.
36-39.   309
Good speech patterns help listening habits grow. Speakers must be made aware of their responsibility to their listeners. Teachers should not insist that children listen to
ill-prepared speakers or to material beyond their understanding. One of the best aids to oral reading is responsiveness
from the listening group.

Draké, Elizabeth and Enevodsen, Jessie V. "Solving the
Problem of Correct Usage." Elementary English 35:
101-03, February 1958.   310

The use of the tape recorder to develop listening abilities is described.

Drake, Francis E.   "How Do You Teach Listening?" Southern Speech Journal 16:268-71, May 1951.   311
Listening, like speech, cannot be taught solely by lecture. A description of teaching listening in college speech classes. Results include the development of good listening habits and increased attention to the content of speech rather than to the mannerisms of the speaker.

Drieman, G. H. J.   "Differences Between Written and Spoken Language." Acta Psychologica 20:36-57, 1962.   312
Graduate students asked to give oral and written analyses of paintings tended toward greater length in the oral and the use of more polysyllabic words in the written.

----.   "Differences Between Written and Spoken Language." Acta Psychologica 20:78-97, 1962.   313
Graduate students, when interviewed in depth concerning their feelings toward oral and written discourse, agreed that speech provided for greater interaction but that greater care was taken in writing.

Drucker, Peter F.   The New Society.   New York: Harpers, 1950, passim.   314
Listening ability needs to be developed by top and middle management and by the workers in industrial situations if communication is to be effective.

Duker, Sam.   "An Annotated Guide to Audiovisual Aids Available for the Teaching of Listening." Audiovisual Instruction 10:320-22, April 1965.   Abstract: Training Research Abstracts 5(3):5, Fall 1965.   315
Seven films, one filmstrip, three taped courses in listening, one taped speech, two sets of phonograph records, and a recorded speech are listed, described, and evaluated.

----.   "Basics in Critical Listening."   English Journal 51: 565-67, November 1962.   Reprinted in Lee, Florence Henry (Editor.)   Principles and Practices of Teaching in Secondary Schools.   New York: McKay, 1965. p. 174-77.   Reprinted in Listening: Readings.   (Edited by Sam Duker.) Metuchen, N. J. : Scarecrow Press, 1966. p. 263-66.   316
Discusses principles involved in the teaching of critical listening at the high school level.

----. "Doctoral Dissertation on Listening." Journal of
    Communication 13:106-17, June 1963.   317
    Classifies 128 doctoral dissertations on listening.

----. "Goals of Teaching Listening Skills in the Elementary
    School." Elementary English 38:170-74, March 1961.
    Excerpts: Burns, Paul C. and Lowe, Alberta L. The
    Language Arts in Childhood Education. Chicago, Ill. :
    Rand McNally, 1966. p. 48-49. Reprinted in Listening:
    Readings. (Edited by Sam Duker.) Metuchen, N. J. :
    Scarecrow Press, 1966. p. 203-10. Also in: Sartain,
    Harry W. and others. English Is Our Language. Third
    Edition. Boston, Massachusetts: D. C. Heath, 1966.
    p. 54-59.   318
    The ten qualities that should be developed in the elemen-
tary school teaching of listening skills are the art of actually
listening, selective listening, skillful listening, critical lis-
tening, courteous listening, attentive listening, retentive lis-
tening, curious listening, reactive listening and reflective
listening.

----. "How Listening Can Be Taught." Instructor 64(9):
    35+, May 1955.   319
    A description of the actual experiences in teaching listen-
ing of a group of elementary school teachers.

----. "In an Age of Communication, Are We Listening?"
    Educational Forum 18:405-09, May 1954. Comment:
    School Review 62:385, October 1954.   320
    The nature of the present-day need for good listening is
discussed.

----. "Learning to Listen." Social Education 18:63-64,
    February 1954.   321
    The role of the social studies teacher in the teaching of
listening.

----. "Listening." Review of Educational Research 31:145-
    51, April 1961.   322
    A review of the research on listening for the years
1958-1960.

----. Listening." Review of Educational Research 34:156-
    63, April 1964. Reprinted in Listening: Readings.
    (Edited by Sam Duker.) Metuchen, N. J. : Scarecrow
    Press, 1966. p. 165-73.   323
    A review of the research on listening for the years

1961-1963.

----. "Listening: A Communication Skill." Educational
    Screen and Audio Visual Guide 42:136-37, March 1963.
                                                          324
    The role of the audio-visual specialist in the teaching of
listening.

----. "Listening and Reading." Elementary School Journal
    65:321-29, March 1965. Reprinted: Schell, Leo M.
    and Burns, Paul C. Remedial Reading. Boston, Mass.:
    Allyn and Bacon, 1968, p. 268-78.   325
    Studies of the relationship between listening and reading.

----, (ed.) Listening: Readings. Metuchen, N.J.: Scare-
    crow Press, 1966.   326
    Excerpts from the literature on listening are reprinted
under the following headings: Nature of Listening; Process
of Listening; Some Relationships with Listening; Research on
Listening; Teaching Listening in the Elementary School; Teaching Listening in the Secondary School; Critical Listening;
Teaching Listening at the College Level; Listening Training
in Business and Industry; Relative Effectiveness of Visual and
Auditory Presentations; Measuring Listening Ability; Voices of
Doubt. Indexed.

----. "Master's Theses in Listening." Journal of Communi-
    cation 12:234-42, December 1962.   327
    One hundred seven theses on listening are listed and
classified.

----. "An Opportunity for Cooperation." Modern Language
    Journal 40:50, January 1956.   328
    The role of the foreign language teacher in the teaching
of listening.

----. "The Rediscovered Art of Listening." Audiovisual
    Instruction 8:744-46, December 1963.   329
    A summary is given of recent research developments in
the area of listening. Some of the developments are the use
of the classroom telephone, speeded speech, and reading improvement by means of simultaneous listening. The opportunities of audiovisual personnel in these areas are stressed.

----. "A Selected Bibliography on the Teaching of Listening
    at the Elementary Level." Journal of Communication
    6:63-69, Summer 1956.   330

An annotated 28-item bibliography.

----. "A Selected Bibliography on the Teaching of Listening
at the Secondary Level." Journal of Communication 5:
7-15, Spring 1955.   331
An annotated 33-item bibliography.

----. "Sharing Experiences." Grade Teacher 71:33+, June
1954.   332
The role of listening in "show and tell," news and current events, etc.

----. "Student Reaction to a Listening Type Examination."
School and Society 81:102-03, April 2, 1955.   333
Graduate students' reactions to a taped oral examina-
tion.

----. "Teacher of Elementary Science and Listening." Science Education 42:341-44, October 1958.   334
The role of the elementary school science teacher in
the teaching of listening.

----. "What We Do Know About Listening." Journal of
Communication 14:245-48, 251-52, December 1964.
                                                          335
Research findings on various aspects of listening ana-
lyzed.

Dumdie, Milton Frederick. The Effects of a Listening Program and a Reading Program upon Listening and Reading Comprehension in a Fourth and Fifth Grade Class.
Master's thesis. Milwaukee, Wisc.: University of Wisconsin, 1961.   336
From an experiment, using 30 fourth and fifth grade
children as subjects, the author suggests that intensive instruction in listening tends to improve reading ability and
vice versa.

Duncan, Charles Howard. The Relationship Between Listen-
ing Ability and Shorthand Achievement. Doctoral disser-
tation. Pittsburgh, Pa.: University of Pittsburgh, 1959.
Abstract: Dissertation Abstracts 20:1640-41, 1959.
                                                          337
Using 552 twelfth grade shorthand students as subjects,
Duncan reports that the correlation between shorthand
achievement and listening ability, as measured by the Brown-
Carlsen Test, was .36. Correlations of subtests of the

Brown-Carlsen with shorthand achievement are also reported.

Dunlap, Vivian H.   Positive Traits of Good Listeners as
    Identified by Teacher Opinion, to be Structured in the
    Curriculum of the Elementary School.   Master's thesis.
    Lawrence, Kan.:   University of Kansas, 1965.   338
    A 50-item questionnaire on the most desirable traits
of good listeners was given to teachers, K through 6, in
ten schools.   There were 95 responses.   The results are
thoroughly analyzed both as a whole and by grade.   The
qualities deemed most desirable by the entire group were:
being alert and accurate in listening to directions; good retention; ability to listen for sequence; sufficient span of attention; listening to others even when not involved in the discussion; response to teacher motivation; courtesy in not interrupting; listening to peers as well as to teacher; ability
to listen even when preoccupied with personal interest; accurate listening; ability to get general idea and to summarize; listening without needing repetition; reactive listening;
receptiveness to new ideas; creative listening; alertness;
and use of listening experiences for relaxation.

Dunn, Joseph and Tyler, Louise L.   "An Experiment in
    Measuring Listening Ability: An Attempt to Discover
    How Effectively Pupils Listen."   Chicago Schools Journal
    37: 272-76, May-June, 1956.   339
    A description of the construction by a committee of a
listening test for the elementary level and of the results of
its first administration.   The text of the test is not given.

Durrell, Donald D. and Sullivan, Helen Blair.   Durrell-Sulli-
    van Reading Capacity Test.   Yonkers, N. Y: World
    Book Co., 1937.   Reviewed: The Nineteen Thirty-
    Eight Mental Measurement Yearbook. (Edited by Oscar
    Krisen Buros.)   New Brunswick, N.J: Rutgers Univer-
    sity Press, 1938.   p. 127-28, and Robinson, Helen M.
    Fourth Mental Measurement Yearbook. (Edited by Oscar
    Buros.)   Highland Park, N.J.: Gryphon Press, 1953.
    p. 600-01.   340
    This is actually a listening test, although it is not called
one.   The primary test is for use in grades 2.5 through
4.5 and the intermediate test is designed for grades three
through six.

Dvores, Florence.   An Effective Program of Listening for
    the Third Grade.   Master's thesis.   Union, N. J.: New-
    ark State College, 1962.   341

Teaching listening in the third grade is described.

Dwyer, Ethel T. Construction of a Listening Test for Kindergarten and First Grade. Master's thesis. Boston: Boston University, 1962.   342
A test based on music was developed. The text of the test is given. Correlations between listening and chronological age are reported as .35 in kindergarten and .11 in first grade. Between listening and mental age .57 in kindergarten and .45 in first grade.

Dwyer, William Michael. An Analysis of the Subject Content of Certain Third, Fourth, Fifth and Sixth Grade Language Arts Textbooks. Master's thesis. Iowa City, Iowa: State University of Iowa, 1960.   343
Five textbook series were examined and their contents were compared to the topics dealt with in a University Demonstration School curriculum.

Dyer, Frederick C. "The Three Levels of Listening." Supervisory Management 9(7):26-28, July 1964.   344
A good listener should have: 1. a receptive ear which "gives the other fellow a chance;" 2. an analytical ear which determines the speaker's purposes and the validity of what he is saying; and 3. a between-the-lines ear that is aware of what is not said as a help in determining the speaker's real attitudes.

Dyer, Henry S. "Testing by Ear." College Board Review 1(23):436-38, May 1954.   345
Description of an aural French test. Text is not given.

Early, Margaret J. Adjusting to Individual Differences in English: Listening. Warren English Project, Bulletin No. 4. Boston: Boston University School of Education, 1954. Excerpts: Journal of Education 137:17-20, December 1954.   346
A comprehensive plan for the teaching of listening.

----. "Communication Arts." Encyclopedia of Educational Research. (Edited by Chester W. Harris.) New York: MacMillan, 1960, p. 306-12.   347
A review of research on listening to November 1957.

----. 'Developing Effective Listening Skills." Frontiers of Elementary Education V. Papers presented at the Fifth Annual Conference on Elementary Education, School of

84   Listening Bibliography

Education, Syracuse University, 1958.   Chapter 9, p.
78-88.   348
Listening is not a discrete skill.   Research indicates
that as reading skills improve, listening skills tend to de-
teriorate.

----.   'Suggestions for Teaching Listening."   Journal of
Education 137(3):17-20, December 1954.   Also in Lis-
tening: Readings. (Edited by Sam Duker.)   Metuchen,
N. J.: Scarecrow Press, 1966. p. 211-18.   349
Various ways of developing purposeful and accurate lis-
tening, critical listening, and appreciative listening.

Eastman, Milton.   "Listen!"   Grade Teacher 81(1):56+, September 1963.   350
Elementary school teachers should not talk continuously.
They should use pleasant, modulated voices, not resort to
tiresome repetition, and be more aware of the physical limi
tations of individual pupils.   If good listening habits are to
be taught, focus must be on listening throughout the day.
A list of activities useful to the teaching of listening is giver

Edelberg, Ann Rita.   "Better Listening Leads to Better
Speech."   Instructor 75(8):127, April 1966.   351
The classroom teacher's example is important in teach-
ing both listening and speech.

Edgar, Kenneth Frank.   The Validation of Four Methods of
Improving Listening Ability.   Doctoral dissertation.
Pittsburgh, Pa.: University of Pittsburgh, 1961.   Abstract: Dissertation Abstracts 22:1084, 1961.   352
Using as subjects 340 fourth through sixth grade children in an eight week experiment, the author found that the
experimental group made a significantly greater gain in listening ability.   The results were measured by an author-
made test.   Listening was taught by practice on taped material: expository, continued story of adventure, uncon-
nected paragraphs, and word lists.   The listening test, the
text of which is given, was designed to measure ability to
observe single details, to keep related details in mind, to
remember a series of details, to follow oral directions, to
use contextual clues, to recognize organizational elements,
to differentiate main and subordinate ideas, and to draw
justifiable inferences.

Edinger, Lois Virginia.   The Effectiveness of Television
Teaching in Developing Pupil Skills of Listening Com-

prehension and Critical Thinking. Doctoral dissertation.
Chapel Hill, N.C.: University of North Carolina, 1964.
Abstract: Dissertation Abstracts 26:1509, 1965.   353
Sixteen history classes, in eight schools, containing 241
pupils, were given the Brown-Carlsen Test as a pre- and
post-test.   Of these pupils, 163 were given television instruction.   At the end of one semester greater gains were
made by those who received television instruction than by
those taught by conventional classroom methodology.

Edith, Sister M. "Developing Listening Skills." Catholic
      School Journal 64(2):72, February 1964.   354
It is helpful to read stories to second grade children as
a means of teaching listening with attention and concentration.   Such reading should be followed by discussion and a
teacher-written chalkboard summary composed by the children.

Edman, Irwin. "The Fairly Good Listener." American
      Scholar 20:109-10, Winter 1950-51.   355
A facetious discussion of those who pretend to listen but
do not.

Effective Listening. A Management Course on the Skill of
      Listening. Columbus, Ohio: Nationwide Insurance Com-
      panies, 1954.   356
This is a discussion of the purpose of listening, the importance of listening to the business man, the nature of poor
listening, and the rules for good listening.

Egan, J.P. "Hearing." Annual Review of Psychology 5:89-
      110, 1954.   357
One hundred fourteen references.

Ehart, Violette Hunt. A Study of the Significance of Se-
      lected Sounds of Speech as Stimulants to Listening and
      Comprehension. Master's thesis. Grand Forks, N.D.:
      University of North Dakota, 1964.   358
The STEP test was altered as follows: one version
had a 70 per cent increase of voiceless plosives--p, t, and
k sounds; another had a 94 per cent increase of fricatives
--f and s sounds; the third had a 59 per cent increase of
nasals, glides, and semi-vowels--m, n, ng, l, and r. No
significant differences were found in test results of 92
speech students among the three altered passages and the
original version of the test. Nevertheless, there was a
tendency in the direction of hypothesized differences.

Ehrmann, Eliezer L. "Listening Comprehension in the Teaching of a Foreign Language." Modern Language Journal 48:18-20, January 1963.   359
This is a description of the emphasis placed on listening in a Hebrew language teaching program. The author suggests that the procedure may have value in teaching other languages.

Eisenstadt, Arthur. "The Employer and the Speech Teacher." Journal of Communication 3:105-09, November 1953.
                                                              360
One of the most important and useful speech skills in industrial situations is listening. This requires training.

Eiserer, Paul E. "Listening as a Tool in Understanding Others." Educational Leadership 12:431+, April 1955.
                                                              361
The teaching of listening is more a matter of good mental hygiene than of specific techniques.

Ekwall, Eldon E. "Listening Skills." Arizona Teacher 54(2): 12-13, November 1965.   362
Teachers must be aware of the need for teaching and learning listening; teachers should give the pupils the same undivided attention they expect; children should not be tricked into listening and should not be expected to listen for too long.

Elfering, Sister Mary Michele. The Value of a Planned Listening Program Correlated with Reading Units in Improving Word Meaning in Grade Two. Master's thesis. Milwaukee, Wisc.: Cardinal Stritch College, 1964.   363
One group received four months' planned listening instruction. There was a significantly greater improvement in listening skills on the STEP test than by the control group.

Elliff, Gertrude. "A Direct Approach to the Study of Listening." English Journal 46:20-27, January 1957.   364
This is a description of an instructional program in listening which emphasizes direct instruction, coordination of speech and listening instruction, and the use of a language laboratory.

Elliott, Charles Ray. An Experimental Study of the Retention of Auditory Material Presented During Sleep. Master's thesis. Chapel Hill, N.C.: University of North Carolina, 1947.   365

Using 40 subjects, this author found no statistically significant results but nevertheless concludes that "the evidence
strongly suggests some retention of auditory materials during sleep."

Elliot, Donald N.   "Review of Auditory Research."   Annual
   Review of Psychology 15:57-86, 1964.   366
   One hundred fifty-five references.

Elson, E. F. , Coladarci, A. P. , and Finis, K.   "The Effect
   of Prestige Labels on Auding Behavior."   (Abstract.)
   California Journal of Educational Research 5:158, September 1954.   367
   Two groups of high school seniors listened to a recorded
meaningless address.   One group was told that the speaker
was a well-known college president and the other that the
speaker was a member of the Parent-Teacher Association.
Students were asked to indicate on a scale how well they understood the "main point."   The speech of the supposed college president was rated more understandable.

Emanuel, Eleanor.   The Listening Abilities of Two Classes
   of Eleventh-Grade American Literature.   Master's thesis.
   Des Moines, Iowa: Drake University, 1962.   368
   Using 50 students as subjects, Emanuel reports that, as
measured by the Brown-Carlsen Test, a group taught lessons
by means of television did not do as well in listening as a
group which was instructed by a teacher in person.

Emmerich, David S. , Goldenbaum, Donald M. , Hayden,
   Dale L. , Hoffman, Linda S. , and Treffts, Jeanne L.
   "Meaningfulness as a Variable in Dichotic Hearing."
   Journal of Experimental Psychology 69:433-36, April
   1965.   369
   An experiment in which two different words were simultaneously given to subjects, one word in each ear.   The results cast doubt on the applicability of Broadbent's (114) findings when meaningful material is used.   Broadbent had used
numbers.

Emslie, Elizabeth A. , Kelleher, Margaret E. , and Leonard,
   Judy D.   A Comparison of Achievement in Silent Reading and Listening in Grade Four.   Master's thesis.
   Boston: Boston University, 1954.   370
   Eight stories were presented to 132 pupils during four
sittings.   One story was read aloud to the pupils and one
was read silently by the pupils at each of the sittings.

There was no significant difference in comprehension, but
poor readers did better in listening than in reading, while
superior readers performed better in reading than in listening.

Enc, Mitat Ahmet. The Effect of Two Different WPM Lis-
     tening Rates on Learning and Retention of Blind School
     Children. Doctoral dissertation. Urbana, Ill.: Univer-
     sity of Illinois, 1958. Abstract: Dissertation Abstracts
     19:2512, 1959. Summary: Enc, Mitat A. and Stolu-
     row, Lawrence M. "A Comparison of the Effects of
     Two Recording Speeds on Learning and Retention."
     New Outlook for the Blind 54:39-48, February 1960.
     Abstract of summary: Kirk, Samuel A. and Weiner,
     B.B. (Editors) Behavioral Research on Exceptional
     Children, Washington, D.C.: National Education Associa-
     tion, 1963. p. 126-27.   371
     Stories were read to 21 blind children in seventh through
tenth grades at 172 and 209 wpm. Efficiency in listening to
the speeded tape increased significantly with practice. Comprehension was satisfactory at both speeds.

Engel, Emily. An Action Study of the Development of Lis-
     tening Skills in Grade Four. Master's thesis. Garden
     City, N.Y.: Adelphi College, 1962.   372
     A fourth grade program for teaching listening.

England, Don W. A Comparison of Certain Skills in Read-
     ing and Listening in Two Fifth-Grade Groups. Master's
     thesis. Columbus, Ohio: Ohio State University, 1953.
                                                            373
     Using 70 subjects, the author found listening to be su-
perior to reading both for comprehension of total meaning
and for noting details.

Enochs, James B. "Listening and Teaching." California
     Journal of Secondary Education 24:434-35, November
     1949.   374
     In teaching it is necessary to listen with mind, heart,
and emotions in order to understand what a child really
means. Sensitive listening builds rapport between teacher
and pupils.

Erickson, Allen G. An Analysis of Several Factors in an
     Experimental Study of Listening at the College Level.
     Doctoral dissertation. Eugene, Ore.: University of
     Oregon, 1954. Summary: "Can Listening Efficiency Be

Improved?" Journal of Communication 4:128-32. Winter
1954.   375
Using 309 college communication students as subjects,
Erickson reports that those groups given 12 weeks of systematic listening instruction showed a significantly greater increase in listening ability, as measured by the Brown-Carlsen Test, than did those groups taking the regular communication sequence.   Correlations with listening are reported as:
reading .67; intelligence .77; and vocabulary .67.   Materials
used in listening instruction included the McCall-Crabb Exercises and Effective Reading by James I. Brown.

Erickson, C.I. and King, Irving. "A Comparison of Visual
and Oral Presentation of Lessons in the Case of Pupils
from the Third to the Ninth Grades." School and Society
6:146-48, August 1917.   376
Experimental findings are reported that show oral presentation to be more effective in grades below the eighth and
reading more effective in grades thereafter.

Erway, Ella Anderson. The Development of Programed Materials for Teaching Cognitive Listening Skills in a Speech
Laboratory in the Beginning Speech Course at Hunter College, New York. Doctoral dissertation. New York:
Columbia University, 1966. Abstract: Dissertation Abstracts 27:3970A-71A, 1967.   377
The preparation and evaluation of a taped programed
course at the college level.

Ethel, Sister M. "Listening for Comprehension." Catholic
School Journal 62(5):21-24, May 1962.   378
This is a description of an eight-unit set of listening exercises that were used 15 minutes daily in a first grade.
They deal with grasping main idea of a passage, following
sequence of ideas, following directions, identifying central
thought, understanding ideas, using context clues to get a
main idea, recognizing relationships, and drawing inferences.

Evans, Annette Vister. Listening Related to Speaking in the
First Grade. Master's thesis. Atlanta, Ga.: Atlanta
University, 1960.   379
Using 26 first grade pupils as subjects, the author re-
ports a correlation of .79 between listening and speaking
ability and .50 between listening and story comprehension.

Evertts, Eldonna L. An Investigation of the Structure of
Children's Oral Language Compared with Silent Reading,

Oral Reading and Listening Comprehension. Doctoral
dissertation. Bloomington, Ind.: Indiana University,
1961. Abstract: Dissertation Abstracts 22:3038, 1962.
                                                              380
A definite and positive relationship was reported between
children's oral language structure and their listening ability,
as measured by the Marten Test. Text of the test is given.

Ewing, H.W. "Finding a Speaking-Listening Index." Quarter-
     ly Journal of Speech 31:368-70, October 1945.   381
This is a description of an effort to arrive at an index
which will determine the degree to which speakers' main
ideas are grasped by the audience.

Fairbanks, Grant, Everitt, W.L., and Jaeger, R.P. "Meth-
     od for Time or Frequency Compression-Expansion of
     Speech." Transactions of the Institute of Radio Engi-
     neers, Professional Group on Audio AU2(1):7-12, Janu-
     ary-February, 1954. Also in: Convention Record of the
     Institute of Radio Engineers, 1953 National Convention
     Part 8 - Information Theory, p. 120-24.   382
The duration of the average speech element or phoneme
of live, connected speech exceeds the minimum duration necessary for perception by the listener. The excess duration
may be referred to as "temporal redundancy." A device for
compressing and expanding speech is described in detail.

     ----,   Guttman, Newman, and Miron, Murray S. "Audi-
     tory Comprehension in Relation to Listening Rate and
     Selective Verbal Redundancy." Journal of Speech and
     Hearing Disorders 22:23-32, March 1957.   383
Experimental evidence is presented which shows that
when speech is compressed and redundant key words are
added, better comprehension results.

     ----. "Auditory Comprehension of Repeated High Speed Mes-
     sages." Journal of Speech and Hearing Disorders 22:20-
     22, March 1957.   384
Experimental evidence is presented which demonstrates
that speech compressed as much as 50 per cent can yield
good intelligibility.

     ----. "Effects of Time Compression of Connected Speech."
     Journal of Speech and Hearing Disorders 22:10-19,
     March 1957.   385
Experimentation with compressed speech showed rapid
decrease in comprehension when compression was greater

Fairbanks, Guttman, Newman, and Miron, Murray S.   91

than 50 per cent.

----,   Everitt, William Littell, and Jaeger,
   Robert Pierson. Recording Device.   U.S. Patent No.
   2,866,650. Washington, D.C.: U.S. Patent Office. 386
   A description of a speech compressor patented May 12,
1959.

----, and Kodman, Frank, Jr. "Word Intelligibility as a
   Function of Time Compression." Journal of the Acoustical Society of America 29:636-41, May 1957.   387
   The process of speech compression is described as follows: "The process of compression involves two stages,
both of which are used in the time compression application.
In the first stage samples of the input signal are extracted
periodically, compressed (divided) in frequency, abutted in
time, and stored.   Time compression is accomplished in the
second stage by reproducing the stored samples at a speed
appropriate for the restoration of the input frequencies."
   It is possible to vary the time compression ratio and
the discard intervals independently.   Intelligibility is affected
by such variances.

Fang, Irving. A Computer-Based Analysis of Television
   News Writing Style for Listening Comprehension. Doc-
   toral dissertation.   Los Angeles, Calif.: University of
   California, Los Angeles, 1966. Abstract: Dissertation
   Abstracts 27:1774A, 1966.   388
   The development and validation of a formula for listen-
ability are described.   ELF (easy listening formula) is based
on the number of syllables above one per word in a sentence.

Farrar, Larston D. "Is Anybody Listening?" Graphic Arts
   Monthly 25(11):52-55, November 1963.   389
   Customers can be antagonized and lost when they are not
listened to by sales personnel.   The right to be listened to
is equated with fair treatment by many customers.   Not listening to instructions about the operation of machinery can
be disastrous.   Clerks do not listen for many reasons; for
example, when they are intrigued by the appearance of the
customer, or when they are flustered, emotionally upset, or
have personal difficulties.

Farrell, Edmund J. "Listen My Children and You Shall
   Read." English Journal 55:39-45+, January 1966. 390
   Reading aloud helps develop critical listening and an in-
terest in reading, but it must be carefully planned and prop-

erly motivated.

Farrow, Vern Leslie.   An Experimental Study of Listening
    Attention at the Fourth, Fifth, and Sixth Grade.   Doctor-
    al dissertation.   Eugene, Ore.: University of Oregon,
    1963.   Abstract: Dissertation Abstracts 24:3146, 1964.
                                                                        391
         The subjects were 317 pupils.   A test, based on
tape recorded stories describing animals, measured listening
attention.   An electric switch was pushed when names of animals were heard.   The correlation between this test and I.Q.
was .15.   The correlation between teachers' judgment of listening attention and I.Q. was .54.   There was a marked improvement in listening attention after the fourth grade.

Fawcett, Annabel Elizabeth.   The Effect of Training in Lis-
    tening upon the Listening Skills of Intermediate Grade
    Children.   Doctoral dissertation.   Pittsburgh: Univer-
    sity of Pittsburgh, 1963.   Abstract: Dissertation Ab-
    stracts 25:7108-09, 1965.   Summary: Elementary Eng-
    lish 43:473-76+, May 1966.   392
    A series of 42 lessons in listening skills dealing with
main ideas, supporting details, sequence, facts, and inference resulted in a statistically significant improvement in
these skills on the STEP Listening Test.   A control group
did not show such improvement.   Subjects were in the fourth,
fifth and sixth grades.   Correlations between listening and
other subject areas and intelligence are reported.   Texts of
the lessons are included.

Fawkes, Barbara and others.   "How Skillful Is Our Communi-
    cation?"   American Journal of Nursing 55:448-50, April
    1955.   393
    The importance of skillful communication by nurses
dealing with patients is stressed.   Listening is one of the
more important facets of communication.

Femania, Winifred and others.   "Skill Sequences in Language
    Arts."   Occupational Education 6:77-100, January 1949.
                                                                        394
    A detailed plan for sequential listening instruction in the
first five grades.

Fergen, Geraldine K.   Listening Comprehension at Con-
    trolled Rates for Children, in Grades IV, V, and VI.
    Doctoral dissertation.   Columbia, Mo.: University of
    Missouri, 1954.   Abstract: Dissertation Abstracts 15:

89, 1955.   395
Material was presented orally at 80, 130, 180 and
230 wpm. Best results were obtained at 130 wpm but there
was satisfactory comprehension at all four speeds. Correlation between mental age and listening is reported to range
from .25 to .46.

Ferris, Margaret Ellis. A Study of the Relationship Be-
     tween Reading Comprehension and Listening Comprehen-
     sion. Master's thesis. Knoxville, Tenn.: University
     of Tennessee, 1964.   396
     A correlational study involving the administration of
the Iowa Reading Test, the Kuhlman-Anderson Intelligence
Test, and the Maurice S. Lewis Listening Test to 389 fourth
grade children. Among the better readers, the correlation between reading and listening was .60; among the poorer readers
the correlation was .06. No sex differences were observed.

Fessenden, Seth A. Designed for Listening: A Speaker-
     Listener Workbook. Dubuque, Iowa: Wm. C. Brown,
     1951.   397
     A useful workbook that can be used at high school and
college levels to teach listening.

----. Effective Listening: Manual. Fifth Edition. Full-
     erton, Calif.: Author, 1968.   398
     A textbook on principles of listening and techniques to
improve listening.

----. "How Can We Teach Listening?" Journal of Com-
     munication 2:86-89, November 1952.   399
     The author advocates that speech teachers be trained
specifically to teach listening.

----. "Levels of Listening - A Theory." Education 75:
     288-91, January 1955. Reprinted in Listening: Read-
     ings. (Edited by Sam Duker.) Metuchen, N.J.: Scare-
     crow Press, 1966. p. 28-33.   400
     Successive levels of listening are reached as one learns:
to isolate sounds; to identify meaning; to integrate with past experience; to inspect the new and its impact on old ideas; to
interpret; to interpolate own ideas; and to introspect while
listening.

Field, Percy A. "The Receiving End of Communication -
     Listening." Proceedings of the 1962 Institute of Tech-
     nical and Industrial Communication. (Edited by Herman

W. Weisman.) Fort Collins, Colo.: Colorado State University, 1962, p. 32-43.   401
A speaker should take into account the possible disabilities of his listeners and be aware that the ear has a maximum capacity for 8000 bits of information per second while
the eye has a maximum capacity for 43×10^6 bits of information per second.

Finch, Mildred M. "Just Listen!" Clearing House 20:534-
36, May 1946.   402
A good listener does not listen only to that with which
he agrees.

Finkbeiner, Edith Joy. A Study of the Relationship Between
the Listening Ability and the Listening Performance of
Ninth Grade Pupils. Master's thesis. Seattle, Wash.:
University of Washington, 1962.   403
Using 269 pupils as subjects, Finkbeiner administered the
Brown-Carlsen Listening Test and a test on a 15-minute lecture which had not been previously announced. The latter
was intended to serve as a test of listening performance under normal conditions. A correlation of .41 was found between the Brown-Carlsen and listening performance. When
intelligence was held constant the partial correlation was .28.
The correlation of school grades with Brown-Carlsen was
.58, with listening performance, .46. The correlation of
intelligence with the Brown-Carlsen was .63, with listening
performance, .33.

Fischer, John H. "English Is Basic," Baltimore Bulletin of
Education 36(2):1-5, November 1958.   404
Children should be taught not only how to listen but also
that they ought to listen.

Fitzgerald, James A. and Fitzgerald, Patricia G. Teaching
Reading and the Language Arts. Milwaukee, Wisc.:
Bruce Publishing, 1965. p. 52-82.   405
Present day conditions require discriminative listening.
Purposeless listening is a waste of time. Various purposes
are listed and discussed.

Flederjohann, William Clarence. A Study of Some Relation-
ships of Visual and Auditory Perception to Reading Com-
prehension. Doctoral dissertation. Los Angeles, Calif.:
University of California, Los Angeles, 1965. Abstract:
Dissertation Abstracts 26:5227-28, 1966.   406
One of three groups was given listening training with

taped versions of "Standard Test Lessons." Another group
was given training in reading the same material. The third
group was given training in both listening and reading. Fifteen to 25 minutes of practice was given each day for four
weeks. All practice was followed by comprehension checks.
The pre- and post-test consisted of three lessons from the
same material given orally and three read, followed by a
comprehension test.

The group trained in listening increased their scores in
both listening and reading; they did significantly better in
both than the group trained in reading. The visual group
had better scores in listening than a control group without
training.

Fleischman, Earl E. "Let's Take Another Look at Interpre-
    tation." Quarterly Journal of Speech 35:447-84. De-
    cember 1949.   407
Interpretive reading needs greater emphasis in the
schools and, concomitantly, skills involved in listening to
such reading need to be taught.

Flemming, Edward L. "A Positive Approach to Interview-
    ing." Federal Probation 18(3):15-19, September 1954.
                                                              408
The importance of listening by counselors during interviews is developed.

Fletcher, Harvey. "The Nature of Speech and Its Interpre-
    tation." Journal of the Franklin Institute 193:729-47,
    June 1922.   409
The manner in which intensity of speech affects intelli-
gibility is discussed in this report of research from Bell
Telephone Laboratories.

Florentine, Sister M. "Children See and Hear and Learn."
    Catholic School Journal 56:237-38, October 1956.   410
"Listening is a child's open door to knowledge." In the
modern elementary schools listening is used extensively to
learn, while in traditional schools listening was not taught;
rather, attention was demanded. Listening involves thinking.

----. "Teaching Listening to Today's Children." English
    Record 7(3):39-40, Spring 1957.   411
Listening takes place constantly during the elementary
school day, and there are many opportunities to teach the
skills of listening by: 1. teachers' becoming better listeners; 2. providing many opportunities for listening; 3. giv-

ing guidance in listening intelligently with discrimination;
4. considering individual differences in the listening program;
and 5. evaluating constantly.

Floyd, William Downing. An Analysis of the Oral Question-
ing Activity in Selected Colorado Primary Classrooms.
Doctoral research study. Greeley, Colo.: Colorado
State College, 1960. Abstract: Abstracts of Field Studies for the Degree of Doctor of Education 22:46-50,
1961.   412
Forty visits to elementary classrooms for the taping of
proceedings are described in an extensive analysis of the
classroom communication process. Teacher-pupil ratio of
questions asked was 95 to 5; of words spoken 71 to 29. Of
the questions asked by teachers, 42 per cent concerned memory for specific facts. Only half of the children's questions
were "information-seeking."

Forbes, Allen E. "Listen Now!" Grade Teacher 78(2):64+,
October 1960.   413
The importance of teaching listening is discussed.

Foshay, Arthur W. "Let's Teach Listening." Exceptional
Children 24:180-81, December 1957.   414
Listening involves attention and receptivity. Children
should be taught to listen for something rather than merely
to "listen to."

Foster, Marriane R. Developing Auditory Skills in Reading
Readiness. Master's thesis. Newark, N.J.: New Jer-
sey State Teachers College at Newark, 1954.   415
The role of listening at pre-reading stages is discussed.

Foulke, Emerson and others. "The Comprehension of Rapid
Speech by the Blind." Exceptional Children 29:134-41,
November 1962.   416
This is a preliminary report of an experiment in preparing and presenting speeded speech materials on tape for
use by blind children. Maximum comprehension was found
at rates as high as 275 wpm. This compares to the average rate of reading of high school seniors at 250 wpm;
average rate of Braille reading of 90 wpm; and average rate
of recordings for the blind of 175 wpm.

Foulke, Emerson. Comprehension of Rapid Speech by the
Blind: Part II. Final Progress Report covering the
period from 1 September, 1961 to 29 February, 1964

on Cooperative Research Project, No. 1370. Louisville,
Ky: University of Louisville, 1964. Summary of Chap-
ter III: Exceptional Children 33:169-73, November
1966. Summary of Chapter IV: New Outlook for the
Blind 61:65-68, March 1967. Summary of Chapter V:
International Journal for the Education of the Blind 16:
11-15, October 1966.   417
Chapter 1
Modifications of the Tempo Regulator, which were made
to increase its reliability at high rates and to make it com-
patible with other equipment, are described.
Chapter 2
Two experiments were performed to evaluate training
methods for the comprehension of "rapid speech." In one
experiment, subjects were trained by listening to uninter-
rupted speech. One group listened at a constant high word
rate of 350 wpm, while the other listened at an initially slow
but increasing word rate. In the other experiment, word
rates were varied in the same way. However, the training
passage was interrupted frequently and subjects were questioned about the material just heard. The effectiveness of
training was evaluated by comparing pre-training STEP Listening Test scores with post-training test scores on an
equivalent form. None of the four training methods yielded
any significant improvement in the ability to comprehend
"rapid speech." However, it was also apparent that some of
the subjects showed superior comprehension of "rapid speech"
without training.
Chapter 3
An experiment was performed to determine the relation
between listening comprehension and the method of compressing speech. One group of subjects heard speech made
rapid by means of the Tempo-Regulator. The other group
heard speech made rapid by playing a record at a faster
speed than the one at which it was recorded. Each group
was further divided into three subgroups, and each subgroup
heard the listening selection at a different rapid word rate
(253, 300, and 350 wpm). Then subjects took a multiple
choice test of listening comprehension, based upon the selection heard. The analysis of variance of test scores showed
the word rate variable to be highly significant. However,
the method used to compress speech was not a significant
variable.
Chapter 4
A two-factor experiment was performed to determine the
influence of the reader's voice quality and reading style upon the comprehension of "rapid speech." Three different

readers recorded a selection and each rendition was reproduced at a normal word rate and at 300 wpm. The six versions were heard by subjects in six experimental groups.
Following this, subjects completed a multiple choice listening test. The analysis of variance showed both the word
rate variable and the reader variable to be significant.
However, no interaction between these variables was found.
This means that, at least in the present case, the comprehensibility of the three readers was not differentially affected by speech compression.
    Chapter 5
    To explore the retention of material presented at ac-
celerated word rates, a two-factor experiment was performed in which word rate and retention interval were
varied. The word rates were 175, 225, 275, and 325 words-
per-minute. The retention intervals were zero days, seven
days, and 30 days. Three hundred fifteen junior high school
pupils were divided into twelve treatment groups; each group
listened to a 2015 word selection reproduced by the speech
compression technique at one of the four word rates used
and was tested after the appropriate retention interval by a
multiple choice test with a reliability of .80. The analysis
of variance revealed an overall significance for both independent variables and for their interaction. The results
suggested that the retention of material learned by listening
to "rapid speech" was not different than the retention of material presented by conventional means.

----.   Comprehension of Rapid Speech by the Blind:
        Part III. Semiannual Report on Cooperative Research
        Project No. 2430, covering the period from March 1,
        1964 to December 31, 1964. Louisville, Ky.: Univer-
        sity of Louisville, 1965.   418
        Plans are discussed for the following types of research:
    1. Prolonged exposure to compressed speech of moti-
vated subjects to determine whether this exposure increases
facility in listening to compressed speech.
    2. A comparison of intelligibility and comprehensibility
of compressed speech.
    3. An examination of the relative distortion of various
speech sounds as a function of the amount of speech compression through spectographic analysis.
    4. An investigation of the value of frequency-selective
filtering of the output of a speech compressor.
    5. Teaching of listening to highly compressed speech
as a "new language."
    6. A survey of reaction to rapid speech by blind col-

lege students.

----.   Comprehension of Rapid Speech by the Blind:
Part III.   Semiannual Report on Cooperative Project,
No. 2430, covering the period from January 1, 1965 to
June 30, 1965.   Louisville, Ky.: University of Louis-
ville, 1965.   419
The present status of several research projects previ-
ously reported.   A new investigation into the determination
of typical oral "reading" rates is briefly described.

----.   Comprehension of Rapid Speech by the Blind:
Part III.   Semiannual Report on Cooperative Project,
No. 2430, covering the period from July 1, 1965 to December 31, 1965.   Louisville, Ky.: University of Louisville, 1966.   420
A detailed report of an investigation of the relationship
between reaction time and ability to comprehend speeded
speech.   Reaction time decreased up to 275 wpm, but not
thereafter.
One hundred introductory psychology students were subjects in an investigation of preferred rate of speech.   A
mean rate of 207 wpm was preferred.
Fifty-one blind college students favored speeded speech.
An investigation is proposed for combining methods of
producing speeded speech.   Investigation into teaching the
comprehension of very rapid speech as a new language is also proposed.

----, and Bixler, Ray H.   The Comprehension of Rapid
Speech by the Blind: Part III.   Interim Progress Report.   Cooperative Research Project No. 2430, covering period from September 30, 1966 to December 31,
1966.   Louisville, Ky.: University of Louisville, 1967.
                                                                  421
The following findings made in completed research projects are reported:
1. When word rate is held constant, variance in vocal
pitch is not influential in comprehension.
2. No advantage was found from reproducing a tape to
be compressed in a direction opposite from the one used in
recording in an effort to increase the intelligibility of word
beginnings.
3. A review of research on compressed speech has
been prepared.
4. A conference on compressed speech was held.
The following current ongoing research projects are

described:

1. Influence of age, grade, and intelligence on the comprehension of time-compressed speech.

2. Listening comprehension as a function of word rate.

3. Compressed speech viewed as a "new language."

4. Spectographic analysis of the relative distortions of various speech sounds in compression.

5. Separation of the effects of word rate and of time-compression.

6. Experimental control of listening difficulty.

7. Influence of neural and anatomical damage to hearing on the comprehension of compressed speech.

8. Comparison of conventional time-compressed speech and dichotic speech with respect to the intelligibility of single words.

A Center for Rate Controlled Recordings has been established.

----, and Sticht, Thomas G. "The Intelligibility and Comprehension of Time Compressed Speech." Proceedings of the Louisville Conference on Time Compressed Speech, October 19-21, 1966. (Edited by Emerson Foulke.) Louisville, Ky.: Center for Rate Controlled Recordings, University of Louisville, 1967. p. 21-28.
422

One hundred subjects listened to speech compressed from 175 wpm to 225, 275, 325, 375, and 425 wpm and were tested for intelligibility and comprehension. Mean intelligibility scores were 93, 91, 89, 85, and 84 per cent respectively, while mean comprehension scores were 73, 66, 67, 56, and 53 per cent respectively. While many questions concerning the best methods remain, a moderate compression (250 to 275 wpm) seems to be practical for blind students.

----, and ----. "A Review of Research on Time Compressed Speech." Proceedings of the Louisville Conference on Time Compressed Speech, October 19-21, 1966. (Edited by Emerson Foulke.) Louisville, Ky.: Center for Rate Controlled Recordings, University of Louisville, 1967. p. 3-20.   423

Research findings on various problems related to accelerated speech are reviewed and classified. Among the problems dealt with are: 1. methods for accelerating speec which include speaking more rapidly, playing a tape or record faster, and sampling which may be done manually, by omissions, by electromechanical means or by computer; 2.

ways of specifying amount of compression which include
fraction of time saved, in terms of acceleration, and word
rate; 3. confusion in terms used, such as compressed, accelerated, speeded, and rapid speech; 4. intelligibility
measures which include reproduction and recognition; 5.
comprehension measures which include tests which may be
standardized, objective, or essay, to measure ability to follow directions, and interviews; 6. factors affecting intelligibility, including methods of compression, sampling, rate of
occurrence of speech sounds, word structure, prior experience of listeners with compressed speech, and the hearing
capacity of the listeners; 7. factors affecting comprehension,
including listeners' age, sex, and intelligence, amount of
compression, method of compression, nature of material,
vocal quality, reading rate of listeners, and prior training
of listeners.

The original word-speed does not appear to be a factor
in intelligibility or comprehensibility of compressed speech.
Increasing the amount of compression has less effect on intelligibility than on comprehension.   There is a high correlation between reading rate and ability to comprehend compressed speech.   No effective procedure of training for listening to compressed speech has yet been developed.

----, and Bixler, Ray H. "Speech Compression." New
     Beacon 47:241-42, September 1963.   424
     A brief description of speech compression is given.
Blind children, aged eleven to fifteen, with no experience
in listening to compressed speech, can listen at the rate of
275 wpm with good comprehension.   Compressed speech may
also be useful in review.

----.   "Summary and Conclusions." Proceed-
     ings of the Louisville Conference on Time Compressed
     Speech, October 19-21, 1966. (Edited by Emerson
     Foulke.) Louisville, Ky.: Center for Rate Controlled
     Recordings, University of Louisville, 1967. p. 149-54.
                                                    425
     Research is needed in these areas: 1. development of
economically feasible sources for compression of speech; 2.
nature of listening and its relationship to reading; 3. measurement of comprehension and intelligibility; 4. most desirable de-
signs for compressed speech experiments; 5. discovery of
organismic variables which may affect the reception of compressed speech; 6. format of accelerated speech and the
possibility that more pause-time may be desirable; 7. tech-
nology of speech compression equipment; 8. development of

uses of compressed speech; and 9. standardization of both
terminology and equipment.

----. A Survey of the Acceptability of Rapid Speech. Tech-
    nical Report. Project No. 2430, Cooperative Research
    Branch, Office of Education, Department of Health, Edu-
    cation and Welfare. Louisville, Ky.: Performance Re-
    search Laboratory, University of Louisville, 1965. Ex-
    cerpts: New Outlook for the Blind 60:261-65, Novem-
    ber 1966.   426
    Short passages of compressed speech were sent to a
random sample of 100 blind college students who were sub-
scribers to the recording services of Recordings for the
Blind.   Fifty-one responses to a questionnaire were received.
A willingness to listen to compressed materials was expressed by 92 per cent.   There was a preference for the
275 wpm rate, but those who had been in college for the
longest period of time expressed a stronger preference for
faster rates--up to 350 wpm. One selection, started at normal rates, and gradually increased, was found to be helpful
by 71 per cent.   There was an expression of preference for
a male voice in recordings, although in the particular material presented here, there was preference for the female
voice. The students stated that recordings were used extensively by them for their "reading." An appendix discusses
the question of which sex is preferable for readers.

----. "Time Compressed Recorded Speech and Faster Aur-
    al Reading." American Association of Workers for the
    Blind Annual, Blindness 1967. Washington, D.C.: The
    Association, 1967. p. 11-20.   427
    Acceleration of speech can be accomplished by:
    1. Increasing the rate of speaking; this has only lim-
ited range and introduces undesired changes in inflection and
in speaking rate.
    2. Changing the speed of reproduction or playback; this
leads to distortion which is disturbing to the listener.
    3. Time compression by sampling and discarding; this
can now be done by an electromechanical device. The sampling is not selective but occurs at random.
    4. Computer; this enables a selection to be made of the
portions of speech to be discarded but is extremely expensive.
    5. The harmonic compressor, which will double the speed
of speech but will have no distortion in vocal pitch; this device has been simulated on a computer but it is now only in
the process of being constructed.

Research by the author and the American Institutes of
Research on the comprehension of compressed speech is described.

Fox, Bernard H. and Robbin, Joseph S. "The Retention of
    Material Presented During Sleep." Journal of Experi-
    mental Psychology 43:75-79, January 1952.   428
Thirty subjects were employed in this experimental
study on learning during sleep. There was no observation
of the subjects while they were sleeping, but there was evidence that learning did take place.

Francis, Sister Clara. "A Frontal Attack on the First Lan-
    guage Art." Catholic Educator 34:799-8, April 1964.
                                                    429
A four-year program to improve teaching of the language
arts. The first year was devoted to listening. For best
results, listening has to be taught. This teaching should
not be confined to an isolated period of the school day.

Franke, Phyllis E. A Preliminary Study Validating the
    Measurement of Oral Reading Rate in Words Per Minute.
    Master's thesis. Iowa City, Iowa: State University,
    1939.   430
A high correlation is reported between the actual wpm
rate of 42 subjects reading 295 words of factual material
and the rate reported by trained observers who listened to
phonographic recordings of the readings.

Frazier, Alexander. "Making the Most of Speaking-and-
    Listening Experiences." English Journal 46:330-38+,
    September 1957.   431
The author gives a series of assignments for use in
teaching listening. They emphasize what is said, why it is
said, and how it is said.

----. "The Teaching of Listening: A Memo to Teachers."
    Elementary English 35:111-12, February 1958.   432
The author suggests that listening can be taught by
means of pupil conversations and by group discussions in
which teachers and pupils analyze the role of the listener
and how it is being fulfilled.

Frederick, Robert W. and Winkler, Pauline A. "A Guide
    to Listening." Education on the Air. Fifth Yearbook
    of the Institute for Education by Radio. Columbus,
    Ohio: Ohio State University, 1934, p. 349-54.   433

A discussion of how cues may be used for effectively listening to a speech.

Free, R. J. "We Measure Growth Together." Educational
    Leadership 4:464-68, April 1947.   434
    A social studies unit should use children's skills in the
language arts, which include listening.

Freeman, Bernice. "Listening Experiences in the Language
    Arts." English Journal 38:572-76, December 1949.
                                                          435
    Student teachers taught listening for a year at a demon-
stration high school of Peabody University. At the end of
the year the pupils concluded that: since we listen to what
we are interested in, we should broaden our interests; listening is courteous; listening requires concentration; it is
possible to listen for organization and structure even when
a subject is not interesting; atmosphere affects listening and
therefore care should be taken in any school situation to prevent distractions and provide atmosphere conducive to learning; moods, home conditions, and events experienced just
prior to the listening experience can affect skill of listening
--pupils should be aware of this and seek to overcome these
effects; anyone can talk but not everyone can listen.

Friedman, Herbert L., Orr, David B., and Graae, Cynthia
    Norris. "Effects of Listening Aids and Self-Pacing on
    the Comprehension of Time-Compressed Speech." Pro-
    ceedings of the 75th Annual Convention of the American
    Psychological Association, 1967. p. 279-80.   436
    Two experiments in improving comprehension of com-
pressed speech. Allowing listeners to see précis of the
material to be heard does not increase the comprehension
scores. Allowing the subject to manipulate his own compressed rate failed to increase comprehension beyond that
shown by a group whose rate was set by the experimenter.

----, ----, Freedle, Roy O. and Norris, Cynthia M.
    Further Research on Speeded Speech as an Educational
    Medium. Silver Spring, Md.: American Institute for
    Research, 1966.   437
    Several experiments designed to test the comprehensi-
bility of speeded speech are reported.
    Concentrated practice (eight to ten hours daily for five
consecutive days) was effective in improving comprehension
at high (475 wpm) rates though not as efficient as spaced
practice over a longer period.

In general, subjects in another experiment did not obtain consistent 90 per cent comprehension at 375 and 425
wpm after sixteen hours of practice.
    In a series of studies retention after one month was as
good for those listening to compressed speech as for those
who listened to taped normal speech.

---- and ----. "Recent Research in the Training of
    Compressed Speech Comprehension." Proceedings of
    the Louisville Conference on Time Compressed
    Speech, October 19-21, 1966. (Edited by Emerson
    Foulke.) Louisville, Ky.: Center for Rate Con-
    trolled Recordings, University of Louisville, 1967. p.
    69-75.   438
    Describes experiments in listening to compressed
speech at rates of up to 475 wpm, performed at the American Institute for Research. Comprehension of compressed
speech may be improved with practice; the limits of comprehension have not yet been reached; compressed speech is a
feasible technique for the educational setting; and further research is desirable to examine individual differences and to
isolate factors in good listening.   .

Friedman, Pacy. A Study of the Listening Ability of Chil-
    dren with Defective Articulation. Master's thesis.
    Minneapolis, Minn.: University of Minnesota. 1958. 439
    The author reports finding, on basis of testing 178 first
through sixth grade children, that those with articulatory defects, but with no basic organic impairment, did significantly less well on listening tests than did those matched children with no articulatory defects. The STEP Test was used
in fourth through sixth grades. An author-made test, the
text of which is given, was used in the first three grades.

Friedman, Robert M. A Comparative Study of the Reten-
    tion Level of Verbal Material Presented Visually and
    Orally: Fifth Grade Pupils. Garden City, N.Y.: Adel-
    phi College, 1959.   440
    Using two fifth grade classes, the author reports that
pupils had better comprehension of material presented orally
than of material they read. Slow readers showed the greatest
difference in favor of oral presentation.

Frohardt, Kenneth E. A Study of the Teaching of Listening.
    Master's thesis. Lincoln, Neb.: University of Nebras-
    ka, 1949.   441
    This is a description of the preparation of a series of

listening projects for use in teaching listening in college
speech classes.

Froman, Robert. "Understand What You Hear." Nation's
    Business 49(10):94-98, October 1961.   442
    Five rules aiding good listening are given and dis-
cussed:
    1. Rephrase your understanding in your own words, and
    whenever possible, check with the source.

    2. When you disagree with an order, but you must ac-
    cept it, take extra care to get it right.

    3. If you find that something you are told is exciting,
    watch for errors of exaggeration in your understanding
    of it.

    4. If you find that something you are told is boring,
    watch for errors of transition.

    5. Concentrate on the unfamiliar items in any message.

Fry, Charles Luther. The Effects of Training in Communi-
    cation and Role Perception on the Communicative Abili-
    ties of Children. Doctoral dissertation. Rochester,
    N.Y.: University of Rochester, 1961. Summary:
    Child Development 37:675-85, September 1966.   443
    The training procedure required speakers to communi-
cate to listeners so that they could correctly identify a particular picture in a series. There were many such series.
Subjects were 64 fifth grade girls. Sixteen were trained as
speakers, sixteen as listeners, sixteen received training in
both speaking and listening, while sixteen were a control
group. Training significantly improved the communication
process but the hypothesis that the kind of training received
would have varying effectiveness was not sustained. No evidence was found that improvement in this particular communication process carried over to other communication
tasks.

Frymier, Jack R. "The Neglected Quarter." High School
    Journal 39:404-06, May 1956.   444
    The author says that the neglected art of listening can
be aided if emphasis is put on the importance of a listener
"doing his share" by being aware of speaker's problems.

Fulbright, Evelyn and Flowers, Anne. "Are You Listen-

ing?" South Carolina Education News 23(8):18-20, May
1967.   445
A selected list of references on listening is discussed.

Fuller, Max E.   "The Communications Teacher Asks Some
    Questions." Journal of Communication 1(1):36-40, May
    1951.   446
The author reports general agreement among teachers
of college communications courses that instruction in listening should be included in their curricula, but he says that
no way has been found to do this.

Fulton, Renee J.   "Language Laboratories Develop the Lis-
    tening Ear." Modern Language Journal 43:224-25, May
    1959.   447
The author says that the distinction between hearing and
listening must be stressed if the learner is to become a perceptive auditor.

Furness, Edna Lue. "Improving Reading Through Listen-
    ing." Elementary English 34:307-11, May 1957.   448
Reading and listening have much in common. It is likely that when a child's listening ability is greater than his
reading ability, he may have untapped reading potential.

----. "Listening: A Case of Terminological Confusion."
Journal of Educational Psychology 48:477-82, December
1957.   449
The term "listening" is inadequate. "Comprehending
aurally" or "auding" are more adequate terms for a process
that includes hearing, listening, recognizing spoken language,
interpreting oral symbols, supplementing meaning, and being aware of facts and assumptions not uttered.   Twelve-
item bibliography.

----. "Listening and Learning." Peabody Journal of Educa-
tion 33:212-16, January 1956.   450
A review of some of the published material on listening.
Thirteen-item bibliography.

----. "Proportion, Purpose, and Process in Listening."
Educational Administration and Supervision 44:237-42,
July 1958.   451
Types of listening are classified as passive, conversa-
tional, exploratory, appreciative, creative, attentive, con-
centrative, and analytical.

----.   "A Remedial and Developmental Program in Listening."   Elementary English 32:525-32, December 1955.
Also in Teaching in the Elementary School (Edited by
Lester D. Crow, Alice Crow, and Walter Murray.)
New York: Longmans Green, 1961, p. 274-82.   452
        The author states that listening disabilities may be
physiological, psychological, or pedagogical.   Causes of and
suggested teaching procedures for each of these types of disabilities are discussed.

Gabor, Dennis.   Broadwidth Compressor and Expansion System for Transmission of Speech.   U.S. Patent No.
3,183,310.   Washington, D.C.: U.S. Patent Office. 453
        A description of a speech compressor patented May 11,
1965.

Gallagher, Frank.   "All Quiet on the 'Listening' Front."
Advanced Management-Office Executive 2(4):28-29, April
1963.   454
        Schools spend 52 per cent of their classroom time
teaching reading but only 8 per cent promoting listening and
speaking skills.   Out of school, however, speaking and listening are increasingly important.   It is a mistake to assume that we know how to listen because we know how to
read.   Non-directive listening is most effective but also
most difficult.

Gallant, Ruth.   The Improvement of Listening Comprehension Skills at the College Level.   Master's thesis. Oxford, Ohio: Miami University, 1959.   455
        Twenty-five college students, who were classed as un-
derachievers, were given listening training consisting of 13
fifteen-minute taped lectures on which they were then tested.
The Brown-Carlsen Test was used as a measure of listening.   The experimental group showed a greater gain than
that of an equated control group, but the difference was not
statistically significant.

Gardiner, Alan H.   The Theory of Speech and Language.
Oxford: Clarendon Press, 1932, passim.   456
        Language arises only from a need to communicate.   At
every stage of the development of language the mutual interaction of speaker and listener is presupposed.

Gardner, D. Bruce.   "If Your Child Doesn't Listen." Today's Health 38(3):14+, March 1960.   457
        To help children learn to listen: one must be sure of

having their attention before giving instructions; one must
speak slowly, clearly, and with patience; use concrete terms
when possible; and be brief. A child who does not listen
well is normal in the same sense that a child who has never
been taught to read is normal, if he cannot read.

Gardner, John W. "The Art of Listening." Saturday Review
    39(22):45-46, June 2, 1956.   458
    A foundation officer must listen under a variety of condi-
tions and circumstances. He cannot be a half-hearted or
passive listener, but he must make careful appraisals of the
speaker and the idea being presented. "One needs to cultivate patience, discipline, and a deeply-rooted interest in
others to listen alertly and intelligently."

Gardner, Neely D. "The Spiral Analysis Method as a Train-
    ing Aid in Learning to Listen." Journal of the Ameri-
    can Society of Training Directors 10(6):13-21, Novem-
    ber-December 1956.   459
    Gardner suggests using diagrammatic representations of
interviews in order to evaluate their effectiveness. An ac-
ceptant attitude, an ability to attend, listening skills, and an
ability to reflect feeling must be developed for successful
interviewing.

Garner, W. R. "Hearing." Annual Review of Psychology 3:
    85-104, 1952.   460
    Eighty-seven references.

Garretson, Robert L. Music in Childhood Education. New
    York: Appleton-Century-Crofts, 1966. Chapter 4 "Ex-
    periences in Listening." p. 66-97.   461
    Intelligent and insightful listening habits are not auto-
matic; they must be carefully developed. Children should
be guided into listening for something specific. Guided listening should include three steps: preparation, presentation,
and follow-up. Topics in listening to music should include
tempo, dynamics, mood, imagery, aural recognition of instruments and recognition of musical components.

Garrigan, Maybelle. "Methods for Improving Appreciation
    for Materials Presented Orally in Grades Four Through
    Six." Oral Aspects of English, Proceedings of the An-
    nual Conference on Reading. Chicago: University of
    Chicago Press, 1955, p. 112-16.   462
    Poor listening may be caused by lack of interest, ma-
terial that is not at the maturity level of the listener, hav-

ing nothing specific to listen to, and the need to have imagi-
nation quickened. The good listener should associate ideas,
organize ideas, react critically and place ideas in his memory for future recall.

Garvey, W.D. Duration Factors in Speech Intelligibility.
    Master's thesis. Charlottesville, Va.: University of
    Virginia. 1949.   463
    Speech was speeded by chopping portions of a tape at
the beginning of each word. Using 66 college students as
subjects, the author found that speech could be speeded as
much as two and one half times without reducing intelligibility below 90 per cent. Only when speed was increased
fourfold did intelligibility fall below 50 per cent. The size
of the chop is the critical factor.

----. An Experimental Investigation of the Intelligibility of
    Speeded Speech. Doctoral dissertation. Charlottesville,
    Va.: University of Virginia, 1951. Summary: "The
    Intelligibility of Speeded Speech." Journal of Experi-
    mental Psychology 45:102-08, February 1953. Summary:
    Quarterly Journal of Speech 39:296-306, October 1953.
                                                                  464
    At a given speed the degree of intelligibility of speeded
speech is significantly higher when the tape is chopped than
when the tape is merely run more rapidly.

----, and Henneman, Richard H. "Practical Limits of
    Speeded Speech." AF Technical Report No. 5917, May
    1950.   465
    A total of 66 male college students served as subjects
in an experiment designed to test the effect on intelligibility
of increasing speech rate by chopping portions of a taped
list of words. The ratio of deleted to retained tape (chop-
ratio) varied from 1cm/2cm to 3cm/1cm, the per cent of
speed-up from 50 to 300, the per cent of word removed by
the chops from 33 to 75, and the per cent of the word remaining on the tape from 67 to 25. The findings were that
speed-ups of 1.5, 1.75, and 2.0 resulted in 95 per cent intelligibility. No significant drop occurred until the speed-
up was 2.5; 50 per cent intelligibility remained at a speed-
up of 3.5.

Gates, Arthur I. "The Mnemonic Span for Visual and Audi-
    tory Digits." Journal of Experimental Psychology 1:
    393-403, October 1916.   466
    For 165 college students, the average recall was 8.2.

digits after visual presentation and 7.7. digits after aural
presentation.

Gates, Louise W. and Meyers, Ruth L. "An Academic
    Evaluation Study of an Industrial Program, 'Effective
    Listening.' " N.S.P.I. Journal 4:6-8, July 1965.   467
    The Basic Systems' taped listening course was admin-
istered to 67 college students in various programs.   There
was significantly greater improvement in listening by that
group than by a control group of 248 students. The difference
persisted after ten weeks. Student reaction was favorable.

Gauger, Paul William. The Effect of Gesture and the
    Presence or Absence of the Speaker on the Listening
    Comprehension of 11th and 12th Grade High School
    Pupils. Doctoral dissertation. Madison, Wisc.: Uni-
    versity of Wisconsin, 1951. Abstract: Speech Mono-
    graphs 19:116-17, June 1952.   468
    Using 302 upper-level high school students as subjects,
Gauger reports that listening comprehension was not significantly different when gestures were used or when the speaker was visible than when no gestures were employed or
when the speaker was concealed by a screen.

Gentilin, Mimi Jane. A Comparative Study of Oral Compre-
    hension After Listening Training. Master's thesis.
    Garden City, N.Y.: Adelphi College, 1963.   469
    On the STEP test, no significant differences were found
in listening improvement between an experimental group of
fifteen fourth, fifth and sixth grade pupils and a control
group of fifteen from the same grades. Listening games
were used to train the experimental group in listening skills.

Gerber, J.C. "What Can High Schools Reasonably be Ex-
    pected to Accomplish in the Skills of Communication?"
    Education 72:456-57, March 1952.   470
    Note-taking skill is an important adjunct to good listen-
ing.

Gibson, Harry L. "Let's Teach Students How to Listen."
    Business Education Forum 19(6):22, March 1965.   471
    Listening skills should be taught specifically in business
education, because oral instructions are much more common in offices than written ones. Courses in office practice
and in typewriting are good places to do this teaching. Specific techniques are suggested.

Gideon, Sara Black. <u>Aural Comprehension or Auding in</u>
<u>Secondary School German.</u> Doctoral dissertation. Uni-
versity Park, Pa.: Pennsylvania State University, 1956.
Abstract: <u>Dissertation Abstracts</u> 17:274-75, 1957. 472
In an experiment involving ten secondary school classes
and 296 pupils, Gideon determined, through the use of a
German language achievement test, an intelligence test, and
the Brown-Carlsen Listening Test, that there was a low but
positive relationship between listening skill in German and in
English.

Giffin, Kim and Hannah, Larry. "A Study of the Results of
an Extremely Short Instructional Unit in Listening."
<u>Journal of Communication</u> 10:135-39, September 1960.
                                                        473
Results of a concentrated four-day unit on listening,
based on <u>Listening and Speaking</u> by Nichols and Lewis,
showed a significantly increased score on listening, as measured by the STEP Test.

Gilkinson, Howard, Paulson, Stanley F. , and Sikkink, Donald E. "Conditions Affecting the Communication of Con-
troversial Statements in Connected Discourse: Forms
of Presentation and the Political Frame of Reference of
the Listener." <u>Speech Monographs</u> 20:253-60, November 1953.   474
Speech students tended to recall more statements that
agreed with their own views than they did statements op-
posed to their views. The order in which pro and con
statements were made had little effect on recall.

----. Effects of Order and Authority in an Argumentative
Speech." <u>Quarterly Journal of Speech</u> 40:183-92, April
1954.   475
Two versions of a speech, one citing eminent authorities as its source of arguments and one giving the same
arguments but without mention of the sources, had no significantly different effect in attitude shift or in retention on 130
college speech students.

Gilham, Mary A. "The Physiologic and Neurologic as Related to Listening to Speech." <u>Projects of the Fourth</u>
<u>Workshop in Basic Communications, University of Den-</u>
<u>ver.</u> (Edited by Edwin L. Levy.) Denver, Colo.: Uni-
versity of Denver Press, 1946, p. 73-77.   476
Good listening focuses on what is said rather than how
it is said. Nevertheless, the manner in which a statement

is made and the conditions under which the listening takes
place have a great impact on listening effectiveness.

Golden, Louis L. , Harris, Marie W. , Marks, Grace M. ,
  and Meagher, Judith A. Teaching the Discrimination
  Between Fact and Opinion in Grades Four and Five.
  Master's thesis. Boston: Boston University, 1962.
                                                      477
This thesis contains an excellent summary of the literature on the teaching of critical thinking. Texts of two forms
of a test for critical thinking and of 20 lessons on this subject are included.

Goldhaber, Gerald Martin. Listener Comprehension of Compressed Speech When the Difficulty Level of the Content
  and the Sex of the Listener Are Varied. Master's thesis.
  University Park, Md.: University of Maryland, 1967.
                                                      478
Using 240 college speech students as subjects, three
passages were read to subgroups. The passages, approximately 2000 words, were of different levels of difficulty, on
the Flesch Readability Formula. The passages were originally read at 140 wpm and compressed to 175, 325, 375, and
425 wpm by use of a Tempo Regulator. A 20-item multiple
choice test measured comprehension. Analysis of variance
showed that male students scored significantly higher than
female students. The mean test scores decreased as the
rate of presentation increased.

Goldstein, Bernard J. The Comprehension of Poetry From
  Recordings. Doctoral dissertation. New York: Columbia University, 1952. Abstract: Dissertation Abstracts 12:434, 1952.   479
Using 400 college students as subjects, the author reports
that the comprehension of recorded poetry reading was the
same when it was read by the author as when it was read
by a trained reader. Comprehension was improved significantly when subjects, while they listened, followed the written text of the poems.

Goldstein, Harry. Reading and Listening Comprehension at
  Various Controlled Rates. Teachers College, Columbia
  University Contributions to Education, No. 821. New
  York: Bureau of Publications Teachers College, Colum-
  bia University, 1940.   480
In an experiment using varying speeds of speech records
and reading moving pictures, the following conclusions were

reached:
1. Listening comprehension in general is superior to reading comprehension.

2. Superiority of listening comprehension is greater when easy materials are used than when difficult materials are used.

3. The relative superiority of listening comprehension is in inverse proportion to intelligence and reading speed of subjects.

4. The relative superiority of listening declines with increased rates of presentation.

5. Reading comprehension is more variable than listening comprehension.

6. There is a decline of comprehension with increased rate both in listening and in reading.

7. This decline is progressive as faster rates are reached.

8. Reading and listening comprehension are highly correlated.

Gooch, Darrell. "Report of the Committee on Elementary and Secondary School Programs." Journal of Communication 1(2):57-59, November 1951.   481
It is suggested that a completely integrated approach to the teaching of English, speech, and communication be started in elementary schools.

Goodman-Malamuth, Leo II. An Experimental Study of the Effects of Rate of Speaking Upon Listenability. Doctoral dissertation. Los Angeles, Calif.: University of Southern California, 1956. Abstract: Speech Monographs 24:89-90, June 1957.   482
Using 487 high school students as subjects, the author reports that for both easy and difficult passages a speed of 150 wpm yields best comprehension. Other speeds used were 125, 175, and 200 wpm. This is a companion study to those of Cartier and Harwood using the same materials.

Gotkin, Lassar G. and Fendiller, Fay. "Listening Centers in the Kindergarten." Audiovisual Instruction 10:24-26,

Gotkin, Lassar G. and Fendiller, Fay   115

January 1965.   483
A tape recorder classroom listening center is advocated
to enable disadvantaged children to hear "school language" as
distinguished from their own.   Great stress is laid on the
need for locating and operating the center so that there will
be minimal distraction.

Gould, Gordon Thomas and Hafer, Frederick Leroy.   Design
    for an Apparatus for Speech Stretching.   Master's thesis.
    Cambridge, Mass.: Massachusetts Institute of Technol-
    ogy, 1950.   484
A group of contiguous band-pass filters separate the im-
put speech according to frequency components.   Each filter
is followed by a full-wave rectifier which acts as a fre-
quency-doubling circuit.   The original speech frequency is
not affected but the pitch is halved.   Possible applications are
suggested.

Goyer, Robert S.   'Oral Communication: Studies in Listen-
    ing." Audio Visual Communication Review 2:263-76,
    Fall 1954.   485
A review and analysis of research already done and of
that still needed in the field of listening.   Forty-six item
bibliography.

Graham, Juston Lair.   The Teaching of Listening Skills
    Through Music Lessons in Fourth and Fifth Grade Class-
    rooms.   Doctoral dissertation.   Greeley, Colo.: Colo-
    rado State College, 1965.   Abstract: Dissertation Ab-
    stracts 26:7114-15, 1966.   486
Daily ten-minute lessons in listening to music were giv-
en for five weeks to 163 pupils.   The Hollow Listening Test
was used as a pre- and post-test.   The experimental group
made significantly greater improvement in listening scores
than did a comparable control group.

Graham, Wayne W. "Time Factor Alteration of Recorded
    Sound While Maintaining Frequency Constants." Pro-
    ceedings of the Louisville Conference on Time Com-
    pressed Speech, October 19-21, 1966.   (Edited by Emer-
    son Foulke.) Louisville, Ky.: Center for Rate Con-
    trolled Recordings, University of Louisville, 1967. p.
    87.   487
A very brief description of a device for compressing
speech, based on the original Fairbanks design.

Grant, David M. and Fitts, Joe W. Jr.   "Communication

Courses in 1952." Journal of Communication 2:31-37,
November 1952.   488
A survey of college communication teaching revealed
that listening was taught in 25 per cent of basic communication courses, in 43 per cent of English courses, and in 15
per cent of speech courses.

Gray, Wallace Allison. Listeners' and Readers' Responses
to Poetry. Doctoral dissertation. New York: Columbia University, 1958. Abstract: Dissertation Abstracts
19:190-91, 1958.   489
In this very superior and concisely reported experimental study 48 college students were used as subjects. Two
poems were presented orally and two were read by the subjects. No differences were found in any area of comprehension between the two methods of presentation.

Green, Marion Evans. An Exploratory Investigation of Listening Ability and Certain Factors Accompanying Listening in Selected Groups of College Students in the University of Tennessee at Knoxville. Master's thesis. Knoxville, Tenn.: University of Tennessee, 1958.   490

Greene, Edward B. "Certain Aspects of Lecture, Reading
and Guided Reading." School and Society 39:619-24,
May 1934.   491
Greene reports that in elementary psychology classes
retention was better on reading assignments for the upper
quartile readers, better on lectures for the lower quartile
readers, and about the same for others. Guided reading
was superior to presentation by lecture.

----. "The Relative Effectiveness of Lecture and Individual
Reading as Methods of College Teaching." Genetic Psychology Monographs 4:457-563, December 1928.   492
On immediate testing after a lecture there was little difference between those having heard the lecture and those
who read the material, but on delayed recall of two weeks
the lecture method was found to be superior. This may be
due to the relative quality of reading and lecture notes.

Greenwich Public Schools. Study Skills: Listening. Greenwich, Conn.: Author, n.d. Summary: Grade Teacher
84(6):122-23+, February 1967.   493
The sequential development of listening skills from kindergarten to grade twelve. Rules for teachers and students,
a checklist for good listening, and the scope of instruction

and suggested activities for each level in each subject area
are given.

Gregory-Panopoulos, John Fred. An Experimental Applica-
     tion of "Cloze" Procedure as a Diagnostic Test of Listen-
     ing Comprehension Among Foreign Students.   Doctoral
     dissertation.   Los Angeles, Calif.: University of South-
     ern California, 1966. Abstract: Dissertation Ab-
     stracts 27:2213A, 1967.   494
The development and validation of a listening comprehension test applying "Cloze" procedures. The Brown-Carlsen,
in an abbreviated form, and the California Reading Tests
were used as criterion measures. Ninety foreign students
were subjects. Text of the test is included. A high reliability and satisfactory validity are reported.

Gresham, Sean. "Hard of Listening?" Supervisory Manage-
     ment 10(4):11-12, April 1965.   495
A good listener approaches the speaker with the idea
that he can learn something from him. Listeners should try
to expand their span of concentration. The listener should
not permit his biases to cause him to lose the point being
made.

Grief, Edwin Charles. Modern Salesmanship. Englewood
     Cliffs, N.J.: Prentice-Hall, 1958, p. 83-85, 165, and
     239-40.   496
The role of listening in salesmanship is described.

Grindle, C.R. "Listen Your Way to Success." Industrial
     Canada 65(7):33-36, November 1964.   497
Listening is an economical way of getting information
and at the same time it leads to better understanding between people. Several barriers to good listening are discussed.

Groff, Patrick (Ed.). "Research Critiques." Elementary
     English 44:405-10, April 1967.   498
Opposing views by Dr. Charles Petrie and Dr. Ramon
Ross on articles by Lundsteen and Fawcett on the teaching
of listening. Dr. Petrie contends that not enough is known
about listening to make it possible to either teach or test it.
Dr. Ross questions the adequacy of the STEP Listening Test
used by Fawcett and the procedure of administering the test
by tape.

Gruszczynski, Sister Mary Lauriana. An Experimental Study

of Functional Reading and Listening Skills in the Fourth
Grade. Doctoral dissertation. New York: Fordham
University, 1957.   499
The Hollow Listening Test was administered to 400 pupils. The author reports that direct instruction was significantly more effective than incidental teaching of listening
skills.

Guthrie, Ruth. "Developing Story Sense in Primary Grades."
Teachers' Science Bulletin in Reading 14: No. 3, February 1953.   500
The author explains the importance of listening in developing a story sense in young children.

Guthrie, Warren. "Training in Listening." (Abstract.)
Journal of the American Society of Training Directors
13(7):6-7, July 1959.   501
Guthrie gives four levels of listening: I can hear, I can
repeat, I will obey, and I participate.

Haakenson, Robert. "Listening - The Much Neglected Key to
the Practice of Communication." National Underwriter
67(31):2+, August 2, 1963. Also in National Underwriter Life Edition 67(35):2+, August 31, 1963.   502
Listening is a common means of communication, yet we
tend to be poor listeners. Downward oral communication in
industry is ineffective because of poor listening. Full attention and objectivity are essential to effective listening.

Haberland, John Andrew. An Investigation of Listening Abil-
ity in College Freshmen. Doctoral dissertation. Evan-
ston, Ill.: Northwestern University, 1956. Abstract:
Dissertation Abstracts 17:303, 1956. Excerpts: "A
Comparison of Listening Tests with Standardized Tests."
Journal of Educational Research 52:299-302, April 1959.
Summary: "Listening Ability in College Freshmen."
School and Society 84:217-18, December 22, 1956. 503
One hundred ten college freshmen were given a battery
of tests consisting of the ACE, Reading Comprehension por-
tion of the Cooperative English Test, Michigan State College
Listening Test (the Dow Test), Stephens College Listening
Test, the Brown-Carlsen Listening Comprehension Test,
Iowa Silent Reading Test, and the Thurstone Temperament
Scale. Correlations among the listening tests and with other
test results are reported. The author concludes that listening tests yield "vastly different" results when correlated with
reading; that these listening tests do not measure the same

thing; that the Brown-Carlsen Test correlates most highly
with the linguistic portions of other tests; that the Stephens
College Test correlates most highly with a grade point average; and that listening ability probably is a combination of
abilities working in association with one another.

----. "Speaker Effectiveness and the Brown-Carlsen Listen-
     ing Test." School and Society 86:198-99, April 26,
     1958.   504
     Haberland reports that there was no significant difference
in test results when the Brown-Carlsen Test was given by a
person with speech training and when it was given by a person without speech training.

Hackett, Herbert. "A Null Hypothesis: There Is Not
     Enough Evidence." Education 75:149-51, January 1955.
     Reprinted in Listening: Readings (Edited by Sam Duker.)
     Metuchen, N. J.: Scarecrow Press, 1966. p. 456-59.
                                                          505
     According to Hackett, there is no evidence that listening
instruction is more than a current fad, that the kind of listening tested in a listening test is in any way related to listening in everyday life, or that knowledge about listening
contributes to the ability to listen.

Hadley, Edythe W. "Techniques of Teaching High School
     Students To Listen." English Journal 40:369-72, Sep-
     tember 1951.   506
     Listening is best taught by taking advantage of everyday
situations. Under proper circumstances children will listen
to each other.

Haehl, Chez J. "Developing Literate Listeners." Projects
     of the Fourth Workshop in Basic Communications. Uni-
     versity of Denver, 1946. (Edited by Edwin L. Levy.)
     Denver, Colo.: University of Denver Press, 1946, p.
     73-77.   507
     To teach listening, one must examine the listening proc-
ess which includes the listening span; examine listening
blockages; and use drills, exercises, and guidance to develop discriminating in listening.

Hall, Robert Oscar. An Exploratory Study of Listening of
     Fifth Grade Pupils. Doctoral dissertation. Los Ange-
     les, Calif.: University of Southern California, 1954.
                                                          508
     This thesis contains an outstanding review and analysis

of previous research to date. On the basis of a study of
441 fifth grade pupils who were extensively tested, the author concluded that: listening scores are not distributed
normally; listening is not a generalized ability but a cluster
of specific abilities closely related to the listening task; in-
tuitive judgments of both teachers and pupils are untrust-
worthy criteria of the actual ability of a pupil to listen; the
relationship between ability to listen and other measurable
differences in ability found to exist in studies of college and
high school students, such as intelligence, reading, and language, are also found in elementary pupils.

Hall, Robert S. "You Can Make Your Boss Listen."
      Nation's Business 48(4):60-64, April 1960.   509
      The following rules are given: 1. catch the interest of
top management; 2. recognize the importance of timing; 3.
conceal pride of authorship; 4. avoid the jargon of the spe-
cialist; 5. present a balanced proposal; 6. learn to compro-
mise; and 7. avoid an unfavorable decision by stalling or re-
tiring when you see that a favorable decision is not forthcom-
ing.

Hampleman, Richard Samuel. Comparison of Listening and
      Reading Comprehension Ability of Fourth and Sixth Grade
      Pupils. Doctoral dissertation. Bloomington, Ind.: Indi-
      ana University, 1955. Abstract: Dissertation Abstracts
      15:1757-58, 1955. Summary: Elementary English 35:
      49-53, January 1958.   510
      Hampleman reports that listening was superior to read-
ing in the fourth and sixth grades; listening superiority was
more marked with easy materials than with difficult ones;
length of passages had no effect on the relative merits of listening and reading; and increase in mental age and, to a lesser extent, in chronological age, decreased the difference
between the two modes of presentation. An excellent review
and analysis of previous research on the relative merits of
oral and visual presentation of material for learning is included.

Hancock, Jewell Hazel Thompson. The Effect of Listening
      and Discussion of Social Values Held by Sixth-Grade
      Children. Doctoral dissertation. Boulder, Colo.: Uni-
      versity of Colorado, 1960. Abstract: Dissertation Ab-
      stracts 21:3377, 1961.   511
      Using 82 sixth grade pupils as subjects, Hancock reports
that social leadership and responsibility, as measured by the
Behavior Preference Record, increased after 24 lessons and

discussions on these subjects.

Hanley, Clair Norton. A Factorial Analysis of Speech Per-
    ception. Doctoral dissertation. Iowa City, Iowa: State
    University of Iowa, 1952. Abstract: Dissertation Ab-
    stracts 12:635-36, 1952. Summary: Journal of Speech
    and Hearing Disorders 21:76-87, March 1956.   512
    Thirty-two auditory tasks were given to 105 college stu-
dents. They were administered in a sound proof room to
groups of seven. A factor analysis identified the following:
verbal facility, pure tone acuity, Seashore Battery factor,
voice memory, resistance to distortion of monosyllables, resistance to masking, unpleasantness, synthesis--where listening was required to piece together fragments of speech and
make a correct response.

Hanna, Regina C. and Liberati, Matilda. A Comparison of
    Silent Reading and Listening by Written Recall and Mul-
    tiple Choice Type Tests in Grade Four. Master's thes-
    is. Boston: Boston University, 1952.   513
    The authors report that on a multiple choice test fourth
grade children showed significantly better results on passages
read orally to them than on passages they read to themselves. On written recall tests, however, the difference was
only slightly in favor of listening. This study is a companion study to that of Kelley and others.

Hannah, Jo Morrison. A Study of Listening from the Ruesch-
    Bateson Theory of Communication. Doctoral dissertation.
    Denver, Colo.: University of Denver, 1961. Abstract:
    Dissertation Abstracts 22:3775, 1962.   514
    Hannah reports that college freshmen understood narra-
tive material better when they listened to it than when they
read it. The opposite was true of descriptive material.

Hansen, Ronald G. An Experimental Investigation of the Ef-
    fects of Different Rates of Speaking on Intelligibility.
    Master's thesis. Columbus, Ohio: Ohio State Univer-
    sity, 1950.   515
    A disc recording was made of 36 subjects reading word
lists at 135, 160, and 184 wpm and at their own natural
speeds. The only statistically significant difference in intelligibility was between readings at the readers' natural speeds
and at the other rates.

Hanson-Good, Rachel Jean. Listening Comprehension of
    Kindergarten Children as Indicated by Partial Recall to

Stories Read to a Child Alone and as a Member of a
Group. Master's thesis. Des Moines, Iowa: Drake
University, 1961.   516
At the kindergarten level children understood stories bet-
ter when they were read to individually than when they were
read to as members of a group.

Harley, Randall. "An Experimental Program in Compressed
    Speech at the Tennessee School for the Blind." Proceed-
    ings of the Louisville Conference on Time Compressed
    Speech, October 19-21, 1966. (Edited by Emerson
    Foulke.) Louisville, Ky.: Center for Rate Controlled
    Recordings, University of Louisville, 1967. p. 63-66.
                                                                         517
A one-month experiment with textbook material com-
pressed to 275 wpm. Subjects, aged eighteen to 21, were
senior high school English students with visual handicaps.
Comprehension test results improved from a range of eighteen to 83 on a 100 point test with a mean of 43, to a range
of 40 to 90 on a 100 point test with a mean of 67. Students' attitudes toward compressed speech were mixed although predominantly favorable for prose and unfavorable for
poetry.

Harris, Daisy Phinazee. The Effectiveness of Listening Ex-
    periences Upon Reading Readiness Levels of Kindergar-
    ten Pupils. Master's thesis. Atlanta, Ga.: Atlanta
    University, 1965.   518
Twenty children were given thirty 15-minute lessons on
listening skills, described in detail. The Metropolitan Reading Readiness Test was used as a pre- and post-test. There
was no significant difference between this group and a comparable control group.

Harris, J. Donald. "Hearing." Annual Review of Psychol-
    ogy 9:47-70, 1958.   519
One hundred eighty references.

Harrison, Carol Franklin Jr. A Study of the Relationship
    Between Speaking Effectiveness and Listening Compre-
    hension in the Single Individual. Master's thesis.
    Missoula, Mont.: Montana State University, 1959. 520
Using as subjects 84 college students who had not had
speech training, the author found a positive relationship between listening ability, as measured by the Dow Test, and
speaking effectiveness.

Harson, Helen Jordan. An Experiment To Determine That the Listening Skills of Sixth-Grade Children Can Be Improved. Master's thesis. Providence, R.I.: Rhode Island College of Education, 1955.   521
Using 50 pupils as subjects, Harson reports that listening ability, as measured by an author-devised test, increased significantly more for members of a group which had been given lessons in listening than for pupils who had not received such instruction. The instruction in listening was for specific details, main ideas, ideas in sequence and directions.

Hartlage, Lawrence C. "Differences in Listening Comprehension of the Blind and the Sighted." International Journal for the Education of the Blind, 13:1-6, October 1963.   522
Fifty blind high school students were paired with 50 sighted students. The groups were tested on listening comprehension by an author-made test based on a prose selection presented by tape recorder. There was no significant difference between the groups on the listening test. The correlation between intelligence, as measured by the Otis Gamma Test of Mental Ability, and listening, was .79 for the blind and .66 for the sighted.

Hartley, Helene. "Just Current Fads?" NEA Journal 39: 697-99, December 1950.   523
Current emphasis on listening instruction is an inevitable outcome of the recognition of the two-way nature of communication.

Harvey, John C. Study of the Durrell-Sullivan Reading Capacity Test as a Measure of Intelligence. Master's thesis. Sacramento, Calif.: Sacramento State College, 1961.   524
Substantial correlations are found between performance on the Durrell-Sullivan test and intelligence, as measured by the California Mental Maturity Test and the Wechsler-Bellevue Scale. There is a letter from Donald D. Durrell in the appendix relating the history of the Durrell-Sullivan Reading Capacity Test. The letter states that this test was originally devised and intended as a listening test.

Harwood, Kenneth A. "A Concept of Listenability." Western Speech 14(2):10-12, March 1950. Reprinted in Listening: Readings. (Edited by Sam Duker.) Metuchen, N.J.: Scarecrow Press, 1966. p. 21-24.   525

Speech intelligibility or audibility is a condition precedent
to listening, but it must not be confused with listening comprehension, which is a function of the listener. Listenability
is a term expressing the comparative ease or difficulty with
which spoken language can be comprehended.

----. An Experimental Comparison of Listening Comprehen-
        sibility with Reading Comprehensibility. Doctoral disser-
        tation. Los Angeles, Calif.: University of Southern Cali-
        fornia, 1950. Abstract: Speech Monographs 18:123-24,
        August 1951.   526
Using 240 tenth grade pupils as subjects, Harwood reports only small differences in intelligibility of passages read
compared to those delivered orally. This was true at various levels of difficulty, as measured by the Dale-Chall Readability Scale. This is a companion study to those of Cartier
and Goodman-Malamuth using the same materials.

----. "Listenability and Rate of Presentation." Speech
        Monographs 22:57-59, March 1955.   527
This is a description of the experimental work of Goodman-Malamuth, which was later incorporated into a thesis.
(q. v.)

----. "Listenability and Readability." Speech Monographs
        22:49-53, March 1955.   528
This is a discussion of the inadequacy of readability
formulas in measuring the degree of difficulty in orally delivered material. Factors to consider in determining listenability are discussed.

----, and Cartier, Francis A. Jr. "On Definition of Listen-
        ability." Southern Speech Journal 18(1):20-23, Septem-
        ber 1952.   529
Listening is defined as attending to sound stimuli in order to comprehend their meanings. Experimental work
should be done on the development of a satisfactory measure
of listenability and terminology in this area should be sys-
tematized.

Hast, Malcolm Howard. The Relative Efficiency of a Sten-
        ographer-Typist in Noise and with One and Two-Channel
        Listening. Master's thesis. Columbus, Ohio: Ohio
        State University, 1958.   530
Employing the method of analysis of variance, the author
reports no significant difference in the efficiency of a sten-
ographer-typist between one- and two-channel listening and

no significantly adverse effect by the presence of noise.

Hatfield, W. Wilbur. "Advances in the Teaching of English."
    NEA Journal 45(2):90-92, February 1956.   531
    "Forty years ago no one but primary teachers preparing
to teach phonics thought of giving instruction in listening,
whereas we now realize that listening is an art as complex
as reading and is improvable through instruction and guided
practice."

----. "Parallels in Teaching Students to Listen and to
    Read." English Journal 35:553-58, December 1946.
                                                     532
    When planning listening instruction much can be learned
from an examination of the ideas used in teaching reading.
One element common to reading and listening is the necessity of a purpose. The student must be aware of the particular purpose of his listening task at any given time.
Some of the purposes of listening are:
    1. Listening for an answer to a definite question.
    2. Listening to a question with the intention of answer-
       ing it.
    3. Listening to form an opinion.
    4. Listening for news.
    5. Listening to an argument in order to answer it.
    6. Listening to directions which one intends to follow.
    7. Listening for unspecified information on a topic in
       which one is interested.

Haugh, Oscar M. The Comparative Value of Reading and
    Listening in the Acquisition of Information and the
    Changing of Attitudes of Elementary Grade Students.
    Doctoral dissertation. Minneapolis, Minn.: University
    of Minnesota, 1950. Summary: Journal of Educational
    Research 45:489-98, March 1952.   533
    Using 539 students as subjects, Haugh reports a corre-
lation of .54 between reading and listening. He found that as
means of changing attitudes listening and reading were not
significantly different in effect but that reading and listening
simultaneously was significantly more effective.

Haun, Ruth. "Creative Listening." Today's Speech 1(2):
    18-20, October 1953.   534
    Active creative listening aids the human creative proc-
ess.

Hauser, Marian Hollingsworth. A Comparison of Children's

Recognition Vocabulary from Visual and Auditory Stimuli.
Master's thesis.   Sacramento, Calif.: Sacramento State
College, 1963.   535
Fifty-four second and third grade children made 640 er-
rors on a visually presented test of 110 words from the
Dolch Basic Sight Word Test.   When the words were pre-
sented orally, 183 errors were made.   Only four per cent
made more errors on the oral than on the visual test.

Havlicek, Larry L.   The Non-Recognition of Auditory Stimu-
    li Presented During Sleep.   Master's thesis.   Lawrence,
    Kan.: University of Kansas, 1959.   536
Using 91 subjects ranging in age from 18 to 28, Havil-
cek reports that he was unable to find any evidence that
learning takes place during sleep as a result of auditory
stimuli.

Hayakawa, S.I.   "On Communication with the Soviet Union."
    ETC.   17:389-400, December 1960.   537
Hayakawa suggests that many Russians be invited to
come to the United States and that we listen to them because,
he says, "The funny thing about human beings, including you
and me and the Russians, is that we tend to respect the intelligence of, and eventually to like, those who listen atten-
tively to our ideas even if they continue to disagree with us."

----.   "How to Attend a Conference."   ETC. 3(1):5-9, Au-
    tumn 1955.   Also in: Our Language and Our World.
    New York: Harpers, 1959. p. 103-110.   538
Education tends to emphasize skills of output while neglecting the skills of input, especially that of listening.   A
good listener refrains from agreement or disagreement until
he is sure what the speaker's views are.   Listening is not
merely a matter of polite silence.   A good listener has empathy with rather than sympathy for a speaker.   A discussion after a speech should be for clarification rather than
for seeking a victory over the speaker.

----.   "Let's Listen to the Russians."   Minutes (Magazine
    of the Nationwide Insurance Companies) December 1961,
    p. 27-30.   539
The author suggests that in dealing with the Russians we
use Carl Rogers' non-evaluative listening.   This leads to
self-discovery of errors, lack of defensiveness, and modera-
tion of dogmatism.   Differences cannot be resolved without
communication.   If we have faith in ourselves we can afford
to listen.

----. "The Task of the Listener." ETC. 7:9-17, Autumn
1949. Also in Mc Grath, Earl James. (Editor.) Communication in General Education. Dubuque, Iowa: Wm.
C. Brown, 1949. p. 103-12.   540
Communication is a mediatory art and can serve to prevent settlement of conflict by force.

Hayes, Mary Therese. Construction and Evaluation of Comparable Measures of English Language Comprehension in
Reading and Listening. Doctoral dissertation. Boston:
Boston University, 1957. Abstract: Dissertation Abstracts 18:1721-22, 1958.   541
The author developed a test based on vocabulary knowledge and sentence comprehension, which is suitable for both
oral and written presentation. The text is not included.
Subjects in this well-done study were 250 second- and third-
grade children.

Hayward, Lillian V. Listening as an Aid to Learning.
Master's thesis. Newark, N. J.: New Jersey State
Teachers College at Newark, 1952.   542
Hayward emphasizes the importance of training in hearing in the teaching of listening skills. An experiment with
two eighth grade classes is described, and it is reported
that measurable improvement in hearing and listening skills
resulted.

Heath, Martha. A Study in Listening: The Relationship Between Interest, Educability and Score in an Objective
Examination Over the Factual Content of an Informative
Speech. Master's thesis. Tallahassee, Fla.: Florida
State University, 1951. Abstract: Speech Monographs
19:159-60, August 1952.   543
Heath reports that she was unable to find a significant
difference in comprehension of a speech between a group
whose interests, as measured by the Kuder Preference
Scale, were dealt with in the speech and a group whose interests were not dealt with. The correlation between listening and intelligence was . 47.

Hedges, Thayne A. The Effect of Auditory Stimuli Presented During the Sleep of Children with Delayed Speech.
Master's thesis. Wichita, Kansas: University of Wichita, 1950.   544
Three mentally retarded aphasic children were subjected
while sleeping to recordings teaching speech sounds. No
measure of state of sleep is reported. There was some in-

dication of speech improvement, but the author points out
that this may have been due to speech lessons given during
the day.

Hedrick, Dona Lea. A Developmental Investigation of Chil-
    drens' Abilities to Respond to Competing Messages
    Varied in Intensity and Content. Doctoral dissertation.
    Seattle, Wash.: University of Washington, 1967. Ab-
    stract: Dissertation Abstracts 28:1926A-27A, 1967.
                                                        545
    Messages containing directions were presented to 120
children from kindergarten to the fifth grade along with distracting messages which varied in intensity and content. Accuracy in following the directions thus presented increased
with age; the relative intensity of the competing message
most affected children from kindergarten through grade two;
and the content of the messages most affected those in the
third grade. No difference was found between boys and
girls.

Hedtke, Florence G. "Methods for Improving Appreciation
    of Materials Presented Orally in Kindergarten Through
    Grade Three." Oral Aspects of Reading. Proceedings
    of the Annual Conference on Reading. Chicago: Uni-
    versity of Chicago Press, 1955. p. 111-12.   546
    The author advocates using conversations to help young
children learn to listen.

Heilman, Arthur. An Investigation in Measuring and Im-
    proving the Listening Ability of College Freshmen. Doc-
    toral dissertation. Iowa City, Iowa: State University of
    Iowa, 1951. Abstract: Speech Monographs 18:302-08,
    November 1951. Excerpts: "Critical Listening and the
    Educational Process." Education 72:481-87, March
    1952. Excerpts: Listening: Readings. (Edited by Sam
    Duker.) Metuchen, N.J.: Scarecrow Press, 1966. p.
    187-88.   547
    The purpose of this study was to develop a series of
six training lessons for improvement of student listening.
Broad objectives of these units were:
    1. To point out to the student a number of listening
        habits which authorities believe make the difference
        between good and poor listeners.
    2. To build up in the student's mind a respect for lis-
        tening as a means of acquiring knowledge.
    3. To explain "projection" and to show the student how
        his own ideas color his reactions to speakers.

4. To provide him with listening situations in which he can discover his own bias as well as that of the speaker.
5. To provide listening situations in which the student can practice recognizing main ideas.
6. To show him how to draw correct inference from facts.

----. "Listening and the Curriculum." Education 75:283-87, January 1955.   548
Educators lean on listening but assume that, unlike playing, speaking, etc., listening requires no instruction. Some unanswered questions about listening are:
1. Can pupils "listen-learn" for 30, 40, or 50 consecutive minutes with efficiency?
2. What are the facts about listening readiness at various levels?
3. Is there eivdence that listening ability can be improved?
4. How are students' concepts related to their learning by listening?
5. How are an individual's emotional responses related to his learning by listening?
6. How does teacher uniqueness inhibit learning by listening?
7. How can listening be evaluated?

Helping Managers Do a Better Job of Listening to Employees. Research Report of the Public Opinion Index for Industry Vol. 23, No. 12. Condensed in Executive Summary of same report. Princeton, N.J.: Opinion Research Corporation, December 1965. Summary: Iron Age 198(15): 21, October 13, 1966.   549
One hundred and thirty engineers, 272 white-collar employees, 803 hourly employees, and 233 of their superiors, employed by a major chemical firm, a household products manufacturer, a midwestern utility, and a large branch store of a major retailer, were surveyed. The study emphasized the importance of listening by management to successful upward communication. Extensive data in the main report.

Henderson, L. J. "Creative Listening." Readings in Personnel Administration. (Edited by Paul Pigors and Charles Meyers.) New York: McGraw-Hill, 1952, p. 186-87. Reprinted from: "Physician and Patient as a Social System." New England Journal of Medicine 212(18):819-23, May 2, 1925.   550

The importance to physicians of good listening is described. A physician should listen to what a patient wants
to tell, does not want to tell, and cannot tell.

Henderson, La Vetta J. "Don't Overlook Our Own Language
    Barrier." Grade Teacher 83(7):24, March 1966.   551
    Culturally deprived children have a language handicap
similar to that of foreign-born students. It helps to teach
listening and organizational skills so that they may learn to
make comparisons and associations, draw inferences, and
solve problems.

Hendrickson, Amanda E. "How to Teach Young People To
    Listen." North Dakota Teacher 27(6):17-18, February
    1948.   552
    Discussion of classroom procedures.

Henmon, V. A. C. "The Relation Between Mode of Presenta-
    tion and Retention." Psychological Review 19:79-96,
    March 1912.   553
    Henmon reports experimental findings showing that "audi-
tory presentation is clearly superior to visual presentation
in immediate memory of adults."

Henneman, Richard H. "The Intelligibility of Highly Speeded
    Speech for Purposes of Auditory Communication." Ab-
    stract. American Psychologist 5:361, July 1950.   554
    Intelligibility remained above 90 per cent for presenta-
tion rates up to 2.5 times the original, using the chop-splice
technique. With a speed-up of 2 times the original, in
which a frequency shift was involved, there was 65 per cent
intelligibility. For continuous speech the intelligibility was
79 per cent, 61 per cent and 37 per cent for 2, 2.3, and 2.8
times the original rate, respectively.

----. "A Technique for the Investigation of the Practical
    Limits of Speeded Speech." American Psychologist 4:
    304, July 1949.   555
    This is an abstract of a paper on the experimental work
done with W.D. Garvey on speeding speech by chopping
small segments from taped speech. It is reported that at
a rate 400 per cent faster than the original there was 40 per
cent intelligibility; at 350 per cent, 60 per cent; at 300 per
cent, 80 per cent; and at 200 per cent, 95 per cent.

----. "Vision and Audition as Sensory Channels for Com-
    munication." Quarterly Journal of Speech 38:161-66,

April 1952.   556
The author states that experimental literature has failed
to give the answer to the relative merits of visual and auditory presentations of learning material. He says that dis-
crepancies in findings are due to differences in types of materials, methods of presentation, intelligibility measures employed, characteristics of the receivers, and environmental
conditions of presentation.

Henry, Richard. "The Integrity of the Listener." Today's
      Speech 5(3):25-28, September 1957.   557
The essence of listening is a willingness to affirm the
integrity of others and to insist on its value.

Henry, William Gannon, Jr. Recognition of Time Com-
      pressed Speech as a Function of Word Length and Fre-
      quency of Use. Doctoral dissertation. Bloomington,
      Ind.: Indiana University, 1966. Abstract: Dissertation
      Abstracts 27:3310A-11A, 1967.   558
This experiment utilized the Language Master to ascertain the degree of word recognition of 25 undergraduate college students. Forty selected words contained from three
to eleven phonemes, and occurred from one to 1000 times
per million words according to the Thorndike-Lorge list.
They were compressed from an original rate of 175 wpm to
six speeds, ranging from 200 to 433 wpm. Increases in
word compression are accompanied by decreased word recognition; recognition is facilitated as word length is increased;
as frequency of usage is increased, recognition is facilitated;
and recognition is facilitated by a combination of length and
frequency of usage.

Herman, Wayne L. Jr. "The Use of Language Arts in So-
      cial Studies Lessons." American Educational Research
      Journal 4:117-24, March 1967.   559
Data collected during five periods in fourteen fifth
grades. Listening took up 76 per cent of the time, writing
2 per cent, and reading 13 per cent. The amount of time
spent listening to the teacher was greater in classes for below average learners. No measure was taken of pupil
achievement.

Heron, W. T. and Ziebarth, E. W. "A Preliminary Experi-
      mental Comparison of Radio and Classroom Lectures."
      Speech Monographs 13:54-57, 1946.   560
No difference was found in comprehension when a lecture was presented live or by radio. However, students

preferred the lecturer.

Hickey, M. Patricia. "They Really Listen Now That They
    Have a Listening Center." Instructor 76(2):85, October
    1966.   561
    A description of a classroom listening center where chil-
dren listen to tapes and recordings over earphones. The
center facilitates education and also entertains.

Higgins, Ivan Duke. An Empirical Study of Listening Re-
    lated to Anxiety and to Certain Other Measures of Ability
    and Achievement. Doctoral dissertation. Los Angeles,
    Calif: University of Southern California, 1964. Ab-
    stract: Dissertation Abstracts 25:745, 1964.   562
    A correlational study report. The correlation between
listening (on the STEP test and the Brown Carlsen Test) and
anxiety (on the Manifest Anxiety Scale and the Text Anxiety
Scale) was very low. Correlation between STEP and Brown-
Carlsen was .58 for men and .53 for women. High reliabilities were reported for both listening tests. One hundred
eighty-one freshmen communication students were subjects.

High, Charles S. A Study of Certain Auditory Functions
    and Abilities in Good and Poor Listeners. Master's
    thesis. Tallahassee, Fla.: Florida State University,
    1952.   563
    Kramar's Listening Test was used to establish two
groups with significantly different listening abilities. No significant differences were found in the performance on the
Seashore Measures of Musical Ability, the Mildred Templin
Speech Sound Discrimination Test, and the digit memory
test from the Wechsler-Bellevue Scale.

Hildebrandt, Herbert W. 'Now Hear This - Some Pointers
    on the Neglected Art of Listening." Supervisory Manage-
    ment 7(1):2-5, January 1962. Reprinted in Listening:
    Readings. (Edited by Sam Duker.) Metuchen, N.J.:
    Scarecrow Press, 1966. p. 389-93.   564
    Time and effort are needed for improvement of listening
habits. Becoming involved and participating help listening.
A good listener asks questions. A speaker's purpose should
be kept in mind by the listener.

Hildreth, Gertrude. 'Interrelationship Among the Language
    Arts." Elementary School Journal 48:538-49, June
    1948.   565
    The close relationship between reading and listening is

charted.   Much poor reading is actually poor language comprehension.

Hildreth, Richard A.   An Experimental Study of Audiences'
    Ability to Distinguish Between Sincere and Insincere
    Speeches.   Doctoral dissertation.   Los Angeles, Calif.:
    University of Southern California, 1954.   566
    Using as subjects 159 members of luncheon service
clubs, Hildreth reports that sincere and insincere filmed
speeches could not be distinguished by audiences.

Hill, Edwin S.   An Analysis of the Results of Special Train-
    ing in Listening Compared to Special Training in Read-
    ing Skills.   Doctoral dissertation.   Bloomington, Ind.:
    Indiana University, 1961.   Abstract: Dissertation Ab-
    stracts 22:3093-94, 1962.   567
    In an experiment using 96 freshman education students,
one group was given training in listening, one in reading,
and one served as a control.   The first two groups gained
significantly more in both reading and listening than did the
control group.

Hill, Priscilla.   An Informal Survey of Listening Skills.
    Master's thesis.   New Britain, Conn.: Central Connecti-
    cut State College, 1963.   568
    A description of a listening test designed for second
graders is given.   Skills which were tested included listening for directions, for word meaning, to draw conclusions,
for immediate recall of details, to identify the main point,
and to identify sequence.   The text of the test and of five
lesson plans for teaching these skills is included.

Hill, Ruth E.   "Listen, Teacher!"   Instructor 75(1):56, Sep-
    tember 1965.   569
    A checklist for teachers to determine how effectively
they teach listening in the elementary school.

Hirsh, I. J.   "Hearing."   Annual Review of Psychology 6:95-
    118, 1955.   570
    One hundred forty references.

Hoffman, Miriam.   "Our Listening Center Livens Language
    Arts."   Elementary School Journal 63:381-85, April
    1963.   571
    This is a description of a listening center made in the
school shop and which enables a number of children to listen
to recordings of literature on earphones.   This kind of ac-

tivity aids in the development of listening skills.

Hogan, Ursula. An Experiment in Improving the Listening
    Skills of Fifth and Sixth Grade Pupils. Master's thesis.
    Berkeley, Calif.: University of California, 1953.   572
    Intensive instruction in listening resulted in improvement
of listening skills as measured by an author-made test.
Children improved in following instructions, making contributions to class discussions, paying attention, focusing discussions on main ideas, making oral reports, and asking questions. A correlation between listening and intelligence of
.60 is reported.

Holleran, Brian Patrick. A Comparison of Oral and Written
    Listening Tests. Master's thesis. Columbus, Ohio:
    Ohio State University, 1966.   573
    When comprehension of 118 subjects was checked after
listening to "good" and "poor" speakers, scores were higher in
both instances on oral than on written tests.

Hollingsworth, Paul M. "Can Training in Listening Improve
    Reading?" Reading Teacher 18:121-23+, November 1964.
                                                         574
    A summary of sixteen studies which support the idea
that instruction in listening will improve reading skills.

----. "Effectiveness of a Course in Listening Improvement
    for Adults." Journal of Communication 16:189-91, Sep-
    tember 1966.   575
    A twelve-week course in listening was given to two
groups of middle management personnel. The sessions lasted
two hours and were based on lectures, films, Nichols' book,
Are You Listening?, and SRA materials. The Brown-Carlsen was used as a pre- and post-test. Statistically significant improvement was made by each group.

----. "So They Listened: The Effects of a Listening Pro-
    gram." Journal of Communication 15:14-16, March
    1965.   576
    The EDL Listen and Read tapes were administered to
fourteen fifth grade pupils at the rate of three per week for
ten weeks. No significant differences between this group and
a comparable control group were found, beyond those expected by chance, on reading achievement, listening comprehension or study skills development. More teacher involve-
ment is necessary to obtain improvement in these areas.

----. A Study to Compare the Effect of Two Listening Programs on Reading Achievement and Listening Comprehension. Doctoral dissertation. Tucson, Arizona: University of Arizona, 1963. Abstract: Dissertation Abstracts 25:3913, 1964. Summary: Journal of Communication 14:19-21, March 1964.   577
Three groups of 97 eighth grade pupils were subjects. One was given ten weeks training in listening, using portions of the Educational Developmental Laboratories' listening program (a taped program, entitled Listen and Read). Another group used the listening skill building portion of the Science Research Associates' Reading Laboratory IIc. The third group continued with its normal school routine. The groups were equated on the basis of intelligence and reading test scores. A post-test in reading and listening, on the STEP test, showed no significant difference.

Hollow, Kevin, Sister M. An Experimental Study of Listening Comprehension at the Intermediate Grade Level. Doctoral dissertation. New York: Fordham University, 1955. Excerpts: "Have We Overlooked Listening?" Catholic School Journal 55(5):147-49, May 1955; "Listening Comprehension at the Elementary School Level." Elementary School Journal 56(4):158-61, December 1955; "Listening." National Catholic Educational Association Bulletin 54(1):285-92, August 1957. Comment: Catholic Educational Review 54:125, February 1956. Excerpts: Listening: Readings. (Edited by Sam Duker.) Metuchen, N.J.: Scarecrow Press, 1966. p. 219-25.   578
This is a description of the construction and validation of a listening test. The text is given. On the basis of testing 532 pupils, the following correlations with listening, as measured by this test, are reported: arithmetic reasoning .56; reading comprehension .55; reading vocabulary .47; intelligence .42; spelling .33; and total language .36. A procedure used in teaching listening skills to 500 fifth-grade pupils in a series of thirty planned lessons is described in detail.

Holmes, Alice L. Development of Effective Listening Skills in a Group of Sixth-Grade Children. Master's thesis. Des Moines, Iowa: Drake University, 1960.   579
A schoolroom study.

Holmes, Jack A. and Singer, Harry. The Substrata-Factor Theory: Substrata-Factor Differences Underlying Reading Ability in Known-Groups. Report of research performed pursuant to contracts with the United States Office of Education. Berkeley, Calif: Holmes and Singer, University of California, 1961. (mimeo.) Reviews: Sam Duker in Journal of Developmental Reading 5:195-97, Spring 1962 and Elementary English 41:921-24, December 1964; George D. Spache in Elementary English 41: 915-20, December 1964. Also in Cooperative Research Monograph, No. 14. Washington, D.C.: U.S. Department of Health, Education and Welfare, Office of Education, 1966.   580

Holmes, in a carefully designed and well executed study, used factor analysis to determine the factors involved in reading. He found a correlation between listening, as measured by the California Auding Test, and speed of reading to be .60. The corresponding correlation with power of reading was reported as .74. Holmes reports that 14 per cent of the variance of speed of reading was accounted for by listening. This was 25 per cent of that portion of the variance which was accounted for by the factor analysis. Of the variance of power of reading 16 per cent was accounted for by listening. This was 21 per cent of the portion of the variance accounted for. In his substrata analysis, Holmes reported that 68 per cent of the variance of the factor of listening in the case of speed of reading could be accounted for by the sub-factors of verbal analysis, range of information, vocabulary in context, Latin and Greek roots, and prefixes. Sub-factors which accounted for 58 per cent of the variance of listening as a factor of power of reading were: musicality, range of information, reasoning, prefixes, Latin and Greek roots, and speed of addition.

Holmes, Marjorie. "Are You Really a Good Listener?" Better Homes and Gardens 27(7):260+, March 1949.
                                                        581

An eight-question multiple choice quiz on how well housewives listen.

Holtzman, Paul D. "Communication Versus Expression in Speaking and Listening." Psychological and Psychiatric Aspects of Speech and Hearing (Edited by Dominick A. Barbara.) Springfield, Ill.: Charles C. Thomas, 1960. Chapter 1, p. 5-26.   582

Communicative listening is defined as that part of a listening event which is motivated toward creation of new associations or actively confirming old associations in the nervous system of the listener.

Expressive listening is that part of a listening event

which is motivated toward production of tension and passively
confirming old associations while resisting new associations
in the nervous system of the listener.

The implications of these definitions to the communication process are discussed.

----. "Do You Listen to Your Child?" Everywoman's Family Circle 57(6):33+, December 1962.   583
The author gives some rules for parents to follow in listening to their children: allow children to express curiosity;
do not put off children's simple requests; remember that
children may not understand the meaning of what you are
saying; and listen to what children really mean rather than
to the literal meaning of the words they use.

Homann, Harold Walter William. The Effect of Recorded
Stuttering on Listening Comprehension. Master's thesis.
Kalamazoo, Mich: Western Michigan University, 1958.
                                                        584
This contains the lecture comprehension portions of two
forms of the Brown-Carlsen Test, one in normal speech and
one with stuttering. Scores were higher on the normal
speech but the difference lacked statistical significance.

Hood, L. C. "Learning to Listen to English." National
Association of Secondary School Principals Bulletin.
39:79-81, September 1955.   585
A brief and cursory summary of some ideas that have
been advanced for teaching listening.

Hook, Julius N. "Developing Good Listeners." Journal of
Education 132:110+, April 1949.   586
An adequate summary of some ideas on teaching listening at the high school level that had appeared in the literature.

----. The Teaching of High School English. New York:
Ronald Press, 1950. Chapter 8, "Creative Listening."
                                                        587
The following techniques are given for improving listening: discussions of listening; suggestions on what to listen
for; note-taking; following instructions; understanding organization; selecting main ideas; critical evaluation; listening
for contradictions and fallacies; and bringing to bear one's
own previous knowledge.

Hopkins, John E. The Brown-Carlsen Test: An Investiga-

138   Listening Bibliography

tion of the Influence of Modes of Presentation, Class
Size, Sex, and Time of Presentation on Listening Comprehension. Master's thesis. Athens, Ohio: Ohio University, 1966.   588
An extensive analysis of listening comprehension of 235
college speech students in twelve classes. No significant
differences were found in relation to sex, mode of presentation (video-tape, audio portion only, and video portion with
placards), class size (varied from twelve to 24), and time
of day (8 a.m., noon, and 3 p.m.). The only significant
differences were in three classes: a video-tape small class
at 3 p.m., an audio-only small class at noon, and an audio-
only small class at 3 p.m.

Horowitz, Milton W. and Berkowitz, Alan. "Listening and
    Reading, Speaking and Writing: An Experimental Inves-
    tigation of Differential Acquisition and Reproduction of
    Memory." Perceptual and Motor Skills 24:207-15, Feb-
    ruary 1967.   589
Under controlled conditions, subjects differed in their
reproductions of The War on Ghosts, depending upon their
mode of acquisition (listening and reading) and their mode of
reproduction (speaking and writing). Listeners produced a
larger corpus, more ideas, fewer omissions of important
units, more distortions, and a stylistically superior reproduction than readers. Reproduction by speaking produced
a larger corpus, less diversity of expression, more additions, more subordinate ideas, and more signals than by
writing. Listening seems, logically and empirically, more
closely allied to speaking, and reading seems more closely
allied to writing.

----, and Newman, John B. "Spoken and Written Expres-
    sion." Journal of Abnormal and Social Psychology 68:
    640-47, June 1964. Excerpts: Newman, John B. and
    Horowitz, Milton W. College Composition and Com-
    munication 16:160-64, October 1965.   590
Two experiments to test differences between spoken and
written expression. These two modes were controlled by
limiting time for preparation and time for exposition, and by
limiting the subjects to two balanced topics. Since each sub
ject spoke and wrote on the two topics, each was his own
control. Spoken expression produces more material (words
phrases, and sentences), more ideas and subordinate ideas,
more ancillary ideas, more communicative signals, and mor
orientation signals. Spoken expression is more repetitious
and more elaborative in all aspects of analysis. These dif-

Horowitz, Milton W. and Newman, John B.   139

ferences between the two modes are related to facility of
utterance, both biologically and psychologically.   The psychological factors include inhibition, deliberativeness, memory for what is said, and a drive to prevent silent intervals.

----, and Berkowitz, Alan.   "Structural Advantage of the
Mechanism of Spoken Expression as a Factor in Differences in Spoken and Written Expression."   Perceptual
and Motor Skills 19:619-25, October 1964.   591
The authors hypothesized that the greater amount of
cognitive and linguistic material produced in speaking than
in writing in response to an open-ended question was due
to greater facility in speaking.   Therefore, an experiment was
performed involving typewriting and stenotyping.   As facility
increased in the writing process by these means, the cognitive and linguistic material increased but still differed significantly from the amount produced by speech.

Horrworth, Gloria L.   "Listening: A Facet of Oral Learning."   Elementary English 43:856-64+, December 1966.
                                                     592
Auding is defined as hearing, plus listening, plus cognizing.   Factors affecting hearing include acuity, binaurality,
masking, and fatigue.   Listening is defined as the process
of directing attention to, and thereby becoming aware of,
sound sequences.   Cognizing encompasses perception, judgment, reasoning, remembering, thinking, and imagining.
Thus, cognizing enables the listener to make comparisons,
note sequence of details, index, catalogue, draw inferences
and conclusions, recognize relationships, abstract main
ideas, and form sensory images.   Listening is not a discrete
skill or a generalized ability but a cluster of specific abilities closely related to those needed in reading.

----.   "The Listening Center."   Maryland Teacher 21(5):10+,
January 1964.   593
As the world becomes noisier, listening habits deterio-
rate.   Passive listening is being taught in the elementary
classroom whereas the need is for critical listening ability.
Listening centers in the classroom, using tapes and response work sheets in all areas of the curriculum, are advocated.   The preparation of the tapes is time-consuming,
but otherwise the use of the center fits in with classroom
work.   Informal evaluation showed the success of the proposed program in the author's classroom.

Hosey, Gladys Valney.   "Better Speech Through Better Lis-

tening." Journal of Business Education 34:172-73, January 1959.   594
Hosey describes the procedure she used in a high school English class. Emphasis was put on listening for such errors as overused words, undesirable expressions, grammatical errors, and mispronounced words. The author says that this procedure has been successful in promoting better speech as well as better listening.

Hoslett, Schuyler Dean. "Barriers to Communication." Personnel 28:108-14, September 1951.   595
In industry those with most authority often do not listen to those with less authority. This may result in the superior acting without full understanding of an issue and without understanding the sentiments of his subordinates.

Houston, Margaret D. A Language Arts Program for a Fourth Grade of Culturally Deprived Children. Master's thesis. Johnson City, Tenn.: East Tennessee State University, 1964.   596
Such children cannot be expected to understand directions immediately, and questions should be welcomed by the teacher. These children have developed non-verbal ways of communication, as they come from a disorganized environment where they have had little experience with real give-and-take conversation.

Howard, George W. "The Art of Listening." Research Development 14(9):30-31, September 1963.   597
Managerial judgment can be exercised only on the basis of information. Listening is useful in gathering such information. A course on listening, consisting of five two-hour sessions, is described.

----. "A Lesson in Listening." Machine Design 36(28):128-31, December 3, 1964.   598
Nichols' ten rules for good listening are presented pictorially. Three types of listening, lecture, conversational and conference, are discussed.

Howe, Doris L. An Exploratory Study Concerning Listening Comprehension and Speaking Effectiveness. Master's thesis. Tucson, Ariz.: University of Arizona, 1960.
                                                                    599
On the basis of tests given to 66 college students, Howe reports a correlation of .43 between speech effectiveness, as judged by a panel of college speech instructors, and listen-

ing, as measured by the Brown-Carlsen Test.

Hoyt, William George. The Effect on Learning of Auditory
    Material Presented During Sleep. Master's thesis.
    Washington, D. C.: George Washington University, 1953.
                                                          600
    In a carefully performed experimental study using 20 stu-
dents as subjects, Hoyt was unable to find evidence that
learning takes place as the result of the presentation of aural stimuli during sleep.

Husni-Palacios, Mary and Palacios, John R. "Auditory Per-
    ception and Personality Patterns of Blind Adults." Jour-
    nal of Projective Techniques and Personality Assessment
    28:284-92, September 1964.   601
    Two hundred and twelve blind subjects were given the
Sound Test, an oral projective test combining human and mechanical sounds. The results differentiated sharply between
those who had outside employment, those who worked in a
sheltered workshop, and those who were unemployed.

Hutton, Charles Lee. A Psychological Study of Speech Rate.
    Doctoral dissertation. Urbana, Ill.: University of Illi-
    nois, 1954. Abstract: Dissertation Abstracts 15:168,
    1955.   602
    Eight passages were taped (55 words) and presented in
original, compressed, and expanded form to two groups of
trained speech people and to one untrained group. They were
asked to estimate the relative rate and duration of the passages. The estimated rate was found to be a logarithmic
function of measured rates. The estimated duration was 1. 2
times the actual duration. "Speech performances with inap-
propriately slow or fast rates were found to be substantially
improved by time compression or expansion toward the most
preferred rate level. When rate was changed by time compression or expansion, the estimated rate and duration
changed correspondingly in appropriate directions and
amounts."

Ihm, De Etta. "The Tape Recorder." Instructor 74(1):118+,
    September 1964.   603
    A listening laboratory in a second-grade classroom is
described.

Immaculate, Sister M. J. "Listening." Catholic Educator
    32:661-62, March 1962.   604
    Teaching of listening has a religious basis. Such teach-

ing is a real challenge to teachers, as home conditions do
not conduce to listening. Children must learn obedience before they can learn to listen or acquire knowledge. Continual drill is necessary in the teaching of listening.

Inglis, Rewey Belle and others. "Report of Committee on
    Place and Function of English in American Life." Eng-
    lish Journal 15:110-31, February 1926.   605
Only 31 of 2983 adults who returned questionnaires about
the uses of English skills felt that listening was the most
important use.

Irvin, Charles E. "Activities Designed to Improve Listening
    Skills." Journal of Communication 4:14-16, Spring
    1954.   606
Twelve specific activities for teaching listening at the
college level are listed and described.

----. An Analysis of Certain Aspects of a Listening Train-
    ing Program Among College Freshmen at Michigan State
    College. Doctoral dissertation. East Lansing, Mich.:
    Michigan State College, 1952. Abstract: Dissertation
    Abstracts 12:704-05, 1952, and Speech Monographs 20:
    122-23, June 1953. Journal of Communication 4:62-64,
    Summer 1954. Summary: "Evaluating a Training Pro-
    gram in Listening for College Freshmen." School Re-
    view 61:25-29, January 1953.   607
Irvin describes in detail a series of seven training units
in listening which he gave to 600 college students. Since he
did not use comparable tests at the beginning and end of the
series, no definite conclusions are reached as to the effects
of these units on listening improvement.

----. "Lend Me Your Ears." Chicago Schools Journal 31:
    265-66, May 1950.   608
The importance of listening is stressed.

----. "Motivation in Listening Training." Journal of Com-
    munication 4:42-44, Summer 1954.   609
College students must be motivated if they are to understand listening training, concentrate on it, and pay attention
to it. Students may be motivated to listen by diverse means
including: belief that listening is a shortcut to knowledge
when they know that examinations are approaching; the idea
that listening skills may broaden the base of conversation;
the thought that listening will improve self-confidence and
personality, and bring financial, social or cultural benefit.

Irvin, Charles E.   143

----. 'Report of the NSSC Listening Committee." Journal
    of Communication 1:66-69, November 1951.   610
    Three methods are used to teach listening: listening
laboratories; coordination of listening and speech instruction;
and direct instruction by lecture.

Iverson, Lee. "Time Compression." International Journal
    for the Education of the Blind 5:78-79, May 1958. 611
    Time compressed speech was demonstrated, at a school
for the blind, to 45 high school students who responded to a
questionnaire. Thirty-nine thought compressed speech should
be used in talking book records; 42 agreed that 25 per cent
compression was not too much.

Jackson, Ann Elizabeth. An Investigation of the Relationship
    Between Listening and Selected Variables in Grades Four,
    Five and Six. Doctoral dissertation. Tempe, Arizona:
    Arizona State University, 1966. Abstract: Dissertation
    Abstracts 27:53A, 1966.   612
    The STEP and Lewis Listening Tests were administered
to 224 pupils at the beginning of the school year. A significant correlation was found between the two tests as well as
between listening and reading, listening and personality adjustment, and listening and school achievement. Children
in small families had higher listening scores than children in
medium and large sized families. Significant improvement
in listening was reported at the end of the school year. Seri-
al placement in family was not found to affect listening
scores significantly.

Jackson, James Harvey. An Experimental Study of Listen-
    er's Evaluations of Speech Content as Compared with
    Speech Delivery. Doctoral dissertation. Los Angeles,
    Calif.: University of Southern California, 1957.   613
    A group of trained speech teachers were unable to make
significantly different evaluations of a filmed speech delivered
by a beginning speech student when they were asked to stress
judgment of delivery, judgment of content, or both delivery
and content.

Jackson, Robert W. B. 'Review of Sequential Tests of Edu-
    cational Progress." Fifth Mental Measurements Year-
    book. (Edited by O. K. Buros.) Highland Park, N. J.:
    Gryphon Press, 1959, p. 62-67.   614
    A generally favorable review of the STEP Listening Tests.

Jacobs, Muriel G. "Are You Listening." Elementary Eng-

lish 27:19-22, January 1950.   615
An interesting description of the use of radio to teach
appreciative listening to an eighth grade.

Jacobson, Homer. "Information and the Human Ear." Journal of the Acoustical Society of America 23:463-71, July
1951.   616
A longer and more thorough explanation is given of the
manner in which the data reported in entry 617 were derived.

----. "The Informational Capacity of the Human Ear." Science 112:143-44, August 4, 1950.   617
The author explains why the capacity of the human ear
is limited to about 8000 bits of information per second.
(See Science 113:292-93, March 16, 1951 for a similar article on the limitation of capacity of the human eye.)

Jayne, Clarence D. "A Study of the Learning and Retention
of Materials Presented by Lecture and by Silent Film."
Journal of Educational Research 38:47-58, September
1944.   618
Using 271 high school pupils as subjects, the author
found that a lecture presentation was more effective in terms
of immediate and delayed recall than a silent film presentation shown without oral comment.

Jeffres, Lloyd A. and Moushegian, George. "Hearing."
Annual Review of Psychology 10:395-414, 1959.   619
One hundred thirty-one references.

Jensen, Jay Robert. A Survey of the Listening Abilities of
a Group of Adolescents. Master's thesis. Salt Lake
City, Utah: University of Utah, 1957.   620
Jensen's conclusions based on test results, are that listening skill is not necessarily affected by a slight hearing
deficiency.

Jensen, Milton B. "An Evaluation of Three Methods of Presenting True-False Examinations." School and Society
32:675-77, November 15, 1930.   621
Using 225 college students as subjects, Jensen reports
that the oral administration of an objective test gave better
results than the visual presentation. Each given separately
was superior to a combined oral and visual presentation.
Students, however, preferred the visual presentation.

Jester, Robert Emile. Comprehension of Connected Mean-

ingful Discourse as a Function of Individual Differences
and Rate and Modality of Presentation. Doctoral disser-
tation. Salt Lake City, Utah: University of Utah,
1966. Abstract: Dissertation Abstracts 27:957A, 1966.
Excerpts: Journal of Educational Research 59:297-302,
March 1966.   622
Three parallel forms of selections from Davis Reading
Tests were presented to 90 subjects: (1) auditorially, (2)
visually, and (3) visually and auditorially simultaneously.
Rates varied from 200 to 400 wpm, in 50 wpm increments.
As rate increased, comprehension decreased, especially after 300 wpm. This was probably due, not to intelligibility,
but to the information-processing capacity of the individual.
Substantial individual differences were found. When material is presented in two modalities simultaneously, the individual selects the modality which is best for him. This sup-
ports Broadbent's conclusion that, as information processing
capacity of the perceptual system is overloaded, it operates
on a single channel system.

Johnson, Eleanor M. "The Improvement of Listening Skills."
    Curriculum Letter, No. 41, Department of School Serv-
    ices and Publications, Wesleyan University, Middletown,
    Conn., 1959.   623
An excellent non-technical review of listening and its
teaching, suitable for use by elementary school teachers who
are not familiar with the subject.

Johnson, Elizabeth Ann. An Investigation into the Relation-
    ship of Listening Comprehension and Speech Discrimina-
    tion in Functional Articulatory Problems. Master's
    thesis. Athens, Ohio: Ohio University, 1963.   624
The only significant correlation between the Brown-Carlsen and the Hutton Semi-Diagnostic Test for Aural Rehabilitation was between Part E (the lecture section) of the Brown-
Carlsen and the Hutton Test. This correlation involved the
test results of the normal control group. No significant correlation was found in the experimental group of high school
students with articulatory defects.

Johnson, F. Craig and Frandsen, Kenneth. "Administering
    the Brown-Carlsen Listening Comprehension Test."
    Journal of Communication 13:38-45, March 1963. 625
The Brown-Carlsen Listening Test, taped, live and on
film, was administered to 2400 freshman students. Best results were obtained from the use of tape. Film yielded the
least satisfactory results. The authors report that the lec-

ture portion of the Brown-Carlsen does not appear to measure the same skills as the remainder of the test.

Johnson, Kenneth O.   A Study of the Effect of an Experimental Course on Listening Comprehension.   Master's thesis.   Minneapolis, Minn.: University of Minnesota, 1948.   Abstract: Speech Monographs 16:351, September 1949.   Summary: "The Effect of Classroom Training upon Listening Comprehension." Journal of Communication 1:57-62, May 1951.   626
Johnson reports that there was a significant degree of improvement in listening skill after four-and-one-half hours of listening practice and instruction.   This improvement was still evident 11 weeks later.   The correlation between listening and reading was .52; between listening and intelligence, .33.

Johnson, Wendell.   "Do You Know How To Listen?" ETC. 7:3-9, Autumn 1949.   Reprinted in Listening: Readings. (Edited by Sam Duker.)   Metuchen, N.J.: Scarecrow Press, 1966. p. 34-42.   627
A general semanticist's views on the nature of the listening act.   The importance of not allowing the speaker's authority, appearance, or manner of speech to influence the listener is stressed.

----.   People in Quandaries.   New York: Harpers, 1946, passim.   628
"Telling one's troubles to a listener who is interested but not critical, sympathetic but not maudlin, can be extremely relaxing and reassuring."

----.   "The Spoken Word and the Great Unsaid." Quarterly Journal of Speech 37:419-29, December 1951.   629
Johnson predicted that speech experts in the future will do more serious investigations of the aspects of listening.

Jones, Edward C.   An Inquiry into the Value of Applying a Readability Formula to Radio News.   Master's thesis. Syracuse, N.Y.: Syracuse University, 1950.   630
Applying the Flesch readability formula to radio newscasts was adequate in predicting the overall listenability but not adequate for predicting the listenability of individual stories.

Jones, Ellis O.   "Confessions of a Professional Listener." Forum 98:119-22, September 1937.   631

A factual account of the "professional listener" in the de-
pression days of the thirties.

Jones, Glenn L. "Listening: A Unified Process." Projects
of the Fourth Workshop in Basic Communications, University of Denver, 1946. (Edited by Edwin L. Levy.)
Denver, Colo: University of Denver Press, 1946. 632
Listening calls for an attitude of eagerness to gain
through listening, intense concentration, and a determination
to follow closely, weigh carefully, and evaluate correctly.
The complexity of these demands accounts for the general in-
effectiveness of listening.

Jones, John Alfred. An Investigation of Scores on the Brown-
Carlsen Listening Test as Correlated with Subjective Instructor Ratings and as Influenced by Media of Presentation. Master's thesis. Seattle, Wash.: University of
Washington, 1961.   633
Jones reports very low correlations between listening-
test results and college instructors' ratings of listening ability. Using two groups of 49 college speech students, he
found no significant differences between a live and a taped
presentation of the Brown-Carlsen Test.

Jones, Mary Elizabeth Hill. A Critical Review of Literature
on Listening with Special Emphasis on Theoretical Bases
for Further Research in Listening. Master's thesis.
Durham, N.C.: North Carolina State College, 1956.
                                                         634
A non-experimental study consisting of a cursory review
of the literature on listening and an original analysis of the
listening process.

Jones, Robert A. and Michael, William B. "The Validity of
a Battery of Tests in Communication Skills for Foreign
Students Attending an American University." Educational
and Psychological Measurement 21:493-96, Summer 1961.
                                                         635
Forty-eight foreign students at the University of Southern California were subjects. The results were compared
to the composite of grades received in a special course on
language skills. The Brown-Carlsen and the criterion
yielded a correlation of .55, which was higher than all but
one of the other measures.

Jones, William Michael. An Exploratory Study of the Effects of Two Media of Presentation on Performance in

Reasoning. Doctoral dissertation. Seattle, Wash.: University of Washington, 1962. Abstract: Dissertation Abstracts 24:434-35, 1963.   636

Material was presented orally and in printed form to 249 college students. Jones found that there was no difference in reasoning performance, as measured by an author-made test, following the two types of presentation.

Joney, Olive L. A Comparison of Reading and Listening in Teaching Factual Material in Grade Four. Master's thesis. Boston: Boston University, 1956.   637

Using passages from history and nature-study textbooks, the author found that listening was superior to reading for 140 fourth grade children. Correlations of .65 between listening and reading and .44 between listening and intelligence are reported.

Jorgensen, Henry. "Did You Transmit a Mental Image?" Montana Education 39(9):22, February 1962.   638

Judson, Lyman Spicer. "Objective Studies of the Influence of the Speaker on the Listeners." Journal of Expression 4:1-11, March 1930.   639

The effectiveness of listening and the degree to which the listener is influenced by the speaker can be determined by the breathing rate of the listener, which will approach the breathing rate of the speaker under optimum conditions.

Kann, Alice M. An Experiment in Listening in a First Grade Classroom. Master's thesis. Shippensburg, Pa.: Shippensburg State College, 1961.   640

Using a teacher-made test, the text of which is given, and the Durrell Sullivan Reading Capacity Test, Kann was unable to find any significant differences between a group of ten children who had been given six weeks of listening instruction and a group of 11 who had not been given such instruction.

Karlin, John Elias. The Factorial Isolation of the Primary Auditory Abilities. Doctoral dissertation. Chicago: University of Chicago, 1942. Summary: Psychometrika 7:251-79, December 1942.   641

Using 200 high school students as subjects, the author concludes that "the conventional auditory acuity tests have little predictive value for auditory behavior in more complex social situations."

Karraker, Mary E.   An Evaluation of the Influence of Inter-
    est and "Set" on Listening Effectiveness in the Basic
    Communication Class.   Doctoral dissertation.   Denver,
    Colo.: University of Denver, 1951.   Abstract: Speech
    Monographs 19:117-18, June 1952.   642
    Karraker reports that listening to materials dealing with
topics of interest to students, as measured by the Kuder
Preference Scale, was not substantially more effective than
listening to other materials.   There is a considerable spread
in listening skills between "A" students and "C" students.
Correlations are reported of .52 between listening and intelligence and .89 between listening and reading, as measured
by the Triggs test.

Kaufman, Irma M.   An Investigation to Ascertain Growth in
    Listening Skills Among First-Grade Children Who Were
    Exposed to a Planned Program in the Area of Listening.
    Master's thesis.   Union, N.J.: Newark State College,
    1966.   643
    Eight weeks of listening instruction for 24 children re-
sulted in significant improvement.   Games and magazine
material were used.

Kavanagh, James Francis.   An Investigation of the Most
    Comfortable Listening Levels for Speech.   Doctoral dis-
    sertation.   Madison, Wisc.: University of Wisconsin,
    1960.   Abstract: Dissertation Abstracts 20:4458-59,
    1960.   644
    This study deals with degrees of loudness of speech and
its effect on the listeners.   A wide individual variation was
found among listeners.

Kavanagh, Robert Z.   Listening: A Problem in Worker
    Effectiveness.   Graduate thesis.   Maxwell Air Force
    Base, Ala.: Air Command and Staff College, Air Univer-
    sity, 1965.   645
    Barriers to listening include: listening only to words
and not to the speaker, bias, boredom, mental or physical
fatigue, improper attitudes, apathy, and pre-judgment.
There are three kinds of responses to listening: 1. "I understand what you are saying;" 2. "I believe what you are
saying;" and 3. "I will act on what you are saying."

Kegler, Stanley Benjamin.   A Comparative Study of the
    Size and Nature of Reading and Listening Vocabularies.
    Doctoral dissertation.   Minneapolis, Minn.: University
    of Minnesota, 1958.   Abstract: Dissertation Abstracts

19:2602, 1959.   646
This study was not primarily concerned with the size of
vocabularies but rather with determining the depth of understanding in listening and reading vocabularies in the eighth,
tenth, and twelfth grades. The claim that high intelligence
is associated with a reading vocabulary that is greater than
a listening vocabulary is not substantiated. Kegler found that
grade level was an important criterion of insight into word
meaning in the case of reading vocabulary but not in the case
of listening vocabulary. There was considerable overlap between grades.

----. 'Teaching to Overcome Pupils' Listening Lag. "
   Clearing House 27:497-99, April 1953.   647
An expository statement concerning the relationship between reading and listening.   The author doubts that there
is much transfer from the teaching of reading skills to listening.

----. 'Techniques in Teaching Listening for Main Ideas. "
   English Journal 45:30-32, January 1956.   648
Kegler suggests that pupils keep a log of their listening
activities. Analysis of these logs will prove helpful as a
pedagogical device.

Keislar, Evan R. , Stein, Carolyn, and Mace, Lawrence.
   "Sequence of Speaking and Listening Training in Beginning French: A Replication Experiment. " American
   Educational Research Journal 3:169-78, May 1966. 649
An experiment with 98 third graders. A group taught to
speak French for one week, followed by one week in learning
to listen to French, performed significantly better on tests
than a group taught to listen the first week and to speak the
second.   This result was found on testing immediate recall
and on testing delayed recall both after one month and   after
three months.

Keliher, Alice V.   "You Are a Good Teacher If You Are a
   Good Listener. " Grade Teacher 42(4):77, December
   1954.   650
The best way to help children learn to listen to their
teachers and to each other is for teachers to be good listeners.

Keller, Paul W.   "Major Findings in Listening in the Past
   Ten Years. " Journal of Communication 10:29-38, March
   1960. Reprinted in Listening: Readings. (Edited by

Sam Duker.)   Metuchen, N. J.: Scarecrow Press, 1966.
p. 145-54.   651
A competent summary of research in listening from
1950 to 1960.

Kelley, Elizabeth V. and others.   A Comparison of Silent
Reading and Listening Through Written Recall and Multiple Choice Tests, Grades 6 and 7.   Master's thesis.
Boston: Boston University, 1952.   652
On both multiple choice and written recall tests sixth
graders showed significantly better results on passages read
orally to them than on passages they read to themselves.
However, the results for seventh grade children did not show
statistically significant difference.   This is a companion
thesis to that of Hanna and others.

Kellogg, Ralph E.   A Study of the Effect of a First Grade
Listening Instructional Program Upon Achievement in
Listening and Reading.   Cooperative Research Project
6-8469.   San Diego, Calif.: Department of Education,
San Diego County, 1966.   Also in: Kellogg, Ralph Ed-
ward.   A Study of the Effect of a First Grade Listening
Instructional Program Upon Achievement in Listening and
Reading.   Doctoral dissertation. Los Angeles, Calif.:
University of California, Los Angeles, 1967.   Abstract:
Dissertation Abstracts 28:395A, 1967.   653
An experiment in the teaching of listening to 822 second-
semester pupils in 33 classrooms.   Forty 20-minute lesson
plans were prepared for the structured teaching of listening,
using paperback books of children's literature for half the
group.   The other classes used an unstructured approach to
the teaching of listening.   One-half the classes were taught
language arts in the traditional manner, while the others
used the language experience approach.
    No pre-tests were given.   The Pintner-Cunningham In-
telligence Test, the Wright Listening Test, and the Stanford
Reading Test were used as post-tests.   Results for boys
and girls were dealt with separately.
    In the traditional language arts classes, boys in the
structured listening classes scored significantly higher, on
both reading and listening, than those in the unstructured
listening classes.   Girls in the structured listening classes
made significantly higher scores only in listening vocabulary.
    In the classes using the language experience approach,
both boys and girls in the structured listening classes made
significantly higher scores in listening and in reading vocabulary.

Also included in this report is a well-developed conceptual model of the teaching of developmental listening, a list of specific skills necessary to informational and to critical listening, a sample lesson plan for the structured approach, and an extensive bibliography.

Kelly, Charles Milburn. "Actual Listening Behavior" of
    Industrial Supervisors, as Related to "Listening Ability,"
    General Mental Ability, Selected Personality Factors
    and Supervising Effectiveness. Doctoral dissertation.
    Lafayette, Ind.: Purdue University, 1962. Abstract:
    Dissertation Abstracts 23:4019, 1963, and Speech Mono-
    graphs 30:183, August 1963. Excerpts: "Mental Ability
    and Personality Factors in Listening." Quarterly Jour-
    nal of Speech 49:152-56, April 1963. Excerpts: Listen-
    ing: Readings. (Edited by Sam Duker.) Metuchen,
    N.J.: Scarecrow Press, 1966. p. 136-42.   654
The Brown-Carlsen Listening Test and the STEP Listening Test correlated more highly with intelligence tests than
with each other. Both listening tests correlated negatively
with employee ratings of supervisory listening behavior.

----. "An Investigation of the Construct Validity of Two
    Commercially Published Listening Tests." Speech Mono-
    graphs 32:139-43, June 1965.   655
A report on the validity and reliability of the STEP and
Brown-Carlsen Listening Tests. On the basis of test data
there is no satisfactory evidence that the STEP test is
valid as it correlates more closely to intelligence and
achievement test results than to other measures of listening.
The Brown-Carlsen Test met the test for validity, but the
new tests are needed.

----. "Listening: Complex of Activities--and a Unitary
    Skill?" Speech Monographs 34:455-66, November 1967.
                                                          656
Published listening tests do not measure a unique skill
as there is no evidence that a unitary skill of listening can
be isolated. Listening test results show low correlation
with each other. Listening training may result in better
test performance but there is no evidence that day-to-day
listening performance is improved by such training. More
research is needed.
    Charles T. Brown's response is included at the end of
the article. While admitting that some of the findings about
listening are confusing, he states that not all knowledge
about listening is a myth, this being the case that Kelly, in

skepticism, advances.

Kelly, J.C. and Steer, M.D. "Revised Concept of Rate."
Journal of Speech and Hearing Disorders 14:222-26,
September 1949.   657
An overall rate is not indicative of the rate of individual
sentences. No relation was found between sentence rate and
the number of syllables per sentence. Sentence rate varied
from 125 to 328 wpm.

Kelly, Marcella R. "Promoting the 'Listening' Habit in Kindergarten and the Primary Grades." American Childhood 43(7):12-14, March 1958.   658
The teaching of listening is generally neglected in kindergarten. The best way to teach it at this level is through rich
experiences, planned practice, and regular exercises on listening with a purpose.

Kelty, Annette P. An Experimental Study to Determine the
Effect of "Listening" for Certain Purposes upon Achievement in Reading for Those Purposes. Doctor's Field
Study. Greeley, Colo.: Colorado State College of Education, 1953. Abstract: Abstracts of Field Studies for the
Degree of Doctor of Education 15:82-85, 1954.   659
The author reports that the skill of selecting details in
reading improved after intensive instruction in listening. However, such instruction failed to help in the selection of main
ideas and the drawing of conclusions in reading.

Kendrick, William M. A Comparative Study of Two First
Grade Language Arts Programs. Cooperative Research
Project 2576. San Diego, Calif.: Department of Education, San Diego County, 1966. Summary: Reading Research Quarterly 2:83-118, Fall 1966.   660
In a comparison between the experience approach and the
traditional approach in teaching language arts, the only significant difference found in listening was in lower economic
social class female students. In that group, there was a
significantly greater achievement by those receiving the traditional method of instruction. The listening test was constructed by the author. The text is not included.

Kibler, Robert Joseph II. The Impact of Message Style and
Channel in Communication. Doctoral dissertation.
Columbus, Ohio: Ohio State University, 1962. Abstract:
Dissertation Abstracts 24:893, 1963.   661
Using 183 college students as subjects, Kibler investi-

gated the effect of message style, mode of presentation
(written or oral), and speaking effectiveness on the communication process.   He reports that when the message style is
extremely easy or extremely difficult, it makes little difference in impact whether the message is spoken or written.

Kielsmeier, Milton.   Learning Differences Between High and
    Low Auding Subjects.   Doctoral dissertation.   Los Ange-
    les, Calif.: University of Southern California, 1960.
    Abstract: Dissertation Abstracts 21:1460, 1960.   662
    Using 61 subjects in an experiment, the author reports
that the better listeners learned more readily, as measured
by immediate recall.   On delayed recall of 24 hours and of
seven days, no difference in learning between the two groups
was found.

King, W. H.   "An Experimental Investigation into the Rela-
    tive Merits of Listening and Reading Comprehension for
    Boys and Girls of Primary School Age. " British Journal
    of Educational Psychology 29:42-49, February 1959. 663
    Using 475 ninth grade pupils as subjects, Hall reports
that boys learned better on oral presentations than on visual
presentations of learning material, whereas girls did slightly better on visual presentation.

Kirschner, Dorothy K.   The Role of Listening in the Sixth-
    Grade Language Arts Program.   Master's thesis.
    Newark, N. J. : New Jersey State College at Newark,
    1954.   664
    Teachers were asked to keep listening inventories for a
total of 70 sixth grade pupils.   This tended to increase the
teachers' awareness of listening problems.   The greatest
shortcoming, according to the inventories, was in the area
of critical listening.   The text of the inventory is included.

Klineman, Janet.   The Effects of Training Sessions on the
    Ability to Comprehend Compressed Speech.   Master's
    thesis.   Pittsburgh, Pa.: University of Pittsburgh, 1963.
                                                          665
    Eleven fifth and sixth grade Braille students were ex-
posed to six 45-minute practice periods of listening to compressed speech at 300 wpm.   The material consisted of
stories chosen for their interest value to this level.   A pre-
and post-test of material taken from the Gates Reading Test
and the Reading Comprehension Section of the Iowa tests
were administered in compressed form at 300 wpm to this
group and to a comparable control group.   The experimental

group made significantly greater gains in the post-test fifteen
days after the pre-test.

Kling, Martin. Auditory and Visual Discrimination. Mas-
    ter's thesis. Berkeley, Calif.: University of California,
    1956.   666
    Two tests were administered to 66 college psychology
students. One was an auditory discrimination test, consisting of 160 simple tones, in which the subjects' task was to
judge whether the second tone was higher, lower, or the
same as the standard. The second was a visual discrimination test, consisting of 120 sine wave patterns, in which the
subject's task was to judge relative frequency. The correlation between the two tests was .03, indicating that independent abilities were measured by the tests.

Klinger, Herbert Nathan. The Effects of Stuttering on Audi-
    ence Listening Comprehension. Doctoral dissertation.
    New York: New York University, 1959. Abstract:
    Dissertation Abstracts 20:3890, 1960.   667
    Using as subjects 96 college speech students, Klinger
found that there was no statistically significant difference in
performance on the STEP Listening Test when it was given
by someone using a normal voice, a mild stuttering voice,
or a severe stuttering voice.

Klumpp, R. G. and Webster, J. C. "Intelligibility of Time-
    Compressed Speech." Journal of the Acoustical Society
    of America 33:265-67, March 1961.   668
    An experiment in which the playback of a tape recorder
was speeded up to a time compression of 0.67. Short
simple messages showed no serious loss in intelligibility.
A word list lost only 10 per cent in intelligibility with a time
compression of 0.75.

Knapp, Peter Hobart. "The Ear, Listening and Hearing."
    Journal of the American Psychoanalytical Association 1:
    672-89, October 1953.   669
    A psychoanalytical analysis of the significance of the hu-
man ear, hearing and listening.

Knower, Franklin H. "Speech: Listening." Review of Edu-
    cational Research 22:108, April 1952.   670
    A review of research on listening for 1948 to 1951.

----,   Phillips, David, and Koeppel, Fern. "Studies in
    Listening to Informative Speaking." Journal of Abnormal

and Social Psychology 40:82-88, January 1945.   671
Experimental findings are reported to the effect that,
where there is equal quality of performance, speaking from
memory is more effective in securing comprehension and retention by the listeners than reading a speech from a text.

Kodman, Francis Jr. An Investigation of Word Intelligibility
as a Function of Time Compression. Doctoral dissertation. Urbana, Ill.: University of Illinois, 1954.   672
An investigation in time compression of taped speech by
discarding portions revealed that intelligibility varied inverse-
ly with time compression and that the percentage of intelligibility exceeded the percentage of signal remaining after the
compression. Minimum signal duration necessary for 100
per cent intelligibility was estimated to be 30 per cent.

Koehn, John J. and Hocking, Charles E. "Emphasis: Listening." Audiovisual Instruction 10:703-04, November
1965.   673
A center with booths and tape recorders for listening instruction is described.

Kohls, Mildred Palmgren. Auding in the Elementary School.
Master's thesis. Sacramento, Calif.: Sacramento State
College, 1965.   674
A daily ten-minute period of instruction in listening was
given to 77 fourth grade pupils for twelve weeks in six different schools. The STEP test was used as a pre- and
post-test. Results showed a significant improvement in both
listening and reading by the experimental group compared to
an equated control group without listening instruction. The
listening lessons dealt with creative, explanatory, interrogative, concentrative, critical, conversational, and apprecia-
tional listening. The text of the lesson plans is included.

Komaiko, Jean R. "The Fine Art of Listening." Parents'
Magazine 36(8):40-41+, August 1961.   675
Instructions that are too extensive and too often re-
peated by parents and teachers lead to poor listening habits.
Good listening is best promoted by example.

Kopp, O.W. "The Evaluation of Oral Language Activities:
Teaching and Learning." Elementary English 44:114-23,
February 1967.   676
The analysis of a child's listening problems should in-
clude hearing, total adjustment, personality, and vocabulary
development. Both formal and informal tests should be

used. The STEP test is appropriate for the fourth grade on,
the Wright Test for grades two to four. Children should set
their own standards for listening performance. The school
environment should be analyzed to see if it is favorable for
good listening.

Korey, Ruth A. "Teaching Children to Listen." Instructor
    58:37, October 1949.   677
A detailed list of proposed activities for teaching listening at the primary, intermediate, and upper grades of the
elementary school.

Kramar, Edward John Joseph. The Relationships of the
    Wechsler-Bellevue and A.C.E. Intelligence Tests with
    Performance Scores in Speaking and the Brown-Carlsen
    Listening Comprehension Test. Doctoral dissertation.
    Tallahassee, Fla.: Florida State University, 1955. Ab-
    stract: Dissertation Abstracts 15:2599, 1955, and
    Speech Monographs 23:93-94, June 1956.   678
One-hundred-ninety speech students were given the A.C.
E., Wechsler-Bellevue and Brown-Carlsen tests. Correlations with the Brown-Carlsen scores are reported: Wechs-
ler .56. A.C.E. .55.

----. A Study of Listening Test Scores on Orally Presented
    Expository Material with the Speaker Seen and with the
    Speaker Not Seen. Master's thesis. Tallahassee, Fla.:
    Florida State University, 1951. Abstract: Speech Mono-
    graphs 19:160, August 1952. Summary: Kramer, Ed-
    ward J.J. and Lewis, Thomas R. "Comparison of Visu-
    al and Non-Visual Listening." Journal of Communica-
    tion 1:16-20, November 1951.   679
Two groups of students sat in an auditorium listening to
a speech. One group listened from behind a screen where
they could not see the speaker; the other sat where they
could see him. Kramar reports that there was no significant difference in comprehension on either immediate or delayed recall. Subjects were 248 college students.

Kraner, Robert Eugene. A Comparison of Two Methods of
    Listening and Reading Training in an Eighth Grade Lan-
    guage Arts Program. Doctoral dissertation. Denton,
    Texas: North Texas State University, 1963. Abstract:
    Dissertation Abstracts 25:1046, 1964. Summary: Edu-
    cational Developmental Reading Newsletter No. 33.
    September 1964. p 3-12.   680
One group was taught listening and reading skills during

the school year with Educational Developmental Laboratories'
tapes and workbooks. The control group was taught through
lectures given by the teacher. The former method produced
significantly better results. Low-ability students were especially benefited by the experimental program. One hundred
twenty-eight subjects. The Brown-Carlsen listening test was
used.

Krawiec, Theophile. A Comparison of Learning and Reten-
    tion of Materials Presented Visually and Auditorially.
    Doctoral dissertation. New York: New York University,
    1945. Summary: Journal of General Psychology 34:
    179-95, April 1946.   681
    This study contains a superior review of listening litera-
ture. It was found that auditory and visual presentation of
nonsense syllables and three-letter words were equally effective. Subjects were 67 college students.

Krueger, David Harry. A Study of the Results of Teaching
    Factors of Listening Comprehension to College Freshmen
    in the Basic Communication II Course. Master's thesis.
    Whittier, Calif.: Whittier College, 1950.   682
    Using 144 college communications students as subjects,
Krueger reports no significant difference in listening, as
measured by Nichols' Minnesota Test, between a group given
a period of listening instruction and a control group. A correlation between listening and intelligence of .41 is reported.

Kurtzrock, George Henry. The Effects of Time and Fre-
    quency Distortion upon Word Intelligibility. Doctoral dis-
    sertation. Urbana, Ill: University of Illinois, 1956.
    Abstract: Dissertation Abstracts 16:1017, 1956, and
    Speech Monographs 24:94, June 1957.   683
    A study of fifty selected words showed these findings:
    1. Intelligibility was unaffected over a wide range of
        time distortion. Fifty per cent was obtained when the
        words had been reduced to approximately one-seventh
        of their original duration. Expansion of duration be-
        yond eleven times the original had slight effect.
    2. Intelligibility was considerably more sensitive to fre-
        quency distortion in the form of division or multipli-
        cation than to time distortion by comparable amounts.
    3. When time and frequency were distorted reciprocally,
        the intelligibility decrement was dominated by the
        frequency distortion, although the effect of duration
        remained appreciable and significant.
    4. Frequency multiplication had less effect on intelligi-

bility than comparable frequency division.

Laird, Dugan and Hayes, Joseph R. "Communications Skills
    or Pink Pills." Training in Business and Industry 3(5):
    22-27, May 1966.   684
    Basic communication courses may teach employees what
they should already know, but if these skills are not known,
and are important on the job, then they should be taught.
Training courses sometimes fail because they are "three-
hour quickies" which pretend to destroy lifetime habits. Few
programs fail when a legitimate need exists, a precise objective is established, and a tested program implemented.
There are few authorities in this area. Few materials are
available for the teaching of listening. Basic System tapes
are the best known single package. Skeptics demand proof
of concrete results from a listening training course.
Courses should include drills which simulate on-the-job conditions. In genuine listening, feelings are perceived and
shared but not necessarily understood. Therefore, listening
courses should include listening for feelings. This is not
easy.

Laird, Donald A. and Laird, Eleanor C. The Technique of
    Handling People. New York: McGraw-Hill, 1954.
    passim.   685
    The following is typical of this down-to-earth discussion:
"Be an honest interested listener. Let the other fellow talk.
Find out about his children, his mortgage and his ulcers.
Find out what makes him tick. As he talks to you and you
listen, he'll hand you the key to his personality. More, you
learn something from everyone to whom you listen."

Lang, Charles H. "Now, Hear This." Supervision 21(9):
    4-6, September 1959.   686
    Listening is an active process. Purpose is important in
listening. Note-taking is helpful, if it is to get details. Do
not let the status of a speaker block good listening. Our educational system should spend more time teaching listening.

----. "Practice Perfects the Fine Art of Listening-Try It!"
    American Business 28(3):26-27+, March 1958.   687
    Approach listening with a positive attitude. Decide ahead
of time whether to listen for main ideas or for details. Do
not interrupt by marshalling arguments against a viewpoint
until a speech has been fully presented. Free yourself to
concentrate. Watch the facial expressions of the speaker.
Budget your spare time listening.

Langford, Frances Stover. The Teaching of Listening in a
    Seventh-Grade Oral Expression Class. Master's thesis.
    Manhattan, Kan: Kansas State University, 1962.   688
    A schoolroom study.

Langholz, Armin Paul. A Study of the Relationship of Lis-
    tening Test Scores to Test Item Difficulty. Doctoral dis-
    sertation. Columbus, Ohio: Ohio State University,
    1965. Abstract: Dissertation Abstracts 26:6912, 1966.
                                                        689
    Changes made in the Brown-Carlsen Test in accordance
with test theory created more discriminating items. An excellent discussion of unpublished listening tests is included.

Lanham, Frank W. "Teaching Listening." American Busi-
    ness Education 16:60-61, October 1959.   690
    Receptive attitude of students toward instruction in lis-
tening will depend in great part on their understanding of the
fact of the great importance to them of good listening. After
a good attitude is established the student should be taught to
use his listening time for fuller understanding and retention
of what he hears.

Lantz, William Carson. An Experimental Study of Listeners'
    Perception of Speech Content as Compared with Speech
    Delivery. Doctoral dissertation. Los Angeles, Calif.:
    University of Southern California, 1955. Abstract:
    Speech Monographs 23:94, June 1956.   691
    Using 152 college students as subjects, Lantz reports
only small differences in performance on tests of content
and on delivery of a 14-minute speech among four groups.
One group was given no specific instructions, one was told
to concentrate on both content and delivery, one was told to
concentrate on delivery, and one was directed to concentrate
on content.

Larke, Alfred G. "How to Learn by Listening." Dun's Re-
    view and Modern Industry 65(2324):43-46, April 1955.
                                                        692
    Individual executives should seize every opportunity to
listen to employees' viewpoints. Sometimes it is more important to be listened to than it is to receive what we are
asking for. Many sales are lost because of excessive talking by salesmen who do not listen.

Larsen, Robert P. and Feder, D.D. "Common and Differ-
    ential Factors in Reading and Hearing Comprehension."

Journal of Educational Psychology 31:241-52, April
1940.   693
This is a report of an experiment showing a superior
performance in reading comprehension over listening comprehension, which was found to be a function of the difficulty
level of the material. Reading ability was superior for those
rated high scholastically. Correlation between reading and
listening comprehension was .62.

Larson, Carl E. (Compiler.) A Selected Source File on
    Speech Communication in Business and Industry. Law-
    rence, Kan.: Department of Speech and Drama, Univer-
    sity of Kansas, 1963.   694
Twenty-one sources of information on industrial communication. Annotated lists of fifteen films, 95 periodical
articles and 38 books. The last two are indexed.
    A survey was made of 300 "business practitioners;" 116
replied. Listening theory in business and industry was
listed, by 24 respondents, as the most important topic for
needed research. This ranked it fifth.

Larter, Marie-Jeanne and Scott, Carol Thacker. Construc-
    tion and Validation of a Listening Test for Grades I and
    II with Evaluation of Listening Exercises. Master's thes-
    is. Boston: Boston University, 1956.   695
A test was constructed which included sections on music,
phonics, listening for main ideas, listening for sequence and
details, and listening to follow directions.

Launderville, Sister Mary Flavian. A Study of the Effective-
    ness of a First-Grade Listening Test as a Predictor of
    Reading Achievement. Doctoral dissertation. Iowa City,
    Iowa: State University of Iowa, 1958. Abstract: Dis-
    sertation Abstracts 19:3172-73, 1959.   696
A reading-readiness test, based entirely on listening,
was found to be as good a predictor of later reading achievement as a conventional reading-readiness test.

Laurent, Marie-Jeanne. The Construction and Evaluation of
    a Listening Curriculum for Grades 5 and 6. Doctoral
    dissertation. Boston: Boston University, 1963. Ab-
    stract: Dissertation Abstracts 27:4167A-68A, 1967. 697
Describes a 10-week course of three 20-minute lessons
per week. Discriminative, critical, appreciative, and correlated listening are stressed. The experimental group of 320
showed a significantly greater gain on the STEP test than a comparable control group. No sex difference was found. The sixth

grade in both groups scored higher than the fifth grade. Listening scores and intelligence scores on the Otis intelligence test were correlated: .73 in the fifth grade and .75 in the sixth. The correlation between reading and listening was .81 for the fifth grade and .74 for the sixth. No evidence that listening training improved reading test scores.

Lawrence, Merle. "Hearing." Annual Review of Psychology 8:29-60, 1957.   698
   Contains 208 references.

Lawton, Robert E. Listening to Rate Controlled Speech: A Technique for Improving Education and Communication in the Air Force and Industry. Graduate thesis. Maxwell Air Force Base, Ala.: Air University, 1967.   699
An excellent review of history, development and research of compressed speech; some speculation as to possible applications. Bibliography contains 165 items.

Laycock, Samuel R. and Russell, David H. "An Analysis of Thirty-Eight How-To-Study Manuals." School Review 49:370-79, May 1941.   700
A total of 217 items were devoted to techniques of listening to lectures.

Lazarsfeld, Paul F. Radio and the Printed Page. New York: Duell, Sloan & Pearce, 1940. p. 3-47, 133-39.
   701
A report of surveys shows that there is a preference for reading by those of higher cultural levels. Poor readers, on the other hand, prefer listening, since the reading process itself demands so much of them that they cannot concentrate on meaning.

Lazarus, Arnold and Knudson, Rozanne. Selected Objectives for the English Language Arts Grades 7-12. Boston: Houghton Mifflin, 1967. p. 1-7.   702
Brief lists of attitudes, understandings, skills, and habits which should be developed in listening. Twenty-six item bibliography.

Leal, Anna Katherine. A Survey of Auding Research. Master's thesis. Austin, Tex.: University of Texas, 1964.
   703
A substantial portion of the literature on listening is analyzed and classified. Ninety-one item bibliography.

"Lean Back and Listen." Business Week 1164:48+, Decem-
    ber 22, 1951.   704
    Listening is essential to upward communication. Listen-
ing and acting on the basis of what subordinates think, not
according to what management thinks, is essential to realistic management.

Leary, Eleanor Denise. The Role of Listening. Master's
    thesis. New Haven: New Haven State Teachers College,
    1959.   705
    A survey showing the techniques used by 68 teachers in
teaching listening at the primary level.

Lebo, Dell and Bruce, Roslyn Sherman. "Projective Meth-
    ods Recommended for Use with the Blind." Journal of
    General Psychology 50:15-38, July 1960.   706
    Review of auditory and tactile techniques. Descriptions
of auditory techniques include the Insight Test; the Verbal
Thematic Apperception Test (VTAT); Sentence Completion;
Word Association; the Azzageddi (Azz) Test; Wilmer and
Husni's Auditory Sound Association Technique; Stone's Audi-
tory Apperception Test; Braverman and Chevigny's Auditory
Perception Technique (APT); Shakov and Rosensweig's Tauta-
phone (Verbal Summation); Bean's Sound Apperception Test
(SAT); and Kunze's Musical Reveries Test.

Lee, Ralph L. "Leadership and Listening." Foundry 87(8):
    120-21, August 1959.   707
    Good leaders usually listen with full attention. Lee sug-
gests that perhaps by listening they get answers that enable
them to be good leaders.

Lefevre, Rita F. The Influence of Personality on the Listen-
    ing Ability of Sixth Grade Children. Master's thesis.
    Washington, D.C.: Catholic University of America, 1956.
                                                        708
    A survey of 354 pupils revealed a significant correlation
of .45 between listening on the Durrell-Sullivan Reading Capacity Test and intelligence, as shown on school records.
Poorly adjusted children were poor listeners.

Lehman, Esther Kendig. A Study of Certain Language Skills
    of Kindergarten Children. Doctoral dissertation. Syra-
    cuse, N.Y.: Syracuse University, 1966. Abstract:
    Dissertation Abstracts 27:4168A, 1967.   709
    A battery of tests included listening comprehension with
items on story plot, details and structure. The listening

test obtained information about children's expressive and receptive language skills.

Lehman, Harvey. "The Oral Versus the Mimeographed
     True-False Test." School and Society 30:470-72, Oc-
     tober 5, 1929.   710
     Lehman found by experiment that oral administration of
a true-false type test was as efficient as visual administration.

Leitner, Margaret Ann. A Study of the Effects of Intra-
     phrase Rate and Pause Time on Information Gain and
     Speaker Image. Doctoral dissertation. Madison, Wisc.:
     University of Wisconsin, 1962. Abstract: Dissertation
     Abstracts 23:2251, 1962.   711
     Using 297 beginning speech students as subjects, Leit-
ner reports that the lengthening and shortening of pauses between words and phrases on taped discourse did not affect
comprehension significantly. Comprehension was significantly effected, however, by increasing the wpm rate of speech.
It was also learned that the pause time was proportional to
the rate of speaking, as was the proportion of total pause
time to the entire speech. The number of pauses tend to decrease as the rate increases.

Lerrigo, Marion O. "Learning to Listen." Today's Health
     29(9):34-35+, September 1951.   712
     Children of pre-reading age need a variety of listening
experiences.

Leshan, Lawrence. "The Breaking of a Habit by Suggestion
     During Sleep." Journal of Abnormal and Social Psychol-
     ogy 37:406-08, July 1942.   713
     In an experiment with no objective measure of sleep,
fingernail biting was inhibited in eight out of 20 subjects by
recorded and oral presentations during "sleep."

Letton, Mildred C. "Classroom Procedures in Improving
     Oral Reading in Grades Seven Through Nine." Oral
     Aspects of Reading, Proceedings of the Annual Confer-
     ence on Reading. Chicago: University of Chicago Press,
     1955, p. 83-87.   714
     An ideal time for instruction and practice in listening is
during oral reading.

----. "The Status of the Teaching of Listening." (Under
     "Educational News and Editorial Comment.") Elementary

School Journal 57:181-85, January 1957.   715
There are some questions about listening which need answering. Is there a sequential growth pattern in listening?
Is a listenability formula possible and desirable? What are
the listening skills and how can they be taught?

Leuba, Clarence and Bateman, Dorothy. "Learning During
    Sleep." American Journal of Psychology 65:301-02,
    April 1952.   716
One subject, whose state of sleep was unverified, learned
during sleep.

Levonian, Edward. "Retention of Information in Relation to
    Arousal During Continuously-Presented Material."
    American Educational Research Journal 4:103-16, March
    1967.   717
Skin-resistance measures were obtained from 83 pupils,
during a showing of a traffic safety film. A questionnaire
on fifteen items presented at specific points in the film was
administered immediately after the film and a week later.
High arousal resulted in better retention but poorer short term
performance. Arousal induction is emotion-independent,
arousal induction may be synchronized to information presentation, and the degree of short-term retention may be the
converse of long term retention.

Lewin, Ilka. "Communication Between the Generations."
    Child Study 30(2):24-26, Spring 1953.   718
Listening is an effective way to convey affection and interest in a family situation.

Lewis, Irving G. A Survey of Management's Attitudes Re-
    garding Oral Communication Needs and Practices in
    Large Industries in Los Angeles County. Doctoral dis-
    sertation. Los Angeles, Calif.: University of Southern
    California, 1954.   719
A survey of oral communication practices in 50 large
industrial organizations showed that listening was a major
factor.

Lewis, Maurice S. The Construction of a Diagnostic Test
    of Listening Comprehension for Grades 4, 5, and 6.
    Doctoral Field Study. Greeley, Colo: Colorado State
    College of Education, 1954. Abstract.: Abstracts of
    Field Studies for the Degree of Doctor of Education 16:
    48-52, 1955.   720
The results of a test based on factors which "experts"

listed as most important showed a correlation between subtests of .27 to .63. Correlations between test and reading
of .67 and the test and intelligence of .67 are reported.
The texts of two forms of the test are included.

----. The Effect of Training in Listening for Certain Pur-
    poses upon Reading for Those Same Purposes. Doctoral
    Field Study. Greeley, Colo.: Colorado State College of
    Education, 1952. Summary: Journal of Communication
    2(2):81-84, November 1952 and 3:115-19, November
    1953. Abstract: Abstracts of Studies for the Degree of
    Doctor of Education 13:93-97, 1952.   721
Listening training of 150 pupils in the fourth through
sixth grades did not make any significant difference in the
comprehension of a main idea, the noting of details, or in
predicting outcomes in reading. The only difference reported
was the immediate recall from a group not given training.

----. "Teaching Children To Listen." Education 80:455-59,
    April 1960.   722
Children learn to listen best in a classroom where the
environment stimulates speaking and listening, is flexible and
permissive, and gives many opportunities for interaction
among pupils and between pupils and teacher.

Lewis, Nettie B. "Listen Please!" Clearing House 30:535-
    36, May 1956.   723
Description of a series of exercises for teaching listening to directions.

Lewis, Penelope B. A Study of the Comprehension of Para-
    graphs Presented Auditorially and Visually Under Condi-
    tions of Divided Attention. Master's thesis. Charlottes-
    ville, Va.: University of Virginia, 1950.   724
An aural presentation of prose material was found to be
superior to a visual presentation when an individual was per-
forming a non-visual psychomotor task which required a
great deal of attention.

Lewis, Robert Fulton Jr. Complementing Instruction in
    Reading Improvement of College Students with Instruction
    in Auding. Doctoral dissertation. Auburn, Ala.: Auburn
    University, 1963. Abstract: Dissertation Abstracts 24:
    3204-05, 1964.   725
One hundred and sixty-four students in a college reading
improvement course were subjects. One group was given a
unit on listening consisting of a lecture and listening prac-

tice, weekly, for nine weeks.   No significant difference was
found in either reading or listening improvement between
this group and a control group which had only reading instruction.

Lewis, Thomas R.   "The Communication Approach in the
    First Course in Speech at the College Level."   Journal
    of Communication 5:113-17, Fall 1955.   726
    A survey showed that a wide variety of approaches were
being used in freshman communication courses.   An emphasis on listening was found in many but not all cases.

----.   "Listening."   Review of Educational Research 28:89-
    95, April 1958.   727
    A review of research on listening from 1955 to 1957.

----, and   Ralph G. Nichols.   Speaking and Listening.   Du-
    buque, Iowa: Wm. C. Brown, 1965.   728
    Revised edition lays additional stress on the need for
teaching listening and contains an extensive analysis of the
categories of listening necessary to the good listener.

Licklider, J. C. R.   "Hearing."   Annual Review of Psychology
    4:90-110, 1953.   729
    Ninety-two references.

Lieb, Barbara.   "How to Be Influenced Discriminatingly."
    Today's Speech 8(2):24-26, April 1960.   730
    Paying attention and hearing words does not constitute
listening.   Neither the "posture theory" nor the "note-taking
theory" assures genuine listening.

----.   The Relationship Between Some Aspects of Communi-
    cative Speaking and Communicative Listening in Fresh-
    men Men and Women.   Master's thesis.   University
    Park, Pa.: Pennsylvania State University, 1960.   Sum-
    mary: Barbara Lieb Brilhart.   Journal of Communica-
    tion 15:35-46, March 1965.   731
    Two groups of 18 students each served as subjects.   The
experimental group gave oral descriptions of, and listened to,
some descriptions of geometric figures of three grades of
complexity.   Brown-Carlsen was also administered.   In general, correlations between ability to describe orally and to
listen to descriptions were not significant.   In the case of
men a significant correlation was found between total listening to descriptions scores and the Brown-Carlsen.

Lieberman, J. Nina. "Listening: Needs, Values, and Impli-
    cations." Elementary English 40:379-81, April 1963.732
    It is the task of the elementary school to teach children
to become aware of others by listening to them, to accept
criticism and to evaluate it in the light of information already
held, and to command others' attention as listeners. Specific
ways of accomplishing this task are suggested.

Lillywhite, Herold. "Communication in Education." Phi
    Delta Kappan 34:67-68, November 1952.   733
    There is a great need for encouragement of research in
the areas of communication, especially in the areas of listening and group behavior.

----. "Communication Problems in a Medical Rehabilitation
    Team." Journal of Communication 6:167-73, Winter
    1956.   734
    Among the difficulties listed are: failure of specialists
to listen accurately and patiently to other specialists and to
parents, and failure of parents to understand correctly remarks made by doctors.

----. "Toward a Philosophy of Communication." Journal
    of Communication 2:29-32, May 1952.   735
    Skills of communication, such as listening, are of con-
cern only when they are connected with the ultimate purposes
of communication.

Lindquist, E.F. "Review of Brown-Carlsen Listening Com-
    prehension Text." Fifth Mental Measurement Yearbook.
    (Edited by O.K. Buros.) Highland Park, N.J.: Gryphon
    Press, 1959, p. 650-51.   736
    A critical review of the Brown-Carlsen Listening Test,
which questions norming procedures, validity, and methods
of administration.

----. "Review of Sequential Tests of Educational Progress:
    Listening." Fifth Mental Measurements Yearbook.
    (Edited by O.K. Buros.) Highland Park, N.J.: Gryphon
    Press, 1959, p. 652-54.   737
    A critical review of the STEP Listening Test especially
regarding method of administration, validity and norming
procedures. Also questioned is the sequential nature of the
tests.

Lindsey, Charles A. A Comparison of Silent Reading and
    Listening as Instructional Media in the Teaching of Cer-

tain Aspects of Language. Doctoral field study. Greeley, Colo.: Colorado State College of Education, 1951. Abstract: Abstracts of Field Studies for the Degree of Doctor of Education 13:99-102, 1951.   738
Three language principles were taught orally to a group of 100 third-grade pupils. Another group was taught by means of written materials. On immediate recall the difference was significantly in favor of the oral presentation, but on one week's recall results were inconclusive, and on a month's recall there were no differences.

----. The Effect of Certain Factors on the Listening Comprehension of Fourth, Fifth, and Sixth Grade Pupils. Doctoral field study. Greeley, Colo.: Colorado State College of Education, 1953. Abstract: Abstracts of Field Studies for the Degree of Doctor of Education 15: 92-98, 1953.   739
This was a study of the effect of interruptions, such as music and announcements over the public address system and the arrival and departure of monitors, on learning by listening. The results were inconclusive.

Linsley, Wm. A. An Experimental Study to Examine the Effect of Note-Taking on Listening Efficiency in the College Classroom. Master's thesis. Peoria, Ill.: Bradley University, 1961.   740
Note-taking increased comprehension and retention in listening to speeches. Subjects were 152 college speech students.

Lippert, Fred G. "The Art of Listening Effectively." Supervision 27(2):13-14, February 1965.   741
Listening requires analysis and judgment to sort out facts and look for meanings beyond the words used. A check chart of listening skills and a case study of a foreman who fails to listen are included.

"Listen Up! You'll Be More Efficient." Steel 160:131, January 2, 1967.   742
A summary of Dr. Ralph Nichols' views on the importance of listening; bad habits in listening.

"Listening, 'A Lost Art.'" School Musician 39(1):92-93, August-September 1967.   743
Active listening involves more than the listener keeping his mouth closed and waiting until he can break in. The purpose of listening should include making the speaker aware

of the importance of his presence, convincing the speaker of
interest in him, and an alliance with his interests when that
is possible. Those bringing up children have an especial responsibility to listen to them.

"Listening: New Approach to Selling." Chemical Week 92
    (1):26, January 5, 1963.   744
    Description of a programmed course in listening for
salesmen, developed by Basic Systems Inc. of New York.

"The Listening Skills." Supervisor's Notebook. Scott
    Foresman Co. No. 979, February 1957, p. 1-4.   745
    This is a good source for a variety of suggested activi-
ties in the teaching of listening.

Loban, Walter D. The Language of Elementary School Chil-
    dren. NCTE Research Report No. 1. Champaign, Ill.:
    National Council of Teachers of English, 1963.   746
    In this longitudinal study, most of the emphasis is on
the language skills other than listening. The STEP test was
administered to 121 eighth graders. There was a "positive
relation between oral language and listening."

Loder, J. Edwin. "A Study of Aural Learning With or With-
    out the Speaker Present." Journal of Experimental Edu-
    cation 6:46-60, September 1937.   747
    A live speaker was found to be more effective on im-
mediate recall than an unseen speaker heard over a loudspeaker. On delayed recall this difference did not exist.

Lodge, Helen. "Reading Teachers Can Learn from Listening
    to the Learners." Claremont College Reading Confer-
    ence Twenty-Fourth Yearbook, 1959, p. 29-33.   748
    "Listening to children is an avenue underused by teachers
in assessing children's needs and thus helping them to meet
their problems. In the area of reading, listening to children
provides insights into the child as a reader, which teaching
practices have been helpful, which need to be strengthened
or changed. Thoughtfully used, such listening can individu-
alize instruction and improve procedures."

Lodge, William J. "Developmental Characteristics of Child-
    hood Related to the Language Arts Curriculum."
    Elementary English 30:106-115, February 1953. Re-
    printed: National Conference on Research in English.
    Child Development and the Language Arts. Chicago:
    National Council of Teachers of English, 1953, p. 17-

26.   749
A teacher of reading who listens well during individual
conferences with pupils can obtain much helpful and useful
information.

Lohnas, Lucille. "Listening Versus Talking." English
    Journal, (High School Edition). 26:479-80, June 1937.
                                                          750
    A list of standards for good listening prepared by junior
high school pupils.

Loper, James Leader. An Experimental Study of Some Ef-
    fects of Time Compression upon the Comprehension and
    Retention of Visually Augmented Speech. Doctoral dis-
    sertation. Los Angeles, Calif.: University of Sourthern
    California, 1966. Abstract: Dissertation Abstracts 27:
    4370A, 1967.   751
    Seven groups of 20 college speech students were subjects.
Fairbanks' 1554 word passage was compressed by 1/3 and
1/2 in both visual and aural modes using a Vari-Vox time
compression device and a skip-frame film printer. No difference was found between aural presentation and simultaneous presentation of aural and visual. Comprehension was
significantly lower as time compression increased.

Lorenz, Robert Birchall. A Comparison of Two Modes of
    Presentation (Traditional; Tape Recorded) Under Two Con-
    ditions of Preparation (Listening Training; No Listening
    Training) in a Basic Audiovisual Course. Doctoral dis-
    sertation. Syracuse, N.Y.: Syracuse University, 1966.
    Abstract: Dissertation Abstracts 27:1284A, 1966.   752
    One half of the experimental group of 28 and of the con-
trol group of 33 were given listening instruction. The listening instruction consisted of a presentation by the instructor,
listening to a tape recording of 4 to 10 minutes in duration,
and taking a test of comprehension of the taped material.
These sessions were held once a week for six weeks and
covered good listening habits, purposes in listening, concentration, indexing, psychological adjustments and mental visu-
alization.
    No significant differences in achievement were found be-
tween the two methods of presentation. There was a significant difference in favor of the listening instructed group in
the course final examination.

Lorge, Irving A. "Review of Brown-Carlsen Listening Com-
    prehension Test." Fifth Mental Measurements Yearbook.

(Edited by O.K. Buros.) Highland Park, N.J.: Gryphon
Press, 1959, p. 651-52.   753
A critical review of the Brown-Carlsen Listening Test
which questions its difference from some subtests on intelligence tests and methods of administration. Lorge says validity is difficult to judge.

----. "Review of Sequential Tests of Educational Progress:
    Listening." Fifth Mental Measurements Yearbook. (Ed-
    ited by O.K. Buros.) Highland Park, N.J.: Gryphon
    Press, 1959, p. 654-55.   754
A critical review of the STEP Listening Test which questions the length of passages used and the nature of data furn-
ished to users.

Los Angeles City Schools. Research Related to Development
    of Listening Skills. Instructional Bulletin No. EC-76.
    Los Angeles, Calif.: Author, 1964.   755
Listening, Purposes of Listening, The Capacity to Listen,
and Teaching of Listening Skills are discussed in the light of
research studies. Seventeen item bibliography.

Lowenfeld, Berthold. Braille and Talking Book Reading: A
    Comparative Study. New York: American Foundation for
    the Blind, 1945.   756
Braille reading of McCall-Crabbe test-material was not
only much slower than listening to the same material on
Talking Book records, but also led to a statistically significant lesser degree of comprehension.

Lown, Arthur. "Some Observations on Speeded Speech by
    Visually-Impaired Students in the Atlanta Public Schools."
    Proceedings of the Louisville Conference on Time Com-
    pressed Speech, October 19-21, 1966. (Edited by Emer-
    son Foulke.) Louisville, Ky.: Center for Rate Controlled
    Recordings, University of Louisville, 1967. p. 61-62.
                                                              757
Of nineteen high school pupils who listened to unaltered
speech, mechanically speeded speech, and time sampled
speech over the telephone, seventeen expressed a preference
for the last. When students were allowed to select their own
rate, it varied from 114 to 352 wpm. No comprehension
test.

Lubershane, Melvin. "Can Training in Listening Improve
    Reading Ability?" Chicago Schools Journal 43:277-81,
    March 1962.   758

Some questions about technique.

Lucas, Aubrey Keith. An Investigation of Auditory Discrimination and Reading Ability. Master's thesis. Hatties-
burg, Miss.: Mississippi Southern College, 1956. 759
Using 88 first to third grade pupils as subjects, Lucas
found no significant correlation between results on the Wepman Auditory Discrimination Test and the Metropolitan Reading Tests.

Luft, Joseph. "Differences in Prediction Based on Hearing
Versus Reading Verbatim Clinical Interviews." Journal
of Consulting Psychology 15:115-19, April 1951.   760
Those who listened to the protocol of a clinical interview
were more effective in interpretation than those who read it.
"The voice in spontaneous speech tends to externalize significant underlying aspects of the personality which may not be
apparent in the content of the speech."

Lundsteen, Sara W. "Defense from the Cooky Cut Mind."
Independent School Bulletin 24(2):22-24, January 1965.
                                                           761
A lack of critical listening leads to blind conformity and
stifles individuality. Teaching of critical listening has been
largely neglected. An experiment in teaching critical listening skills to 400 fifth and sixth grade pupils is described.

----. "Listening, Reading and Qualitative Levels of Thinking in Problem Solving." Vistas in Reading. International Reading Association Conference Proceedings, Vol.
11, Part I, 1967. (Edited by J. Allen Figurel.) Newark, Del: International Reading Association, 1967. p.
45-54. Also in California Journal of Educational Research 18:230-37, November 1967.   762
Eighty-six sixth graders were given a 48-item test of
qualitative levels of thinking. Based on incomplete problem
stories, there were 12 multiple-choice items about possible
completions for each of four stories. Half of the group read
the test and the other half listened to an oral presentation.
The correlation between test results on the listening and
reading presentations was .39. A factor analysis yielded
four clusters, suggesting separate factors: abstract reading
ability, concrete listening quality, functional listening quality,
and functional reading quality.
"The relatively small relationship between listening and
reading factors and the qualitative levels may lend some support to the theoretical concept of a constellation of listening

abilities, as well as reading abilities, related to qualitative
levels of thinking as measurable."

----. "Procedures for Teaching Critical Reading and Listening." Ginn and Company Contributions in Reading,
No. 34. Boston: Ginn, 1964.   763
Instruction in critical listening and reading is important
because mass media tend to produce conformity; abilities in
critical reading and listening are not acquired automatically
but must be taught; many prejudices, misconceptions, and
stereotypes are acquired as early as the third grade; and
the amount of time devoted to reading and listening is increasing. Critical thinking while reading and listening is
defined as the process of examining written and spoken materials in the light of related, objective evidence, comparing
them with some standard, criterion, or consensus, arriving
at a conclusion, and acting upon the judgment made. There
is a high correlation between critical listening and critical
reading. Specific techniques for teaching critical reading
and listening are discussed.

----. Teaching Ability in Critical Listening in the Fifth and
Sixth Grades. Doctoral dissertation. Berkeley, Calif.:
University of California, 1963. Abstract: Dissertation
Abstracts 24:5247, 1964. Summary: "Teaching and
Testing Critical Listening in the Fifth and Sixth Grades."
Elementary English 41:743-47+, November 1964. Read-
ing and Inquiry. International Reading Association Con-
ference Proceedings, Vol. 10, 1965. (Edited by J. Al-
len Figurel.) Newark, Del.: International Reading Asso-
ciation, 1965. p. 306-08. Excerpts: California Journal
of Educational Research 16:210-16, November 1965.
Listening: Readings. (Edited by Sam Duker.) Metuchen,
N.J.: Scarecrow Press, 1966. p. 283-84, 285-90, 291-
301, 302-08. Elementary School Journal 66:311-15,
March 1966.   764
A description of a set of lessons suitable for teaching
critical listening skills to intermediate grade children and a
test of critical listening. Text of the lessons and test is included.

Lunnen, Vera L. "Listening Games." Instructor 74(5):32,
January 1965.   765
Thirteen games suitable for practice in auditory dis-
crimination and listening briefly described.

Lynch, James J. and Evans, Bertrand. High School English

Textbooks: <u>A Critical Examination.</u> Boston: Little
<u>Brown, 1963. p. 405-96.</u>   766
A content analysis of fourteen series. Of a total of
26,141 pages, 424 were concerned with listening, 2063 dealt
with speaking.

McBrian, Donna Jeanne Benson. <u>An Experimental Study of</u>
   <u>the Effectiveness of a Planned Program Designed to Teach</u>
   <u>Certain Listening Skills.</u> Master's thesis. St. Paul,
   <u>Minn.:</u> Macalester College, 1962.   767
Using the Kuhlman-Anderson as a test of intelligence,
the Iowa Basic Skills as a test of reading and the STEP as
a test of listening, McBrian gave a series of 21 lessons in
listening to 164 fifth grade pupils. No significant differences
were found to have occurred as a result of the lessons.

McBroom, Patricia. "Compressed Speech Helps." <u>Science</u>
   <u>Newsletter</u> 88:214, October 2, 1965.   768
A device used for speech compression by the Department
of Defense, which compressed up to 500 wpm with intelligibility for persons without practice, is described. The compressed speech is heard in one ear while the discards are
heard in the other. The highest speed for intelligible speech
may be equal to the highest comfortable reading rate.

McCarthy, Dorothea. "Home Influences." National Conference on Research in English. <u>Factors That Influence</u>
   <u>Language Growth.</u> Chicago: National Council of Teach-
   <u>ers of English, 1953, p. 8-16.</u>   769
The importance of home influence on language development is especially vital in the area of listening, as this is
the language skill first called upon in school.

McClarty, Edward Leon. <u>Auding Ability Related to Achieve-</u>
   <u>ment in Two Telecourses.</u> Doctoral dissertation. Stan-
   <u>ford, Calif.:</u> Stanford University, 1957. Abstract:
   <u>Dissertation Abstracts</u> 18:531-32, 1958.   770
Using 195 college students as subjects, McClarty gave
lessons in psychology and economics live and on television.
He found no correlations between gains on criterion tests and
listening, as measured by the Brown-Carlsen Test. Because
there was a high relationship between listening and pre-test
scores on economics and psychology, the author concludes
that listening, as measured by this test, is closely related
to general information.

McClendon, Paul Irving. <u>An Experimental Study of the Re-</u>

lationship Between Note-Taking Practices and Listening
Comprehension of College Freshmen During Expository
Lectures. Doctoral dissertation. Iowa City, Iowa:
State University of Iowa, 1956. Abstract: Dissertation
Abstracts 16:1736-37, 1956, and Speech Monographs 24:
95 June 1957. Summary: Speech Monographs 25:222-
28, August 1958, and Pauk, Walter "Does Note-Taking
Interfere with Listening Comprehension?" Journal of
Developmental Reading 6:276-78, Summer 1963.   771
Using 678 freshman communication students as subjects,
the author reports no significant differences between groups
taking no notes, taking notes only on main ideas, taking
notes on details, and taking notes in a customary manner.

Maccoby, Eleanor E. and Konrad, Karl W. "Age Trends in
    Selective Listening." Journal of Experimental Child Psy-
    chology 3:113-22. May 1966.   772
Groups of kindergarten, second, and fourth grade children listened to words spoken simultaneously, one by a male
voice and one by a female voice. The words were presented
binaurally and dichotically. Children were asked to report
the words spoken by one of the voices. The number of correct reports increased with age; the number of reports of
words spoken by the unwanted voice decreased with age, and
the scores were higher at all age levels for the dichotic
presentation. More errors were made on one-syllable than
on multi-syllable words. Performance improved with practice.

McConnell, Ethel Marie. A Study of Listening at Fourth and
    Sixth Grades Based Upon STEP: Listening, Including a
    Study of the Literature. Master's thesis. DeKalb, Ill:
    Northern Illinois University, 1966.   773
The STEP Listening Test, The Metropolitan Reading Test,
and the California Test of Mental Maturity were administered
to 409 fourth grade and to 181 sixth grade pupils. The sixth
grade pupils had significantly higher listening scores than the
fourth grade, but the difference was not as large as the difference in reading scores. An item analysis of the STEP
test shows: "STEP: Listening is probably from 39 to 58 per
cent efficient in measuring skills which are unique to listening . . ." This test may be a better indicator at the fourth
than at the sixth grade level. Correlations of .59 were
found between listening and reading at the fourth grade level
and .73 at the sixth grade level. Listening-Intelligence correlations were .54 and .62.

McCormack, Sister Mary Eulogius. An Experimental Study
    of the Effect of a Concentrated Program of Listening
    Comprehension Skills on Reading Comprehension of First
    Grade Pupils in Selected Schools in Massachusetts.
    Master's thesis. Milwaukee, Wisc.: Cardinal Stritch
    College, 1962.   774
    A well-performed experimental study showed that a group
of 44 students given systematic listening instruction over a
period of six months gained significantly over a control group
in total reading, reading sentence comprehension, and paragraph comprehension. Texts of tests used and of some exercises for teaching listening are included.

McCracken, Lawrence. "--And the Unique Art of Listening
    Too!" Commerce Magazine 46(12):19+, January 1950.
                                                          775
    Report on a survey by a public relations firm which lists
a number of situations in which listening is stressed in industrial relations between management and worker.

McDavid, Thomas O. "How to Listen Effectively." Business
    Management 23(1):44-45+, October 1962.   776
    Lateral communication in business and industry offers
little difficulty in listening. In downward communication,
there is a great loss of information; as much as 80 per cent
in three sequential transmissions. Poor listening is caused
by: 1. assuming that the subject is uninteresting; 2. mentally criticizing speaker's delivery; 3. becoming over-stimulated; 4. listening only for factual data; 5. trying to outline
everything; 6. permitting speaker to speak inaudibly; 7.
tuning out messages that border on the technical; 8. being
allergic to certain distasteful words or phrases; 9. pretending to listen; 10. letting one's mind wander.

McDonald, Adelbert O. The Teaching of Listening at the
    Ninth-Grade Level. Master's thesis. Lawrence, Kan.:
    University of Kansas, 1960.   777
    Using 78 students as subjects, and the Brown-Carlsen
test as a measure of listening, McDonald reports that the
group given ten listening lessons showed a statistically
[significantly greater gain on a retest than did the control
group.

McDonald, Douglas Francis. The Construction and Evalua-
    tion of Objective Tests of Oral Language Skills. Doctor-
    al dissertation. Boston: Boston University, 1957. 778
    Experimental data is reported showing little difference

in recall of material heard and read by fourth-grade children. In the fifth and sixth grades the recall was greater
for reading.

MacDonnell, Sister M. Patrina. An Experimental Study
    of the Effect of Intensive Training in Listening Skills
    on Reading and Spelling Achievement in Grade One.
    Master's thesis. Milwaukee, Wisc.: Cardinal Stritch
    College, 1962.   779
Using in her thesis the materials developed by McCormack, MacDonnell found that, as a result of three months
of systematic listening instruction, the experimental group
made significantly greater gains in reading and listening, but
not in spelling, than the control group.

McKee, Norma. "Susan, Touch Your Toes."   Texas Outlook
    51(5):58, May 1967.   780
The use of the intercom loudspeaker from the principal's
office for practice in listening is described. Children's
names were used, and specific directions were given for the
individual to carry out. This was found to be a very effective way of increasing listening skills in the first grade.

McKee, Paul. "The Nature and Scope of the Language
    Arts." National Elementary Principal 20:235-56, July
    1941.   781
McKee advocates a greater degree of attention to listening in the elementary school curriculum. He states that
pupil achievement in this area is much lower than is generally thought and that this situation grows worse as the educational level advances.

McLain, Julie Rhinehart. "A Comparison of Two Methods
    of Producing Rapid Speech." International Journal for
    the Education of the Blind 12:40-42, December 1962.
                                                              782
A 2105 word fictional passage from a textbook was
played at a time compression of .46 to   58 visually handicapped seventh grade students. One half heard the passage
compressed by the Tempo Regulator, while the other half
heard the same passage played faster. A significant difference in comprehension was found in favor of the speech compressed by the Tempo Regulator.

McPherson, Irene. The Effect of Direct Practice in Listen-
    ing on Certain Reading Skills. Master's thesis. Gree-
    ley, Colo.: Colorado State College of Education, 1951.

783
The improvement on a reading test by a group of 65 second grade pupils who had been given 30 practice exercises in listening was statistically significant when compared to results from a control group of the same size.

Macrorie, Ken. "Teach Listening?" College English 12:
220-23, January 1951.   784
The author advocates that everything possible be done to improve students' listening skills, though the best way to teach listening may not yet have been established by research. A good argument is given for the importance of listening.

Madden, Theodore Martin. The Effect of Instruction and Practice in Certain Skills Through the Media of Reading and Listening upon Various Aspects of Proficiency in Reading and Listening. Doctoral dissertation. Tucson, Arizona: University of Arizona, 1959. Abstract: Dissertation Abstracts 20:2178-79, 1959.   785
Using 200 sixth grade pupils as subjects and the STEP tests as measures of listening and reading, Madden reports that both listening and reading instruction produced higher reading test scores but that neither produced higher listening test scores.

Maize, Ray C. "A Military Program in Communications." Journal of Communication 2:57-63, May 1952.   786
Maize found that listening plays a very small role in the communications instructional program in the Air Force.

Maloney, Louise Ann. Auditory Discrimination and Its Relation to the Reading Program. Master's thesis. Normal, Ill.: Illinois State Normal University, 1960. 787

Maloney, Martin. "Semantics: The Foundation of All Business Communication." Advanced Management 19(7):26-29, July 1954.   788
The need is stressed for projective and attentive listening rather than marginal listening.

Manion, Orville Gayle. An Application of Readability Formulas to Oral Communication. Doctoral dissertation. Ann Arbor, Mich.: University of Michigan, 1953. Abstract: Dissertation Abstracts 13:452, 1953, and Speech Monographs 21:151, June 1954.   789

   This item contains an excellent review of the literature
on readability formulas as applied to oral communication.
From experimental data presented, Manion concludes that
sentence length, prepositional phrases, number of definite
words, number of unfamiliar words, and word length in syllables are not useful measures of listening difficulty.

Many, Wesley Allen. The Comprehension of Identical Ma-
     terials Presented Under Reading and Listening Conditions.
     Master's thesis. Iowa City, Iowa: State University of
     Iowa, 1953. Summary: Reading Teacher 19:110-113,
     November 1965.   790
     Using 352 sixth-grade children as subjects and the Pratt
Test as a measure of listening, Many reports that visual
presentation was significantly superior to oral. A correlation between listening and reading of .68 is reported.

Marcatante, John. "Listening in an Integrated Program."
     High Points 41:64-66, May 1959.   791
     A description of a listening program at the junior high
school level based on listening to records, making logs of
listening experiences, and practicing listening for details.

Marcoux, J. Paul Albert. The Integration of Speaking and
     Listening with Twelfth Grade Literature in Calais. Mas-
     ter's thesis. Boston: Boston University, 1959.   792
     A descriptive study.

Markgraf, Bruce Richard. An Observational Study Determin-
     ing the Amount of Time That Students in the Tenth and
     Twelfth Grades Are Expected to Listen in the Classroom.
     Master's thesis. Madison, Wisc.: University of Wiscon-
     sin, 1957. Excerpts: Listening: Readings. (Edited by
     Sam Duker.) Metuchen, N.J.: Scarecrow Press, 1966.
     p. 90-94.   793
     Twenty high school students were followed through their
school day. They were expected to listen 46 per cent of the
time; to work and study 48 per cent. Of the listening time
66 per cent was devoted to teachers. In English classes
students were expected to listen 97 per cent of the time.

----. A Survey of Listening Pedagogy in American Teacher-
     Training Institutions. Doctoral dissertation. Madison,
     Wisc.: University of Wisconsin, 1960. Abstract: Dis-
     sertation Abstracts 21:699-700, 1960. Summary: Jour-
     nal of Communication 12:33-35, March 1962. Excerpts:
     Listening: Readings. (Edited by Sam Duker.) Metuchen,

N.J.: Scarecrow Press, 1966. p. 311-20.   794
The results of 839 questionnaires returned by speech,
education and English departments in 406 teacher-training
colleges showed that 88 speech courses, 92 education
courses, and 118 English courses had units on listening.
Many other details are given.

Marks, Alvin, Cathcart, Robert, and Michael, William B.
    "The Prediction of Gains in Mean Performance in Vari-
    ous Measures of Communication Skills Relative to Type
    of Curriculum Pursued." Journal of Experimental Edu-
    cation 31:303-06, March 1963.   795
Three college freshman curricula were offered: one
semester of English composition followed by one semester of
speech; one semester of speech followed by one semester of
English composition; and a two-semester sequence in the language arts. STEP Reading, Listening, and Writing Tests,
ACE Critical Thinking, and the verbal subtest of SCAT were
used as pre- and post-tests for students in each of the curricula. There was no control group. All subjects gained
significantly on each of these tests, but there was no significant difference among the three curricula.

Marks, Edmond and Noll, Gary A. "Procedures and Cri-
    teria for Evaluating Reading and Listening Comprehension
    Tests." Educational and Psychological Measurement 27:
    335-48, Summer 1967   796
A mathematical model which determines whether a particular test item measures either reading or listening comprehension.

Marsden, W. Ware. A Study of the Value of Training in
    Listening to Achievement in Reading. Doctoral field
    study. Greeley, Colo.: Colorado State College of Edu-
    cation, 1952. Abstract: Abstracts of Field Studies for
    the Degree of Doctor of Education 14:50-52, 1953. 797
Using 232 elementary school pupils as subjects, Marsden reports that the group given systematic listening instruction gained significantly more in reading, as measured by
the Gates Test, than did a control group.

----. A Study to Determine the Effect of Training in Lis-
    tening upon Ability to Listen. Doctoral field study.
    Greeley, Colo.: Colorado State College of Education,
    1953. Abstract: Abstracts of Field Studies for the De-
    gree of Doctor of Education, 15:111-13, 1954.   798
Using 100 fifth and sixth grade pupils as subjects,

Marsden reports that systematic instruction in listening resulted in significantly greater gains in listening than when
no such instruction was given. Measurements were made
by the oral administration of the Chicago Reading Test.

Marshall, Clair Jones. Development and Experimental Eval-
     uation of a Program of Listening Instruction for Grade
     Two. Master's thesis. Columbus, Ohio: Ohio State
     University, 1963.   799
     A carefully designed study showing that a 13-week pro-
gram resulted in a significant improvement of listening
skills by 25 pupils. A modification of the listening test developed by Larter was used.

Mart, Melvin. The Relationship Between Achievement and
     Verbal Communication of Secondary School Children.
     Doctoral dissertation. New York: Columbia University,
     1963. Abstract: Dissertation Abstracts 24:4527, 1964.
                                                          800
     A correlational study of relationships between the STEP
Listening Test, the California Mental Maturity Test, scholastic index, age, and sex. Subjects were 109 seventh-grade
pupils.

Marten, Milton E. The Relationship Between Expressed In-
     terests and Listening Skills of Children in the Sixth
     Grade. Doctoral dissertation. Bloomington, Ind.:
     Indiana University, 1958. Abstract: Dissertation Ab-
     stracts 19:2295-96, 1959.   801
     Using 45 students as subjects, Marten found no relation-
ship between interest inventories and pupils' skills in listening to materials dealing with those interests. A correlation
of .65 is reported between listening and intelligence.

Martin, Adrian W. Factors in the Relationship Between
     Listening Comprehension and Academic Achievement of
     the Senior Class of June 1958, East High School. Master's
     thesis. Des Moines, Iowa: Drake University, 1958.   802
     The following correlations with listening, as measured
by the Brown-Carlsen Test, are reported: California Reading Test, .60, academic achievement .54, language grades
.51, and social studies grades .44.

Martin, William Ivan Jr. A Comparative Study of Listening
     Comprehension and Reading Comprehension in the Teach-
     ing of Literature to Seventh-Grade Pupils. Doctoral
     dissertation. Evanston, Ill.: Northwestern University,

1961. Abstract: Dissertation Abstracts 23:2806-07,
1963.   803
Using 113 pupils as subjects, Martin found no significant
difference in comprehension of passages read and of passages
listened to. Pupil interest was an effective influence on both
reading and listening comprehension. Length of passages,
level of difficulty, and literary style did not affect the significant relationship found between reading and listening comprehension.

Mason, Harry M. "Improvement of Listener Performance in
    Noise." Speech Monographs 13(2):42-46, April 1946.
                                                        804
An experimental study in which listening instruction consisted solely of practice. Listening training was found to be
of little value.

----. "Understandability of Speech in Noise as Affected by
    Region of Origin of Speaker and Listener." Speech
    Monographs 13(2):54-58, April 1946.   805
Reports a finding that intelligibility is greater for persons from the same region as the speaker than for inter-
regional listeners.

----, and Garrison, Barbara K. "Intelligibility of Spoken
    Messages: Like and Disliked." Journal of Abnormal and
    Social Psychology 46:100-03, January 1951. Abstract:
    American Psychologist 4:395, August 1949.   806
Using 40 advanced-psychology students as subjects, the
authors found that aurally transmitted three-word sentences
intended to represent "liked" activities were transcribed
more accurately than those "disliked." It is suggested by
the authors that in this instance this may be due to greater
familiarity with the words in the "liked" messages.

Matthews, Sister John Louis. An Experimental Study of the
    Effects of Training in Listening Comprehension on Read-
    ing Comprehension in the Third Grade. Master's thesis.
    Milwaukee, Wisc.: Cardinal Stritch College, 1958. 807
A ten-minute listening lesson given during reading periods for six months failed to result in an increase in either
listening or reading significantly greater than that shown by
a control group.

Matthews, Thomas LeRoy. A Comparison of Aural and Vis-
    ual Presentation of Materials Under Conditions of Dis-
    traction. Master's thesis. Charlottesville, Va.: Uni-

versity of Virginia, 1950.   808
Forty subjects, who were required to watch dials while
receiving aural and visual messages, showed better comprehension of the aural than of the visual messages.

May, Thomas Stephen. The Effect of an Indoctrination of
    Techniques of Viewing and Listening on the Achievement
    of Students in a Televised Zoology Course. Master's
    thesis. University Park, Md.: University of Maryland,
    1963.   809
A 45-minute briefing to 99 students about to take a tele-
vised college course on skills involved in listening and view-
ing resulted in no statistically superior final performance
when compared to a control group. However, the students
believed the briefing had been helpful.

Meerloo, Joost A.M. Conversation and Communication.
    New York: International Universities Press, 1952,
    passim.   810
An excellent presentation of a psychiatrist's view of the
importance of listening in the communication process.

Melrose, Jay. The Temporal Course of Changes in the
    Amount of Vocal Disturbance Produced by Delayed Audi-
    tory Feedback. Doctoral dissertation. Urbana, Ill.:
    University of Illinois, 1954. Abstract: Dissertation Ab-
    stracts 15:169, 1955.   811
When one's own speech is fed back immediately or after
a very short time interval, speech is seriously impaired.
When there is a longer lapse of time between the original
speech and the feedback, the effect is not as marked.

Mercer, Jessie. "Listening in the Speech Class." Bulletin
    of the National Association of Secondary School Princi-
    pals 32:102-07, May 1958.   812
Training in listening is an aid to discipline. The author
stresses the importance of pupils listening to each other.

Merrihue, Willard V. Managing by Communication. New
    York: McGraw Hill, 1960.   813
While only a few pages deal specifically with listening,
the general principles expounded in this book are highly relevant for the student of listening in business and industry.

Mersand, Joseph. "Developing Competence in Listening in
    Secondary Schools." Speech Teacher 7:289-301, Novem-
    ber, 1958.   814

An excellent and well-documented review and summary
of the literature on listening.

----. "How to Train Pupils to Listen." Scholastic Teacher,
    85(8):9T, November 4, 1964.   815
Six rules for effective listening:
1. Teacher should be aware of the importance of listening.
2. Pupils should not be required to listen too long at
one stretch.
3. Specific directions for listening are helpful.
4. Listening should be taught both directly and indirectly.
5. Courteous habits of speech and listening should be
developed in students.
6. No opportunity should be lost to show the importance
of listening.

----. "Listening - Neglected Skill." Professional Growth
    for Principals (An Arthur C. Crofts publication.) Janu-
    ary 1958, p. 1-4.   816
Questions to ask teachers about the teaching of listening
are discussed. Short items by Alexander Frazier ("Listening School-Wide"), Donald E. Bird ("Listening in the Lower
Grades"), Edwin C. Sutton, Jr. ("A Junior High School Project in Progress"), and Sid F. Moore ("Check Lists for High
Schools"), are included as is a list of available reprints.

----. "Teaching Listening in High School." Bulletin of the
    National Association of Secondary School Principals
    42:123-30, May 1958.   817
The teaching of listening through the use of recordings,
radio, and motion pictures is advocated. Guides to presentations made through these media are described.

----. "Why Teach Listening?" English Journal 40:260-65,
    May 1951. Reprinted: The Recording as a Teacher's
    Tool. A Bulletin for Parents and Teachers, Folkway
    Records and Service Co., 117 West 46th Street, New
    York, 1955.   818
The spoken word is becoming more and more powerful
as a medium of communication; therefore, listening must be
taught. Teaching should be for comprehension and for critical evaluation. Radio and recordings are valuable aids in
teaching this skill. Types of listening are listed.

Merson, Edna May. The Influence of Definite Listening Les-
    sons on the Improvement of Listening and Reading Com-
    prehension and Reading Vocabulary. Doctoral disserta-
    tion. College Park, Md.: University of Maryland,
    1961. Abstract: Dissertation Abstracts 22:3120-21,
    1962.   819
    Twelve fourth-grade classes were taught 45 planned les-
sons in listening, the texts of which are given. The classes
failed to show any greater improvement in listening, as
measured by the STEP Listening Test, or in reading, as
measured by the Iowa Test of Basic Skills, than did control
groups. In the opinion of teachers involved, however, the
lessons were useful to both reading and listening.

Merwin, Mary F. Listening Games. Scranton, Pa.:
    Acadia Press, 1962. (Accompanied by a Teacher's Edi-
    tion.)   820
    This book presents 52 games for the improvement of
listening skills in kindergarten, first grade, and in special
classes. Each game is accompanied by a diagrammatic page
which is used to answer the requirements of the lesson or
"game."

Metropolitan School Study Council. Tips and Games for the
    Classroom Teacher of the Elementary Language Arts.
    New York: Author, 1958.   821
    A description of successful procedures in teaching the
various language arts, including listening.

Meyer, Bernrdine. "They Have Ears But Hear Not." Catho-
    lic Business Education Review 12(4):37-39, June 1961.
                                                          822
    Good listening requires alert senses, physical comfort,
and a receptive mind, as well as controlled emotional responses. Good listening should be for ideas rather than for
words.

Meyer, John Leonard. An Experimental Study Determining
    the Effects of Direct Instruction in Listening upon Tenth
    Grade Students. Master's thesis. Madison, Wisc.:
    University of Wisconsin, 1963. Summary: Meyer,
    John L. and Williams, Frederick. Speech Teacher
    14:299-304, November 1965.   823
    Sixteen practice listening sessions did not result in any
significant difference in listening improvement on the Brown-
Carlsen test between a control group of 120 and the experimental group of 60. A correlation of .68 between intelli-

gence and the listening pre-test and of .58 between intelligence and the post-test is reported.

Michael, William B. and others. "Gains in Various Measures of Communication Skills Relative to 3 Curricular Patterns in College." Educational and Psychological Measurement 23:365-74, Summer 1963.   824
The experiment described in Marks (795) was repeated with the same results. Correlations of .70 were found between reading and listening. It is suggested that other measures were needed to ascertain the value of the alternate courses.

Miller, Eleanor Almy. The Relation of Hearing Comprehension to Reading Comprehension in Grades Three and Four. Master's thesis. Boston: Boston University, 1941.   825
Using 217 pupils as subjects and the Durrell-Sullivan Reading Capacity Test, Miller reports that listening was superior to reading in both grades, particularly in vocabulary. The difference was less in the fourth grade than in the third.

Miller, Ernest Coleman. Effects on Learning of Variations in Oral Presentation. Doctoral dissertation. Denver, Colo.: University of Denver, 1954.   826
Twenty-seven taped lectures were delivered to 972 newly enrolled Air Force cadets. An analysis of variance revealed no significant differences in the results of pre- and post-tests attributable to variations on style difficulty (ranging from eighth grade to college graduate levels as measured by Flesch and Dale-Chall formulas) or to variations in speed of delivery of the lectures (ranging from 95 through 165 wpm).

Miller, Fred Robert. An Experiment to Determine the Effect Organization Has on the Immediate and Delayed Recall of Information. Master's thesis. Oxford, Ohio: Miami University, 1966.   827
There was a significant difference in the scores of 69 high school seniors on a comprehension test between groups hearing a well organized speech and groups hearing a poorly organized speech with the same content. The well-organized speech showed the best results.

Miller, G.A. and Licklider, J.C.R. "The Intelligibility of Interrupted Speech." Journal of the Acoustical Society of America 22:167-73, March 1950.   828
It is possible to interrupt speech waves as many as

10,000 times a second without affecting intelligibility. A
smaller number of interruptions can, however, affect intelligibility.

Miller, G.A. "The Masking of Speech." Psychological Bul-
    letin 44:105-29, March 1947.   829
    A very lucid explanation of the concept of masking of
speech. Masking depends on its intensity relative to the intensity of the speech being masked, its acoustic spectrum,
and its temporal continuity.

Miller, James Nathan. "Listen for a Change." Empire
    Magazine 16(30):30-33, July 25, 1965. Digest: "The
    Art of Intelligent Listening." Reader's Digest 87(521):
    83-86, September 1965.   830
    A popularly written argument for the importance of good
listening in the conversational process.

Miller, Julie F. "Listening with the Heart." Parents Maga-
    zine 29(8):32-33, August 1954.   831
    A short, sentimental appeal that the childish ability to
"listen with the heart" not be lost.

Miller, Nathan. "Listening to Learn." See and Hear 1:71-
    75, February 1946.   832
    Out-of-school listening is important in detecting bias,
prejudice and propaganda.

Mills, Barriss. "Communication Versus Composition."
    Education 72:501-08, March 1952.   833
    Little is being done about the teaching of listening, al-
though it is listed in the statement of objectives in many
communications courses.

Mills, Donna M. "Interrelating Reading and Listening in
    Grades Four Through Eight." Reading and the Language
    Arts. Proceedings of the Annual Conference on Reading.
    Chicago: University of Chicago Press, 1963. p. 59-62.
                                                         834
    Listening and reading call for the same mental proc-
esses. Physical aids and attitudes helpful to listening are
listed, as are goals for listening and appropriate activities
for teaching listening skills.

Mingoia, Edwin. "Possible Causes of Underachievement in
    Reading." Elementary English 39:220-23, March 1962.
                                                         835

The Durrell-Sullivan Reading Capacity Test was administered to 128 fourth through sixth grade pupils. Bright children were found to be achieving one and a half to two years below their level of listening comprehension. The data for these conclusions are not given.

Mirrielis, Lucia B. "How Do Your Pupils Listen?" Montana Education 23(9):30, January 1947.   836
Daily listening exercises, modeled after written workbook exercises in reading, should be included in the elementary school curriculum.

Mobray, G.H. "Simultaneous Vision and Audition: The Comprehension of Prose Passages with Varying Levels of Difficulty." Journal of Experimental Psychology 46: 365-72, November 1953.   837
An experiment is reported in which two different prose passages were presented simultaneously in both visual and auditory form. The passages used were at varying levels of difficulty measured by the Flesch formula. The easy material was most difficult to grasp when materials of differing levels of difficulty were presented simultaneously. The auditory channel showed significantly greater disruption of performance than the visual.

Moe, Iver L. Auding as a Predictive Measure of Reading Performance in Primary Grades. Doctoral dissertation. Gainesville, Fla.: University of Florida, 1957. Abstract: Dissertation Abstracts 18:121-22, 1958. Excerpts: Listening: Readings. (Edited by Sam Duker.) Metuchen, N.J.: Scarecrow Press, 1966. p. 118-23
                                                       838
Moe reports on experimental findings that show that listening test scores and mental age together are better predictors of reading performance than either one alone.

Moldstad, John Alton. A Study of the Relative Effects of Film Narration Listenability Difficulty on the Learning of Factual Information and the Development of Incidental Vocabulary. Doctoral dissertation. Bloomington, Ind.: Indiana University, 1953.   839
Using the Dale Readability formula, Moldstad prepared three forms of film commentary of varying degrees of difficulty. He found no difference in comprehension or in the development of vocabulary among the groups hearing different versions.

Molitoris, Anna. Listening: Its Relationship with Reading
   and Arithmetic Achievement. Master's thesis. Normal,
   Ill.: Illinois State Normal University, 1963.   840
   The Stanford Achievement Tests for reading and arithmetic and the STEP test for listening, were used as pre- and
post-tests for this study. In the interval, listening instruction was given during one school year. Subjects were 36
sixth-graders; there was no control group. Very high correlations are reported between listening scores and reading and
arithmetic scores.

Monroe, Marion. Children Who Cannot Read. Chicago: University of Chicago Press, 1932.   841
   Monroe reports that a lack of precise auditory discrimination is more common among poor readers than among
others.

----. "Let's Teach All the Language Arts." Teaching
   Trends. Chicago, Ill.: Scott Foresman, 1961. p. 5-8.
                                                           842
   A chart and table show the overlapping skills involved
in speaking, writing, reading and listening. It cannot be assumed that teaching a child to read and write will automatically make him a good speaker and listener. All the language arts need to be taught, and none should be left to
chance or incidental attention. Listening involves forming
mental images. Good listening habits aid pupils' progress in
reading. The first step is to define the aims and purposes
of teaching listening.

Moore, Eva A. "Listening Is a Skill." English Journal
   42:378-81, October 1953.   843
   Listening to ideas differs from listening for ideas. A
good listener is more than a sponge. Sometimes not listening is a good thing.

Morkovin, Boris V. "Growth Through Speaking and Listening." Elementary English 26:129-31+, March 1949.
                                                           844
   Listening is not a new idea. Children do not learn to
listen automatically, but they can be taught to listen. Reading stories, announcements, telephone conversations, radio,
nature sounds, and keeping a listening log are some of the
activities to use in teaching listening.

Morris, June. "Relative Efficiency of Reading and Listening for Braille and Large Type Readers." Conference

Report, *American Association of Instructors of the Blind*, June 26-30, 1966. Washington, D.C., 1966. p. 65-71.   845
Several 2,000-word selections of varying levels of difficulty dealing with science, social studies, and literature, were administered to 1152 legally blind elementary and secondary school pupils, in Braille, large print, and by tape recording. Part of the group read or heard the passages once, while others read or heard the same passage on three successive days. Multiple choice comprehension tests were administered.

In every case the three-day groups learned more than the one-day groups. High school students learned significantly more in social studies and literature by reading than by listening. There was no difference in the science learning. Among elementary school pupils there were no significant differences between learning by listening and by reading. If time spent was taken into account, listening was the more efficient way of learning.

Morrison, James H. "How to Talk - and Listen - Better." *Factory* 117(6):91-93, June 1959.   846
Four rules of good listening are given: listen, and act like it; listen and look like it; listen and understand; and listen completely.

Moser, Henry M. and Dreher, John J. "Effects of Training on Listeners in Intelligibility Studies." *Journal of the Acoustical Society of America* 27:1213-19, November 1955.   847
Training of subjects is shown to be an important factor in intelligibility studies.

Murphy, George. "We Also Learn by Listening." *Elementary English* 26:127-28, March 1949.   848
Children should be taught to listen purposefully, accurately, critically and responsively. A detailed list of suggested activities is included.

Murphy, Mary Ellen. *Current Practices for Developing Listening Skills in the English Programs of Selected Junior High Schools of Iowa.* Master's thesis. Des Moines, Iowa: Drake University, 1965.   849
The results of a questionnaire sent to 150 junior high school teachers in 28 Iowa cities are reported. There were 96 responses. Only one teacher used a standardized listening test (STEP). Informal teacher-made tests were used by

28 teachers. Direct teaching of listening was reported by
79 teachers. Of these, 49 taught listening as part of other
units. The most commonly taught skill was note-taking (27).
A copy of the questionnaire is included.

Murphy, Sister Miriam Melda. A Study of the Inter-Rela-
    tionship Among Listening Comprehension, Intelligence
    and Interest. Master's thesis. Washington, D.C.:
    Catholic University, 1958.   850
    Describes the construction and validation of a listening
test suitable for the eighth grade. The text is included.

Murphy, William Carl. A Study of the Relationships Be-
    tween Listening Ability and High School Grades in Four
    Major Academic Areas. Doctoral dissertation. Tusca-
    loosa, Ala.: University of Alabama, 1962. Abstract:
    Dissertation Abstracts 23:3693, 1963.   851
    In a study employing the Brown-Carlsen Listening Test,
the following correlations between scores on that test and
school grades were reported: English .53, social studies
.41, science .52, and mathematics .49.

Murray, Elwood. "What Are the Problems of Communica-
    tion in Human Relations?" Journal of Communication
    1:23-26, May 1951.   852
    It is the essence of true democracy that communication
is a two-way process, which implies listening at both ends.

Muth, Cecilia. "Learning Through Listening." Baltimore
    Bulletin of Education 34(4):39-46, June 1957.   853
    A useful report of various procedures employed in the
teaching of listening.

Myers, Ruth L. and Gates, Louise W. Effective Listening
    and Cognitive Learning at the College Level. Muncie,
    Ind.: Ball State University, 1966.   854
    Basic Systems' Effective Listening tapes were adminis-
tered to 67 college students selected from psychology and
other classes. The post-test which is part of this course
was administered to these students and to a control group.
At the end of ten days both groups were asked to summarize
a class lecture by stating main points and supporting reasons, omitting irrelevant details. Ten weeks later a test
similar to the original post-test was administered. Except
in the case of the lecture summary, the performance of the
experimental group was significantly better than that of the
control group. No significant relationship was found between

the study of listening and academic grades. Students in the
experimental group said that they considered the listening
course worthwhile.

The authors concluded that the Effective Listening course,
although designed for industry, did work in a college setting,
"probably because it utilized some of the best of our current
learning theory." "However, the instrument does not teach
the variety of listening skills required of college students."

Nafziger, Vivian Beulah. Listening: Relationship with Reading and Spelling Achievement. Master's thesis. Normal,
Ill.: Illinois State Normal University, 1962.   855

Napier, Grace D. Listening Research Bibliography. Washington, D.C.: American Association of Instructors of
the Blind, 1967.   856
Lists 100 references.

Nashville Public Schools. "Experiences in Listening."
(Mimeographed) Nashville, Tenn., 1951.   857
An extensive and extremely useful list of various tech-
niques used in the teaching of listening.

----. "Listening Abilities of Pupils in the Nashville Public
Schools." (Mimeographed) Nashville, Tenn., 1950.
                                                          858
A very useful report of a survey, on a schoolwide basis,
of listening practices and abilities.

Nathan, Ernest D. "The Listening Spirit and the Conference
Leader." Training Directors Journal 18(1):22-30, January 1964.   859
Perceptive listening is defined as a cognitive effort involving primarily the sense of hearing reinforced by other
senses and leading to understanding. When this is accompanied by a sincere desire to understand it becomes more
than a sensory process. The success of a conference leader
depends on his effectiveness as a listener. 24-item bibliography.

Needham, Arnold E. "Experiments in Permissive Listening."
College Composition and Communication 3(3):6-9, October 1952.   860
Describes a college communications course in which listening experiences were selected by the students.

Needham, Arthur. "Listening Exercises with a Purpose."

Education 75:311-15, January 1955.   861
Four steps in the teaching of listening are described:
listening to and following oral instructions; detecting the main
point of a talk; listening to one's self on tape; and listening
for language usage.

Nelson, Harold E. and Moll, Karl R. "Comparison of the
    Audio and Video Elements of Industrial Films." Journal
    of Communication 1:62-66, May 1951.   862
A combination of the audio and video portions of a film
was more effective than either audio or video alone. The
conclusion is drawn that the best possible integration of these
two modalities is desirable.

Nelson, Harold E. The Effect of Variations of Rate on the Re-
    call by Radio Listeners of "Straight" Newscasts. Doc-
    toral dissertation. Iowa City, Iowa: State University of
    Iowa, 1947. Summary: Speech Monographs 15:173-80,
    1948.   863
A total of 250 college students listened to recorded simulated newscasts given at rates varying from 125 to 250 wpm.
No significant difference in recall was observed, but the students found 175 wpm the most acceptable rate.

Neville, Mark A. "Listening Is an Art: Practice It." Ele-
    mentary English 36:226-33, April 1959.   864
Listening involves disciplined attention. Effective listening takes place only with proper motivation. Two aids to the
teaching of listening are instructions in note-taking and immediate evaluation after a listening experience.

----. "Methods for Improving Appreciation of Materials Pre-
    sented Orally in Grades Seven Through Nine." Oral
    Aspects of Reading. Proceedings of the Annual Confer-
    ence on Reading. Chicago: University of Chicago Press,
    1955. p. 116-20.   865
"To be unprepared to listen is an educational sin; yet
few of our students are without this sin."

Neville, Mary H. The Effect of Silent Reading, Oral Read-
    ing, and Listening on Accuracy and Comprehension in
    Beginning Reading. Master's thesis. Calgary, Alberta:
    University of Alberta, 1965.   866
In this study, 93 first-graders were assigned to 31
matched triads. Three treatments were administered. In
individual tests, one group read a prepared passage silently;
one group read the same passage aloud; the third group lis-

tened to the passage read to them with normal intonation by
the experimenter. Each subject then read the same passage
orally. This tested accuracy of word identification and ability to answer oral comprehension questions.
There was no significant difference between the two reading groups, but the listening group identified significantly
more new words and had a significantly higher comprehension.

"New Hope for Audiences." National Parent-Teacher 48:16-
    17, April 1954.   867
A listener's duty is to attempt to understand what a
speaker is saying while withholding his own opinions. Then
in order to accept or reject ideas advanced by the speaker,
he matches what the speaker has said with his own ideas,
knowledge, insight, and experience.

Newman, E.B. "Hearing." Annual Review of Psychology 1:
    49-70, 1950.   868
    Lists 105 references.

Nichols, Lois K. "Increasing Listening Skills with Tape-
    Recorded Lessons." Audiovisual Instruction 11:544,
    September 1966.   869
A set of tapes giving directions for doing simple tasks
was heard by a first-grade class in a campus school. Children paid attention constantly as they didn't know when the
next direction was coming; since directions were given only
once, the children had to concentrate in order to react successfully. Transfer to regular classroom listening seemed
apparent.

Nichols, Ralph G. "Are You Listening?" Kentucky School
    Journal 43(9):32-34, May 1965.   870
Summary of an address to the Public Relations Society
of America, giving ten rules for good listening.

----. "The Art of Listening." Administration in Extension.
Selected papers presented at the Sixth National Coopera-
tive Extension Administration Seminar, Madison, Wisc.,
August 16-27, 1959. (Edited by Robert C. Clark and
Roland H. Abraham.) Madison, Wisc.: University of
Wisconsin, 1960. p. 185-201.   871
The necessity for listening in everyday activities is
stressed. The role of listening in management is described,
and ten bad listening habits are discussed. Nine-item bibli-
ography.

----. "Do We Know How to Listen? Practical Helps in a
    Modern Age." Speech Teacher 10:118-24, March 1961.
    Also in Education for World Leadership: A Yearbook of
    Addresses from the 1960 Convention of the National
    School Boards Association, Chicago, Ill., April 24-27.
    Evanston, Ill.: National School Boards Association,
    1960. p. 388-98.   872
    Guides to effective listening: find areas of interest;
judge content not delivery; hold your fire; listen for ideas;
be flexible; work at listening; resist distractions; exercise
your mind; keep your mind open; and capitalize on thought
speed.

---. Factors Accounting for Difference in Comprehension
    of Materials Presented Orally in the Classroom. Doc-
    toral dissertation. Iowa City, Iowa: State University of
    Iowa, 1948. Abstract: Speech Monographs 15:154-63,
    1948. Excerpts: Listening: Readings. (Edited by Sam
    Duker.) Metuchen, N.J.: Scarecrow Press, 1966. p.
    135, 189-90, 321-24.   873
    This pioneering and ground-breaking thesis on listening
is the most frequently referred to of any on the subject.
Two hundred college freshmen listened to six ten-minute lectures dealing with various curricular areas. In addition to
being tested for comprehension and retention of material in
the lectures, the subjects were given a battery of tests in
various areas of skill and aptitude. Students submitted answers to questionnaires about their listening habits and procedures. The 20 lowest and highest students were interviewed in depth. In the judgment of these college freshmen,
factors involving mental set and possession of certain skills
were more important to listening ability than factors involving susceptibility to distractions or emotional maladjustment.
Correlations of listening with intelligence of .53 and of listening and reading of .46 are reported.

----. "He Who Has Ears." NEA Journal 45(1):15-16, Janu-
    ary 1956. Reprinted: Education Digest 2:37-39, April
    1956 and PEO Record 66:18-19, April 1956.   874
    Lists four basic principles of listening: 1. The listener,
not the speaker, is primarily responsible for any learning
which may take place. 2. A speaker's point must be fully
understood before it can be accurately judged. 3. The contribution of note taking to efficient listening depends upon the
utilization of the notes taken. 4. Sustained attention to oral
discourse depends upon the listener's continual mental manipu-
lation of its content.

Nichols, Ralph G.   197

----. "Interscholastic Contests in Listening." School Ac-
      tivities 21:259, April 1950.   875
The author suggests that interscholastic contests be held
in reading and listening in order that the introverted student
may have an opportunity to engage in competition.

---. "Listening." American Educator Encyclopedia 6:
     2109B-09F. Lake Bluff, Ill.: United Educators Inc.,
     1959.   876
Explains ten guides to good listening and lists these
four steps in teaching listening: 1. Give a listening test.
2. Discuss the test results individually. 3. Analyze each
student's listening performance in terms of a list of ten bad
listening habits. 4. Replace bad habits with good habits
through practice sessions.

----. "Listening Ability and Success." Minnesota Medicine
      39:236, April 1956.   877
The need for listening in industry is being recognized by
inclusion of listening instruction in training courses of large
corporations.   It seems likely that within a few years listening ability will be considered in the hiring of industrial personnel.

----. "Listening Habits Which Impede Communication."
      What's New in Home Economics 22(2):109, February
      1958.   878
A short quiz based on a list of ten bad listening habits.

----. "Listening Instruction in the Secondary School."
      Bulletin of the National Association of Secondary School
      Principals 36:158-74, May 1952. Excerpts: Listening:
      Readings. (Edited by Sam Duker.) Metuchen, N.J.:
      Scarecrow Press, 1966. p. 240-59.   879
This is an excellent review and analysis of previous research in listening.   The author lists five objectives for listening instruction: developing respect for listening as a
medium for learning; eliminating poor listening habits; developing necessary basic skills; increasing markedly the
ability to listen to difficult informative speech; and coordi-
nating listening assignments with assignments in speech,
reading and writing.

---. "Listening Is a 10-Part Skill." Nation's Business
     45(7):56-60, July 1957. Digest: "Nine Tips on Being a
     Good Listener." Management Review 46(9):47-49, Sep-
     tember 1957, Science Digest 21(12):53-56, October 1957,

and <u>Hospital Management</u> 86(2):135-37, August 1958.
                                                            880
    Lists ten points involved in effective listening: experi-
ence with difficult materials; interest in topic; adjustment to
speaker; expenditure of energy by listener; adjustment to the
listening situation even when this is an abnormal or uncom-
fortable one; adjustment to emotion-laden words; adjustment
to emotion-arousing points; recognition of central ideas;
utilization of notes; and reconciliation of more rapid thought
speed with listening.

----.   "Listening Is Good Business." <u>Manager's Magazine</u>
        34(2):31-40, Spring 1959.   881
        Ten bad listening habits are discussed.

----.   "Listening Is Good Business." Schrader, Albert W.
        and Odiorne, George S. (Editors) <u>Personnel Manage-
        ment...New Perspectives.</u> Bulletin 29, Bureau of In-
        dustrial Relations, The University of Michigan School of
        Business Administration, Ann Arbor, Michigan: Univer-
        sity of Michigan, 1961. p. 69-87.   882
        The author estimates that in a five-level downward com-
munication in business and industry, only about 20% of the
message survives.   In listening, it is important to antici-
pate the speaker's next comment, identify elements and make
mental summaries.   Motivated practice is the key to teaching listening.   A ten-question quiz is included.

----.   "Listening: Questions and Problems." <u>Quarterly
        Journal of Speech</u> 33:83-86, February 1947.   883
        The author suggests 14 areas for useful research in lis-
tening.

----.   "Listening: What Price Inefficiency?" <u>Office Execu-
        tive</u> 34(4):10-11+, April 1959.   884
        Both downward and upward communication in business
are less efficient than they might be because of ineffective
listening.   Ten poor listening habits are listed and discussed.

----.   "Materials for Courses in Communication." <u>Quarter-
        ly Journal of Speech</u> 38:465-69, December 1952.   885
        Unpublished tests of listening comprehension are being
used successfully at Stephens College, Michigan State College, University of Denver, and Florida State University.
The only published test listed is the Brown-Carlsen.

----.   "Needed Research in Listening Communication."

Nichols, Ralph G.

Journal of Communication 1:48-50, May 1951.   886
Twenty areas lending themselves to research in the area
of listening are classified under problems in measurement,
problems in pedagogy, problems in identification and description, and studies of causal factors.

----. "Poor Listening Is Costing You Money." Commerce
56(12):18-19+, January 1960.   887
A description of ways in which effective listening is important to efficient management.

----. "The Teaching of Listening." Chicago Schools Journal
30:273-78, June 1949. Digest: Education Digest 15(1):
34-36, November 1949.   888
A comprehensive discussion of previous research about
the teaching of listening and suggestions of ways to make listening more effective.

----. "Ten Components of Effective Listening." National
Elementary Principal 37(5):21-26, February 1958. Also
in: Education 75:292-302, January 1955.   889
An excellent summary and of present knowledge about listening.

----. "This Business of Listening." American Trade Association Executives Journal 8(1):31-41, January 1956.
                                                     890
Listening training is given to employees and executives
on an organized basis in many industrial organizations, including American Telephone, General Motors, Ford, Dow
Chemical, Thompson Products, and Western Electric. Results obtained in the parallel skill of reading suggest hope-
fully that listening will also be improved.

----. "What Can Be Done About Listening?" Supervisor's
Notebook (a Scott Foresman Service Bulletin.) 22(1):1-4,
Spring 1960.   890a
Ten poor listening habits are listed: calling a subject
dull, criticizing a speaker, getting over-stimulated, listening only for facts, trying to outline everything, faking attention, tolerating distraction, choosing only what is easy, allowing emotion-laden words to interfere with listening, and
wasting differential between speech and thought speed.

----, and Brown, James I. "A Communications Program in
a Technical College." Quarterly Journal of Speech 34:
494-98, December 1948.   891

Description of a revision of a freshman composition
course. Its new format made it a communications course
with sections on listening, speaking, writing, reading, exposition, and persuasion. Students are enrolled in those sections
in which tests show they are weakest.

----, and Cashman, Paul H. "The Approval Factor in Lis-
    tening." Education 80:268-71, January 1960.   892
Not only should teachers express their belief in the importance of listening, they should actually listen to their pupils.

----, and Keller, Robert J. "The Measurement of Communi-
    cation Skill." Junior College Journal 24:160-68, Novem-
    ber 1953. Summary: Nichols, Ralph G., Brown, James
    I., and Keller, Robert J. "Measurement of Communi-
    cation Skills." A University Looks at Its Program.
    (Edited by R. E. Eckert and R. J. Keller.) Minneapolis,
    Minn.: University of Minnesota Press, 1954, p. 118-
    23.   893
A detailed description of the teaching of listening at the
University of Minnesota.

----, and Lewis, Thomas R. Listening and Speaking.
    Dubuque, Iowa: Wm. C. Brown, 1954.   894
    Text with exercise material. Has chapters on: listen-
ing to learn; ten components of effective listening; detecting
patterns of speech composition; four systems of note-taking;
concentration; and appreciative and critical listening.

----, and Stevens, Leonard A. Are You Listening? New
    York: McGraw-Hill, 1957. Excerpts: "Listening to
    People." Harvard Business Review 35(5):85-92, Sep-
    tember-October 1957; Journal of Communication 8:8-10,
    Spring 1958; Reader's Digest 71(426):65-67, October
    1957; American Salesman 3(1):67-72, September 1957;
    and Pageant 13(8):48-51, February 1958. Favorably re-
    viewed by Hugh Gyllenhaal in Management Review 47(2):
    92-93, February 1958. Review: Library Journal 82:
    2825-26, November 1, 1957.   895
    The first full-length book on listening. Contents: The
Missing "L" in Learning-Listening; Listening's Profits and
Pleasures; How Listening Controls Talking; If Only Someone
Would Listen; Do You Know How People Talk?; The Archi-
tecture of What We Hear; The Ears Can Concentrate; Emo-
tional Filters; Six Bad Habits; Paper-and-Pencil Listening;
Listening to High Pressure; Executive Must Listen; The
Salesman: Fast Talker or Fast Listener; Why Work Confer-

ences Need Good Listening; The Family Listening Circle;
and Listening in School.

----, and Stevens, Leonard A.   "Learning to Listen While
    Listening to Learn."   A Complete Course in Freshman
    English.   (Edited by Harry Shaw.) New York: Harper,
    1959. p. 271-80.   896
    Gives six steps for improving listening: 1. Regard
listening as an opportunity to learn.   2. Realize that listening is faster and more efficient than reading.   3. Use listening as a way of understanding difficult literature.   4.
Give listening assignments in connection with students'
speeches in class.   5. Realize that listening makes speakers express themselves better.   6. Realize that listening
will be important after one leaves school.

----, and Stevens, Leonard A.   "Listening with the Inner
    Ear."   Think 24(6):11-13, June 1958.   Also in Science
    Digest 44(3):1-6 September 1958.   897
    Listening is defined as the ability to understand and re-
call the spoken word.   This process is a skill which can be
improved through training.   Because of poor listening habits,
office files bulge with unnecessary written memoranda.

----, and Stevens, Leonard A.   "You Don't Know How to
    Listen."   Colliers 132(4):16-19, July 25, 1953.   Also
    in: University of Minnesota Agricultural Service Com-
    munications Bulletin No. 6, 1953.   Condensed: Catholic
    Digest 18(2):20-24.   898
    A popularized account of the importance of listening and
of ways to become a better listener.

Nicholson, Harold.   "On Human Misunderstanding."   At-
    lantic Monthly 180(1):113-14, July 1947.   899
    A whimsical account of the frequent breakdown of com-
munication between a speaker and his audience.

Niles, Doris.   "Teaching Listening in the Fundamentals
    Course."   Speech Teacher 6:300-04, November 1957.
                                                             900
    The speech teacher should think of talking-listening
rather than of talking and of listening.   Listening should be
taught specifically and with pre-planning.

Niles, Lyndrey Arnand. An Experimental Investigation of the
    Relative Effectiveness of Written Outlines in Oral Com-
    munication. Master's thesis. University Park, Md.:
    University of Maryland, 1965.   901
    No difference in comprehension was found among groups
of college freshmen receiving outlines of a discourse in advance or making outlines as they listened, and those not having or making outlines. Attitude change, in both directions,
was greater among the group receiving outlines of the discourse they were about to listen to.

Niles, O.S. and Early, M.J. "Adjusting to Individual Dif-
    ferences in English: Listening." Journal of Education
    138:41-55, December 1955.   902
    A comprehensive and useful treatment of the nature of
listening and its teaching. Includes a table of listening
skills; ways to teach accurate, critical, and appreciative listening; a list of helpful recordings, pamphlets, and audio
visual aids; and references to curriculum bulletins dealing
with listening.

Nilsen, Thomas Robert. The Communications Survey: A
    Study of Communication Problems in Three Office and
    Factory Units. Doctoral dissertation. Evanston, Ill.:
    Northwestern University, 1953. Abstract: Dissertation
    Abstracts 14:423-24, 1954.   903
    Although this study says little about listening as such,
it is invaluable to a student of listening because of its pene-
trating analysis of the communication process.

Noel, Elizabeth. "Good Listening: New Proficiency in the
    Language Arts." See and Hear 2(32):46, April 1947.
                                                              904
    Skill in listening is needed to detect ready-made atti-
tudes, half-truths, invalid conclusions, over-generalizations,
and misinterpretations of data.

Nolan, Carson Y. "Audio Materials for the Blind." Audio-
    visual Instruction 11:724-26, November, 1966.   905
    An experiment is reported in which visually handicapped
children were given material in literature, social studies,
and science to read in Braille and to listen to at 175 wpm.
Elementary school pupils learned equally from both. Sec-

ondary school pupils learned more from Braille, but when
an equal amount of time was spent on reading and listening,
the learning was greater from listening.

----. "Listening and Reading in Learning." Proceedings
   of the Louisville Conference on Time Compressed
   Speech, October 19-21, 1966. (Edited by Emerson
   Foulke.) Louisville, Ky.: Center for Rate Controlled
   Recordings, University of Louisville, 1967. p. 67-68.
                                                          906
   In a southern residential setting consisting of dual
schools for white and Negro visually handicapped children,
the Negro children consistently made lower scores than did
white children on the STEP test, up to 45 percentile points
at one grade level. "This finding does not present much
encouragement to those who might wish to use commonly
available auditory materials in attempts to overcome educational deficits for such groups."
   In a study involving 1152 legally blind elementary and
secondary school pupils, it was found that at the elementary
level, listening and reading each resulted in equal retention
for both Braille and large-type readers. At the secondary
level, science material was retained equally in listening and
reading, but reading was superior in social studies and literature. On a time-spent basis, listening was two or three
times as efficient as reading.
   There has been a very small acceptance of auditory instructional materials by teachers of the blind. It is unlikely
that they will be any more receptive to compressed speech
materials unless convincing evidence of their value is presented. The teaching of listening skills at the elementary
school level is urged.

----. "Reading and Listening in Learning by the Blind."
   Exceptional Children 29:313-16, February 1963.   907
   A study of 14 blind students from each of grades seven
through ten showed that learning by listening was more efficient than learning by reading Braille.

North, Robert D. "An Evaluation of the STEP Listening
   Test for the Independent School Testing Program."
   Educational Records Bulletin 72:61-67, July 1958.   908
   This is a report on the administration of the STEP Listening Test to pupils from the fourth to twelfth grades in 26
schools. North doubts the validity of the tests since, he
says, 70 per cent of their content is a duplication of intelligence and achievement test items. He regards the tests as

too easy for the levels designated.   Correlations and detailed data are reported.

"Now Hear This."   Nation's Business 54(8):78-80, August
      1966.   909
      The Basic Systems taped course in listening has been
taken by 100,000 people in 200 companies.   It is generally
regarded very highly by executives who have had experience
with it.

Nye, Irene.   "We Taped Our Way Through the Year."   Ari-
      zona Teacher 54(2):18-19, November 1965.   910
      A fourth-grade program for teaching listening with tape
recorders is briefly described.   No data are given, but the
Lewis listening test showed a statistically significant improvement after one semester.   The gain in listening skills was
maintained during the second half of the school year, when
no formal listening training was given.

Oberembt, Sister M. Doris.   A Study of the Relationship
      Between Physiological Reactions of Listeners and Their
      Attitudes Toward Stuttering.   Master's thesis.   Vermil-
      lion, S.D.:   University of South Dakota, 1964.   911
      The Iowa Scale of Attitude Toward Stuttering was admin-
istered to 24 college students.   Their galvanic skin response
while listening to a tape of the speech of four stutterers was
also measured.   No statistically significant correlation between the two measures was reported.

O'Connor, Olwyn.   "The Art of Listening."   Educational
      Screen and Audio-Visual Guide 38:523, October 1959.
                                                                       912
      Audio-visual equipment and materials are "naturals" for
teaching effective listening skills.

Odom, Charles L. and Miles, Ray W.   "Oral Versus Visual
      Presentation of True-False Achievement Tests in the
      First Course in Psychology."   Educational and Psycho-
      logical Measurements 11:470-77, Autumn 1951.   913
      Using two groups of 100 college students as subjects,
the authors report better results on an oral true-false test
than on a written one.

O'Donnell, Robert J.   A Workbook to Improve Accurate and
      Critical Listening in the Junior High School.   Master's
      thesis.   Boston: Boston University, 1955.   914
      The workbook formulated in this thesis contains selec-

tions to be heard orally. These are followed by questions
for recall and for selection of main ideas to promote accuracy, and questions on fact and opinion, relevancy, slanted
information, and generalizations to promote critical listening.

Olsen, James. "How to Help Your Pupils Pay Attention."
    Grade Teacher 84(1):148-50, September 1966.   915
    Listening skills require active training. Admonitions to
"pay attention" are of little value. Skills that should be
taught include listening for main ideas, listening actively,
and critical listening.

O'Neill, John Joseph. Contributions of the Visual Compo-
    nents of Oral Symbols to the Speech Comprehension of
    Listeners with Normal Hearing. Doctoral dissertation.
    Columbus, Ohio: Ohio State University, 1951. Abstract:
    Speech Monographs 19:119-20, June 1952.   916
    An experimental study showed that 32 college speech stu-
dents were more proficient in listening to consonants, vowels,
words, and phrases, when they could see the speaker at
close range than when they did not see him.

Ongman, Edward Earl. Construction of a Listening Compre-
    Hension Test for the Sixth, Seventh and Eighth Grades.
    Master's thesis. Chicago: Chicago Teachers College,
    1960.   917
    The test constructed by Ongman is unique because a por-
tion of it contains background noises. The text is given.

O'Reilly, Francis J. "Listening." English Journal 16:548-
    50, September 1927.   918
    The author complains about the paucity of materials
available for the teaching of listening.

Ormsby, Bill. "A Businessman's Guide to the Fine Art of
    Listening." Canadian Business 33:82-86, February
    1960   919
    Effective listening is essential to success in business.
White collar workers have to listen during 40% of their working day but operate only at 25% of effectiveness in that area.
Executives can most efficiently tap ideas of subordinates by
sympathetic listening.

Orr, David B. and Friedman, Herbert L. "The Effect of
    Listening Aids on the Comprehension of Time-Com-
    pressed Speech." Journal of Communication 27:223-
    27, September 1967.   920

Allowing subjects to study précis and key word lists before listening to compressed speech did not aid comprehension.

Orr, David B. "A Note on Rapid Listening." Phi Delta
Kappan 46:460, May 1965.   921
Listening is a skill that can be improved significantly.
Compressed speech can be heard at 300 wpm without loss of
comprehension and at 425 wpm with 80% comprehension.
Compressed speech has many potential uses.

----. "Note on Thought Rate as a Function of Reading and
Listening Rates." Perceptual and Motor Skills 19:
874, December 1964.   922
The author suggests that thought speed will not exceed
the speeds at which a person has listened or read, and that
eye movements limit maximum reading speed to not more
than 700 wpm.
"Exploratory research...in the comprehension of highly-
speeded (but pitch normal) connected discourse is of interest.
For example, auditory comprehension began to fall off rapidly as the auditory rate exceeded normal reading rate. Further, however, the use of very rapid auditory material as a
pacing procedure while reading, resulted in significant increase in reading speed, without loss of comprehension.
These tentative findings, when confirmed by current work,
may support the notion that the rate of processing of connected discourse is normally habituated but is trainable."

----, Friedman, Herbert L., and Williams, Jane C.C.
"Trainability of Listening Comprehension of Speeded Discourse." Journal of Educational Psychology 56:148-56,
June 1965.   923
Describes an elaborate and well designed experiment related to the effects of practice on listening to compressed
speech. The subjects were college freshmen and sophomores.
Speeds used were 175, 325, 375, 425, and 475 wpm. Practice resulted in considerable improvement in the ability to
comprehend speeded speech. A control group without practice failed to show a similar improvement. The experimental group showed improvement in both speed and comprehension on the Nelson Denny Reading Test. The potential uses
of compressed speech in education are stressed.

Overstreet, Bonaro H. "After This Manner Therefore Listen." Wilson Library Bulletin 20:597-98, April 1946.
                                                      924

It is erroneous to assume that talking is a more active
process than listening. Good listening aids the quality of
speaking.

Owen, Jason Camillous. A Study of the Prognostic Value of
   Certain Measures of Intelligence and Listening Compre-
   hension with a Selected Group of Elementary Pupils.
   Doctoral dissertation. Columbia, Mo.: University of
   Missouri, 1957. Abstract: Dissertation Abstracts 19:
   484, 1958.   925
   The California Reading Test, California Test of Mental
Maturity, Lorge-Thorndike Intelligence Test, the Durrell-
Sullivan Reading Capacity Test, and the Van Wagenen Listening Vocabulary Tests were administered to 160 second-
through fourth-grade pupils. Besides reporting a number of
correlations, Owen states his conclusion that a combination
of listening and intelligence tests yields the best prediction
of reading achievement.

Oyster, Mary Mercedes. The Value of Certain Oral Techniques in Developing an Understanding of Prepositions
   Met in First-Grade Reading Texts. Master's thesis.
   Greeley, Colo.: Colorado State College of Education,
   1947.   926
   Oral instruction, involving listening, is an effective way
of teaching prepositions to young children.

Packer, Frederick C. Jr. "Learning to Listen." Harvard
   Educational Review 14:197-201, May 1944.   927
   Better listening habits lead to better speech. The use
of recordings to teach better listening at the high school
level is advocated.

Page, Paul R. "The Value of Listening." School Musician
   22(6):5-6, February 1951. Part II 22(8):12-13, April
   1951.   928
   Suggestions for teaching listening to music in elementary
schools and in junior and senior high schools. Such listening is important for enjoyment; recognition of musical structure, form, and quality; and creative music development.

Palmer, Brother Michael. A Study of the Relationship Between Reading Comprehension and Listening Comprehension of Selected High School Freshmen. Master's thesis.
   Chicago, Ill.: DePaul University, 1966.   929
   Describes a correlational study in which STEP Reading
and STEP Listening and the Otis were administered to 329

pupils. The following correlations are reported: I.Q. and reading .57; I.Q. and listening .55; listening and reading .62. For the high intelligence group, a correlation of .79 between listening and reading is reported; for the average group .33, and for the low group .54.

Parke, Margaret B. "Children's Ways of Talking and Listening." Childhood Education 29:223-30, January 1953.
930
     The teaching of listening in elementary schools should not be left to chance. Use of the Caliphone is advocated.

Paton, Wenda Carter. The Development of Musical Listening Acuity in the Kindergarten Child. Master's thesis. New Haven, Conn.: Southern Connecticut State College, 1965.   931
     After a series of lessons, 16 kindergarten children showed a 15% improvement in musical listening on a modified form of the Seashore Measures of Musical Talent Test. Three lessons a week were given for two months. Children were taught to listen for the following: "up and down, loud and soft, same and different in rhythm, long and short in time, and same and different in timbre or musical quality."

Patterson, Kenneth M. A Survey of Listening Taught in USAF and Business Management Schools. Graduate thesis. Maxwell Air Force Base, Ala.: Air Command and Staff College, Air University, 1965.   932
     A questionnaire was sent to 85 Air Force Bases and to 42 businesses to ascertain whether listening was taught in in-service courses and, if so, what procedures were employed. Replies were received from 60 Air Force Bases and 30 businesses.
     Thirty-three bases and 10 businesses reported the teaching of listening. The emphasis was on teaching comprehensive and critical listening and on note-taking. The most common methods used were lectures and films. Most courses ran for two to five hours.

Patterson, Marcus Dean. An Experimental Investigation of the Effect of Practice on Multi-Channel Listening. Master's thesis. Athens, Ohio: Ohio University, 1961.
933
     Patterson reports that a limited amount of practice in listening to a simultaneous presentation of two messages on tape did not result in a performance superior to that of those who had no practice.

Paulson   Stanley Fay.   Experimental Study of Spoken Com-
    munications: The Effects of Prestige of the Speaker and
    Acknowledgment of Opposing Arguments on Audience Re-
    tention and Shift of Opinion.   Doctoral dissertation.
    Minneapolis, Minn.:   University of Minnesota, 1952. Ab-
    stract: Dissertation Abstracts 13:270-71, 1953.   934
    The subjects, 978 college speech students, heard re-
corded speeches.   One version gave only one-sided arguments;
another gave both sides.   Half the students heard these
speeches credited to a college sophomore.   The others heard
them credited to a college professor.   Upper classmen tended to shift their opinion on the "college professor" version.
Generally, the speech that presented both sides was most effective.

Payne, Ethel T.   "Improvement of Listening Skills." Balti-
    more Bulletin of Education 27:73-74, March-May 1950.
                                                          935
    In planning for the promotion of growth in listening, a
faculty committee gave attention to: 1. the establishment of
a consciousness of the need for such growth through statistical information on the amount of time spent in listening and
an analysis of the listening habits and skills of pupils; 2.
listening in relation to propaganda; 3. listening for enjoyment; 4. setting up objectives; and 5. planning of teaching
procedures.

Pear, Norman August.   A Study of the Relative Effect on
    Listening of Two Different Methods in Question Forma-
    tion.   Doctoral Research Study.   Greeley, Colo.:   Colo-
    rado State College, 1964.   Abstract: Dissertation Ab-
    stracts 25:5158, 1965.   936
    When two groups, totaling 239 subjects, were given the
STEP Listening Test, no significant differences were found.
Only one group was given extensive instruction and practice
in developing relationship concepts and in identifying material as descriptive, exploratory, narrative, or argumentative.
Both groups showed a statistically significant improvement
in listening between pre- and post-tests.

Perkins, Flora C.   "How to Listen Persuasively." Today's
    Speech 8(1):6-7+, February 1960.   937
    A humorous view of listening to a husband who happens
to be a speech professor.   It is urged that one listen carefully but also be careful in listening.

Perrin, Noel.   "The Unwilling Ear or How to Miss Fun."

Vogue 135(8):82-83, April 1960.   938
A humorous, popularized account of the need for listening.

Peterfreund, Stanley. "Why Listen to Employees?" Supervisory Management 10(9):18-20, September 1965.   939
The most important factor in good upward communication is the establishment by the supervisor of a climate in which employees feel they can express their thoughts and ideas without having to wonder if anyone is listening. Listening to employees is good for morale, but it also can provide information to help the supervisor solve problems and become aware of the status of employee morale.

Peters, Raymond W. "Management Looks at Communication Again." Journal of Communication 2:5-9, November 1952.   940
There is a growing recognition by management of the necessity of listening with intelligence and understanding to what employees have to say.

Peters, Robert W. "The Effect of Acoustic Environment upon Speaker Intelligibility." Pensacola Joint Project, Ohio State University Research Foundation and U.S. Naval School of Aviation Medicine, 1954. Joint Project Report No. 26. The Bureau of Medicine and Surgery Project N.M. 001 064.01.26.   941
When speakers were subjected to diverse acoustic signals while speaking, intelligibility of speech was influenced by the type of signal. For example, nonsense words had less effect on intelligibility than words related to the speaker's message.

Peterson, Carolyn. A Curriculum for the Teaching of Listening in the Elementary School and a Study of Its Effectiveness. Master's thesis. Claremont, Calif.: Claremont College, 1963.   942
Using 51 fourth-grade pupils as subjects and the STEP Test as a measure of listening, Peterson reports on a controlled experiment. No significant differences were found between the control group and a group which had been given 15-minute lessons on listening daily for four months.

Peterson, Gordon E. The Significance of Various Portions of the Wave Length in the Minimum Duration Necessary for the Recognition of Vowel Sounds. Doctoral dissertation. Baton Rouge, La.: Louisiana State University,

Peterson, Gordon E.   211

1939.   943
    An experiment is described in which an attempt was
made to ascertain whether the particular portion of the wave
length of a vowel was significant in the recognition of short
portions of a vowel sound. Over 50 per cent was reported
at an interval of .0031 of a second giving approximately
.298 of a cycle. It was determined that there was a difference in intelligibility among different segments of a vowel
wave length.

Peterson, Robert D. Relationship Between Listening Compre-
    hension and Scholarship; A Comparison of Eighth Grade
    Boys and Girls in Amos Hiatt Junior High School, Des
    Moines. Master's thesis. Des Moines, Iowa: Drake
    University, 1961.   944
    The author used 282 subjects who took a battery of tests
including the Brown-Carlsen Listening Test. Correlations
between listening and reading of .75, and English grades of
.52, and social studies grades of .60 are reported.

Petrie, Charles Robert Jr. An Experimental Evaluation of
    Two Methods for Improving Listening Comprehension
    Abilities. Doctoral dissertation. Lafayette, Ind.:
    Purdue University, 1961. Abstract: Dissertation Ab-
    stracts 22:2511-12, 1962. Summary: Central States
    Speech Journal 15:6-12, February 1964. Excerpts:
    Listening: Readings. (Edited by Sam Duker.) Metuchen,
    N.J.: Scarecrow Press, 1966. p. 325-32, 333-49, 350-
    51, 352-53, 354-61 and in Speech Monographs 30:79-91,
    June 1963.   945
    This item contains an excellent bibliography and com-
plete review of the literature. The author is critical of the
quality and inconclusiveness of previous research dealing
with listening. Using the Brown-Carlsen Test and the Goyer
Test of the Organization of Ideas as pre- and post-tests,
he compares three groups. One group had no special instruction, one had four 50-minute periods of speech instruction, and one had four 50-minute periods of listening instruction. No significant differences were found.

----. "A Plea for Caution." Newsletter of the Business
    and Professional Speaking Interest Group, SAA. August
    1962, p. 1-4.   946
    Listening has been "over-sold." Enthusiasm has re-
placed valid and reliable research. There is no experimental verification of the success of listening training programs.

----. "Reply to a Plea." Newsletter of the Business and
   Professional Speaking Interest Group, SAA. November
   1962, p. 4-5.   947
   There is little scientific knowledge about the listening
process and even less about how to teach it. More basic
research is needed.

----. "What We Don't Know About Listening." Journal
   of Communication 14:248-52, December 1964.   948
   The inadequacy of existing research on listening and the
need for more rigidly designed experimentation in this field
are stressed.

Petty, Walter T. "Listening: Directions for Research."
   Elementary English 39:574-77, October 1962.   949
   Petty suggests some areas of research in listening.
What is the effect of "set" in listening? What effect does
the emotional status and personality of the listener have?
Can listening affect the personality or values of the listener?
What is mature listening? What are the readiness factors in
listening? What is the effect on listening of the controlled
vocabulary used in reading instruction? What are the transfer effects of listening to sounds and music, to listening to
speech?

Phifer, Gregg. "Propaganda and Critical Listening."
   Journal of Communication 3:38-42, May 1953.   950
   Listening should be an active rejecting as well as receiving process. True critical listening will lead to genuine
self-government. Ability to recognize propaganda in written
matter does not carry over to listening. Measuring devices
to test critical listening are needed.

Phillips, David C. Some Factors That Make for Effective
   and Ineffective Conversation. Doctoral dissertation.
   Madison, Wisc.: University of Wisconsin, 1946. Summary: Speech Monographs 16:203-13, September 1949.
                                                    951
   A detailed analysis of good and poor conversations
among Stephens College students. Listening in conversations
must be based on sympathy, intelligence, patience, full attention, and restraint.

Phillips, J. Donald. Your Listening Can Be Improved!
   Hillsdale, Mich.: Hillsdale College, 1964.   952
   A number of succint hints are given on the importance

of listening and how one's listening can be improved.

Pierce, Anne E. Teaching Music in the Elementary School.
   New York: Holt, 1959. p. 118-20.   953
   Goals are listed for the teaching of listening to music
for grades K to 6.

Pigors, Paul. Effective Communication in Industry. New
   York: National Association of Manufacturers, 1949,
   passim.   954
   Meaning can be the heart of communication only when it
is truly a two-way process, which requires effective listening.

Pillsbury, Walter B. and Mender, Clarence L. The Psychology of Language. New York: Appleton, 1928.
   Chapter 8, "Language Receptors--Reading and Listening."
   p. 129-51.   955
   This chapter gives greater emphasis to reading than to
listening. The excellent discussion of the reception of communication, however, has relevance for the student of listening.

Planty, Earl and Machover, William. "Upward Communications: A Project in Executive Development." Personnel
   28:304-18, January 1952.   956
   For good upward communication the listener must realize
that the same set of facts does not necessarily lead to the
same conclusion in the employee's mind as in management's.
Management must try to ascertain the real causes of com-
plaints, even if they are not stated explicitly. Subordinates
tend to tell the superior what they think he wants to hear.
Subordinates are alert to visible and other non-verbal signals. Upward communication is never highly effective if it
stresses the upward motif.
   Listening must be objective. Opinions should be sought
before rather than after management's proposals are made.
If listening takes place with a certainty that the listener is
right and the subordinate is wrong, little will be accomplished. Listening implies action. Blowing off steam is not
enough; necessary adjustments must be made. Do not appear to agree if you do not intend to take corrective action.

Plavnick, Max. "From Passive Listening to Active Participation." Music Educators' Journal 50(4):135-38, Febru-
   ary-March 1964.   957
   If music appreciation programs are to lead to a love

for music instead of being a pro forma bow to cultural development, active listening must be taught. An intelligent
understanding of music must be developed so that the listener
can hear what the composer wrote and can know how to direct his attention. A fifth-grade program for teaching active
musical listening is described.

Plessas, Gus Peter. Reading Abilities and Intelligence Fac-
    tors of Children Having High and Low Auding Abilities.
    Doctoral dissertation. Berkeley, Calif.: University of
    California, 1957. Excerpts: California Journal of Edu-
    cational Research 14:90-94, March 1963, and Elementary
    School Journal 63:223-26, January 1963.   958
Using 414 eighth-grade pupils as subjects, Plessas administered the California Auding Test as a measure of listening and a number of reading and intelligence tests. He reports that students in the upper quartile in listening were also better readers. Correlations of listening with various
factors are reported: with spatial relations .18; numerical
reasoning .61; logical reasoning .73; verbal concepts .66;
and language factors, .68.

Pollack, I. "Hearing." Annual Review of Psychology 12:
    335-62, 1961.   959
    Lists 204 references.

Pope, Curtis Lamar. A Survey and Evaluation of Current
    Theories of Writing for the Eye and for the Ear. Mas-
    ter's thesis. Iowa City, Iowa: State University of Iowa,
    1949.   960
An examination and review of instructional materials for
writing for newspapers, radio, advertising, public speaking,
and general prose publications with respect to communication theory and readability leads the author to the conclusion that most authors find differences between the stylistic
requirements of material to be read and material to be
heard. However, the differences were not found to be substantial.

Postman, Leo J. The Time Error in Auditory Perception.
    Doctoral dissertation. Cambridge, Mass.: Harvard
    University, 1946.   961
A carefully performed, controlled experiment determined
an absence of time error in the case of pitch but a considerable time error in connection with loudness.

----, and Rozensweig, Mark R. "Practice and Transfer

in the Visual and Auditory Recognition of Verbal Stimuli."
American Journal of Psychology 69:209-26, June 1956.
                                                          962
Recognition of both visual and auditory stimuli, when
presented with verbal stimuli, is increased by training of
subjects. The transfer effects from visual training to auditory recognition were found to be more pronounced than the
reverse.

Posz, A. Conrad and Dow, Clyde W. "Do You Irritate
    Your Students?" Journal of Communication 8:186-89,
    Winter 1958.   963
A total of 145 Michigan State University freshmen were
asked to list the ten most common listening habits and the
ten most irritating habits of their instructors. While the order was not the same, there was a close correspondence between the two lists.

Potter, Mary and Thurlow, Dorothy. "Listening in the Lan-
    guage Arts." Elementary English 40:757+, November
    1963.   964
A description is given of a program for training first-
and second-grade children in listening by means of tape recordings. The skills of following directions and self-check-
ing of phonics were emphasized.

Potter, R. "How to Listen to a Lecture." Good House-
    keeping 120(2):25, February 1945.   965
Seven ways to improve a lay person's listening to a lecture are discussed.

Poulton, E.C. "Simultaneous and Alternate Listening and
    Speaking." Journal of the Acoustical Society of America
    27:1204-07, November 1955.   966
Simultaneous repetition of oral messages was found to
be less accurate than repetition immediately after the message was heard. Speeding up the messages had some effect
on the accuracy of the repetition.

----. "Two Channel Listening." Journal of Experimental
    Psychology 46:91-96, August 1953.   967
Sixteen British Navy enlisted men were asked to listen
to two simultaneous messages. Intelligibility was better
when they were instructed to listen to one of the messages
than when they were required to listen to both.

Prater, Helen Mason. The Effect of a Listening Program

upon Listening Achievement and Reading Comprehension.
Master's thesis. Knoxville, Tenn.: University of Tennessee, 1965.   968
Thirty 4th-grade pupils were given 24 structured lessons
on informational, appreciative, creative, and critical listening for a period of 12 weeks. The STEP Listening and Iowa
Silent Reading were used as pre- and post-tests. The experimental group made significantly greater gains in both
reading and listening than did a comparable control group.
Texts of the lessons are included.

Pratt, Eleanor. "Listening Attitudes and Reading Readiness."
American Childhood 40:24, September 1954.   969
Providing a large number of listening opportunities in
pre-school years is a definite aid to the acquisition of reading-readiness skills.

Pratt, Lloyd Edward. The Experimental Evaluation of a
Program for the Improvement of Listening in the Ele-
mentary School. Doctoral dissertation. Iowa City, Iowa:
State University of Iowa, 1953. Abstract: Dissertation
Abstracts 13:1118-19, 1953. Summary: Elementary
School Journal 56:315-20, March 1956. Excerpts: Listening: Readings. (Edited by Sam Duker.) Metuchen,
N.J.: Scarecrow Press, 1966. p. 226-29, 230-33, 234-
37.   970
In a carefully performed and controlled experiment in 40
sixth-grade classes, Pratt found that lessons in listening
over a period of five weeks resulted in an improvement in
listening skills, as measured by an author-made test, which
was greater than that shown by the control group. Lessons
and two forms of the test used are included.

----, and Greene, Harry A. Training Children to Listen.
Monograph for Elementary Teachers, No. 80. White
Plains, N.Y.: Row Peterson, 1956.   971
This is an excellent, short treatment of the teaching of
listening, which would be of value in the orientation of
teachers who wish to begin to teach listening.

"Pre-Induction Needs in Language Communication and Reading." Education for Victory 2(11):1+, December 1,
1943.   972
In this statement of basic language skills needed by serv-
icemen, emphasis is placed on oral communication skills, including listening.

Prince, Bernice L. A Study of Classroom Listening Ef-
    fectiveness in Basic Communications and Its Relation to
    Certain Other Factors. Master's thesis. Denver, Colo.:
    University of Denver, 1948.   973
    Using 28 students as subjects, Prince reports a number
of correlations with listening.

Pronovost, Wilbert. The Teaching of Speaking and Listen-
    ing in the Elementary School. New York: Longmans
    Green, 1959.   974
    Although this textbook is devoted primarily to speech, the
important role of listening is presented forcefully throughout.

Publicover, Phyllis R. Listening Efficiency of College Stu-
    dents with High Frequency Hearing Loss. Master's
    thesis. Logan, Utah: Utah State Agricultural College,
    1954.   975
    Contrary to the findings in several other studies, Publi-
cover's report shows that students with moderate hearing
loss had greater difficulty with the Brown-Carlsen Listening
Test than did those with normal hearing.

Pulliam, Charles R. A Plan for Teaching Listening at Ben-
    jamin Franklin Junior High School, Springfield, Illinois.
    Master's thesis. Charleston, Ill.: Eastern Illinois Uni-
    versity, 1961.   976
    This is a plan for the teaching of listening, which was
not implemented as part of the study. Objectives of such a
program as solicited from "experts" are listed.

Purcell, Theodore V. "Observing People." Harvard Busi-
    ness Review 33(2):90-100, March-April, 1955.   977
    A successful foreman must observe his employees ac-
curately. This involves listening to each person. "Of all
the sources of information a foreman has by which he can
come to know and accurately 'size up' the personalities of
the people in his department, listening to the individual employee is the most important."

----. The Worker Speaks His Mind on Company and Union.
    Cambridge, Mass.: Harvard University Press, 1953,
    passim.   978
    One of the principal complaints of workers is that their
superiors will not and do not listen to them.

Putt, Robert C. "Listening Skills Can Be Taught." New
    York State Education 51(8):20-21, May 1964.   979

Quigley, Rt. Rev. Msgr. Thomas J. "The Relationship of
    Reading and Listening to the Communication Arts."
    National Catholic Educational Association Bulletin 54(1):
    209-12, August 1957.   980
    "It has always been the mark of an educated man that he
listens well..."

Radloff, Marge Rowe. An Experimental Study in Instruction
    in Listening. Master's thesis. De Kalb, Ill.: Northern
    Illinois State College, 1956.   981
    Using 47 ninth-grade pupils as subjects, Radloff per-
formed an experiment in which one group was given instruction in listening. There was no significant difference between
the groups on the Brown-Carlsen Test. An extensive discussion of the nature of listening and a student self-evaluation
chart on critical listening are included.

Ragan, William B. Modern Elementary Curriculum. New
    York, Dryden Press, 1953, p. 238-64.   982
    In a unified language arts program it is essential that
instruction in listening be included.

Rankin, Paul T. The Measurement of the Ability to Under-
    stand Spoken Language. Doctoral dissertation. Ann
    Arbor, Mich.: University of Michigan, 1926. Abstract:
    Dissertation Abstracts 12:847, 1952. Excerpts and sum-
    maries: "The Importance of Listening Ability." English
    Journal College Edition 17:623-30, October 1928; "Lis-
    tening Ability." Proceedings of the Ohio State Educa-
    tional Conference, Ninth Annual Session. Columbus,
    Ohio: Ohio State University, 1929, p. 172-83; "Lis-
    tening Ability: Its Importance, Measurement and Devel-
    opment." Chicago Schools Journal 12:177-79, January
    1930 and 12:417-20, June 1930. Excerpts: Listening:
    Readings. (Edited by Sam Duker.) Metuchen, N.J.:
    Scarecrow Press, 1966. p. 25-27, 51-62, 124.   983
    This is the first major study dealing with listening. It
has been cited principally because of the statement that listening is the most frequently used communication skill, since
it comprises 42 per cent of communication time as compared
to reading, 15 per cent; talking, 32 per cent; and writing,
11 per cent. While these data were obtained from a small
sample, the findings have been confirmed by later writers.
Using a self-written test, the text of which is included, Rankin also surveyed the listening abilities of fifth- and sixth-
grade children. After extensive analysis, Rankin concluded
that reading and listening were closely associated, but that

the correspondence was far from perfect.

Raper, Katherine A. A Study of Listening. Master's thesis.
    Iowa City, Iowa: State University of Iowa, 1951.   984
    Using 33 sixth-grade children as subjects, Raper gave
one group six lessons in listening over a three-week period.
There was no difference in either reading or listening improvement between the experimental and control groups at
the end of this period.

Ratchford, Alice Hannon. An Analysis of the Research on
    Listening at the Elementary School Level. Master's
    thesis. Scranton, Pa.: Marywood College, 1964. 985

Ratcliff, J.D. "Learn While You Sleep." Look 14(6):46-53,
    March 14, 1950.   986
    This popularly written article presents "evidence" of
people's ability to learn during sleep.

Rathgaber, Sister Jean Marie. A Comparison of the Listen-
    ing Ability of Blind Students and the Listening Ability of
    Sighted Students in the Intermediate Grades. Doctoral
    dissertation. New York: Fordham University, 1965.
    Abstract: Dissertation Abstracts 27:420A, 1966.   987
    Scores made on the STEP Listening Test by sighted chil-
dren were found to be significantly higher than scores of
visually handicapped children. Scores were higher for both
groups at 175 wpm than at 225 wpm. There was a significant positive correlation between listening test scores and
intelligence for both groups. There was no significant difference between the scores of blind children attending integrated schools and those attending schools for the blind.
A total of 304 children served as subjects.

Rayl, Cleo. "Islands of Deafness." Journal of Business
    Education 22(3):17-20, November 1946.   888
    The author suggests that developing one's skill in lis-
tening before starting to study shorthand is helpful.

Reasoner, Charles F. The Development of a Series of Tele-
    vision Scripts Dealing with the Language Arts Practices
    in Elementary-School Classrooms. Doctoral disserta-
    tion. New York: Columbia University, 1961. p. 292-
    351.   989
    One of the nine television scripts, entitled "The Lost
Signal," is concerned with listening skills.

220   Listening Bibliography

Rebach, Howard Martin. A Study of the Effects of a Critical
     Set on Listening Comprehension. Master's thesis. Uni-
     versity Park, Md.: University of Maryland, 1964.   990
     A questionnaire on attitudes toward Negroes was adminis-
tered to 210 college speech students. A liberal speech test on de-
segregation was then given, followed by an objective test on the
content of this speech. Contrary to the hypothesis being tested,
those with the most extreme views scored the highest on the test.

Redding, W. Charles. "The Most Important Problems of
     College Courses in Communication." Journal of Com-
     munication 1(1):30-35, May 1951.   991
     Redding states that there is a desperate need for studies
establishing correlations between the communication skills of
reading, listening, speaking, and writing.

Redfield, Charles E. Communication in Management. Chi-
     cago: University of Chicago Press, 1953, passim. 992
     Listening is important to management for dealing suc-
cessfully with workers in conferences and interviews.

Reeves, Harriet Ramsey. The Effect of Training in Listen-
     ing upon Reading Achievement. Doctoral dissertation.
     Tallahassee, Fla.: Florida State University, 1965. Ab-
     stract: Dissertation Abstracts 26:7181, 1966.   993
     Twenty fourth-grade classes were pre- and post-tested
on the STEP Listening Test. The experimental group was
given listening lessons for 15 weeks. Two lessons of 15
minutes each were given weekly during the reading period,
using the Gates-Peardon Reading Exercises. No significant
differences in either listening or reading were found. A
correlation of .72 between reading and listening is reported.

Reidford, Phillip Arthur. Reading Comprehension Improve-
     ment as a Function of Speech Compression Training.
     Master's thesis. Urbana, Ill.: University of Illinois,
     1965.   994
     Subjects for this study were 40 undergraduates who vol-
unteered for a non-credit course in reading improvement for
poor readers. The experimental group were trained on
speech compression levels from 40 to 65%; the control group
from zero to 40%. The Fairbanks speech compressor was
used. Reading material was presented as a pre- and post-
test on the Perceptoscope at 185, 240, 320, and 485 wpm.
Improvement was shown by all subjects at the first three
rates. No significant differences were found between sexes,
between those having and those not having a written text to

follow while listening to the compressed speech, or between
the experimental and control groups. The author concludes
that the improvement in reading may have been due to motivation rather than to the training, which consisted of twelve
40-minute practice sessions.

Renwick, Ralph Jr. "A Listening Course for High School
    Seniors." Speech Teacher 6:59-62, January 1957. 995
    A clear and detailed description of teaching units for a
twelve-week course in listening, with emphasis on teaching
comprehension and critical evaluation.

Reynolds, Larry Joe. Auditory Comprehension of Com-
    pressed Material. Master's thesis. Salt Lake City,
    Utah: University of Utah, 1966.   996
    Passages from the Davis Reading Test were presented
to six groups of fifteen college students each, under the following conditions:
    Treatment 1: three presentations at 197.5 wpm.
    Treatment 2: four presentations at 263 wpm.
    Treatment 3: four presentations at 200, 250, 300, and
        350 wpm.
    Treatment 4: four presentations at 350, 300, 250, and
        200 wpm.
    Treatment 5: five presentations at 329 wpm.
    Treatment 6: six presentations at 395 wpm.
    The mean number of correct responses on a 45-item
multiple choice test were 17, 22, 19, 18, 12 and 8 respectively. There was a significant difference at the .01 level
in the results between Treatments 3 and 4 and between
Treatments 5 and 6.

Rice, Gwen. "The Sound Barrier." Ohio Schools 43(2):28-
    29, February 1965.   997
    Inattention and half-listening are common in classrooms.
Good listening habits are learned from doing, not from
scolding. Listening practice materials should be made interesting.

Richard, Cecile M. A Comparison of Silent Reading Com-
    prehension and Listening Comprehension by Means of
    Standardized Tests. Master's thesis. Boston: Boston
    University, 1956.   998
    Using 35 fourth- through eighth-grade pupils as subjects,
Richard administered reading and listening tests. The only
significant difference was found in favor of listening on difficult passages.

Rickheim, Carol Margaret Ware. An Experiment in Listening at the Fourth Grade Level. Master's thesis. Mankato, Minn.: Mankato State College, 1965.   999
    Thirteen children were given listening instruction five
days a week for five months. The STEP test was used as a
pre- and post-test. Listening materials were based on encyclopedia articles. The gains made by the experimental
group were significantly greater than the gains made by a
comparable control group.

Rider, M.R. "Is Listening a Lost Art?" New York State
Education 33:704-05, June 1949.   1000
    Story-telling is advocated as a valuable device in the
teaching of good listening.

Riggle, Ruth S. Ways to Improve Listening Skills in the
Second Grade. Master's thesis. Danbury, Conn.:
Danbury State College, 1966.   1001
    A 20-week course in listening is described. Substantial
changes were shown on the Botel Reading Inventory, used as
a pre- and post-test. No test of significance is reported.
Teacher observation also revealed substantial improvement
in academic and social aspects.

Ringle, Charles Edward. A Consideration of Increased Listening Comprehension as a Result of a Unit on Listening
with Ninety-Three Tenth Grade Students in the Speech
Fundamentals Course at Wayne (N.J.) High School,
Spring, 1964. Master's thesis. Montclair, N.J.:
Montclair State College, 1964.   1002
    A 12-lesson unit on listening was included in a high
school speech class. The Brown-Carlsen Test was used as
a pre- and post-test. The improvement in listening ability
was not statistically significant.

Rivers, Wilga M. "Listening Comprehension." Modern
Language Journal 50:196-204, April 1966.   1003
    Teaching comprehension of spoken speech is of primary
importance if the communication aim of foreign language
teaching is to be achieved.
    Two levels of activity, both of which must be taught,
are necessary to listening to a foreign language: the recognition level, involving word identification, and the selection
level, involving extracting the gist of the message.

Robbin, Joseph Sigmund. An Experiment Demonstrating the
Retention of Learning Material Introduced During Sleep.

Master's thesis. Washington, D.C.: George Washington University, 1951.   1004
In a study that made no provision for an objective measure of sleep, a significant amount of learning was reported to have taken place as a result of oral stimuli during sleep.

Robins, James Edward. A Study of the Effects of Syntactic Structure on the Immediate Recall of Speeded Speech Materials. Doctoral dissertation. Washington, D.C.: George Washington University, 1967.   1005
Twenty college students listened to ten experimental sentences compressed to 325 wpm. Using the Yngve model, they were asked to reproduce the sentences immediately after listening to them. It was found that the number of omissions was as reliable a measure as the number of omissions, additions, transpositions, and substitutions combined.
The superiority of "progressive" over "regressive" sentence structure, which has been found to exist in listening at natural rates, was maintained. The magnitude of the superiority was less than when speech was speeded.
"There appears to be a definite promise for using syntactic structure to optimize the communication economies wrought by speeded auditory presentation of verbal material."

Robinson, H. Alan. "The Directed Listening Activity." Report of the 13th Annual Conference and Course in Reading. Pittsburgh, Pa.: University of Pittsburgh, 1957, p. 79-87.   1006
The author develops a plan for teaching listening parallel to directed reading activity composed of readiness, concept development, listening, discussion, and re-listening when possible.

Robinson, Karl F. "Review of 'Effective Listening.'" Speech Teacher 12:172, March 1963.   1007
A favorable review of a film on listening prepared by E.C. Buehler and William Conboy.

Robinson, Margaret. "Attention Giving Versus Attention Getting." Wisconsin Journal of Education 89(3):17, November 1956.   1008
The need of teaching listening to overcome indifference and inattention is explained.

Robinson, R.M. and others. "Reading and Listening Skills." Yearbook of the National Council for Social Studies, 1933, p. 105-38.   1009

The author discusses the importance to the student of social studies of a variety of listening skills.

Robinson, Ruth. Why They Love to Learn. Charlotte,
    N.C.: Author, 1960. p. 150-51.   1010
    Concentrated, deliberate effort should be made to develop the skill of listening from the first grade on. A logical way of building a child's listening skill is to let him tell something to the class which he has just learned through listening.

Rockwell, Leo L. "The Fourth R Is an L." College English 1:61-67, June 1939.   1011
    An integrated language arts program should include listening. Audiometer tests, oral vocabulary tests, and tests in determining meaning from context and in locating central thoughts are helpful.

Roethlisberger, F.J. Management and Morale. Cambridge,
    Mass.: Harvard University Press, 1941, passim. 1012
    In this description of the "Hawthorne Experiment," constant emphasis is put on the importance of listening by industrial supervisors.

----, and Dickson, W.J. Management and the Worker.
    Cambridge, Mass.: Harvard University Press, 1947,
    passim.   1013
    A skilled industrial interviewer must be able to listen efficiently to not only what is actually said but to what is intended to be said and to what is intended not to be said.

Rogers, Carl R. and Roethlisberger, F.J. "Barriers and
    Gateways to Communication." Harvard Business Review
    30:46-52, July 1952.   1014
    The importance of listening with understanding and of withholding evaluation is stressed.

Rogers, George Walter. Lecture Listening Skills: Their
    Nature and Relation to Achievement. Doctoral dissertation. Columbus, Ohio: Ohio State University, 1959.
    Abstract: Dissertation Abstracts 20:4165, 1960.   1015
    A filmed lecture, which was stopped at various points for testing purposes, and the Brown-Carlsen Test were administered to 113 college students who were taking a study skills course. A factor analysis was performed. A general listening ability factor was isolated.

Rogers, John Robert. The Derivation of a Formula for
    Predicting the Comprehension Level of Material to Be
    Prsented Orally. Doctoral dissertation. Austin, Tex.:
    University of Texas, 1952.   1016
    A formula, which is a modification of the Dale-Chall
formula, is developed for measuring the difficulty of oral material presented to children. A valuable table showing elements in the various readability formulas is included. There
is a 67-item bibliography.

Rolfe, Mary Eugenie. Some Indications of the Relationship
    Between General Semantics and Listening. Master's
    thesis. Denver, Colo.: University of Denver, 1951.
                                                        1017
    Listening is "about synonymous with the general semantic
principle, consciousness of abstracting." It follows that material from both fields may be helpful to the student of listening.

Rose, Ervin. A Comparative Study of the Brown-Carlsen
    Listening Comprehension Test and Three Tests of Read-
    ing Comprehension. Doctoral dissertation. New York:
    New York University, 1958. Abstract: Dissertation Ab-
    stracts 19:2007, 1959.   1018
    Using 157 tenth-grade pupils as subjects, Rose reports
the following correlations with the Brown-Carlsen Test:
California Reading Test, .55; Traxler High School Reading
Test, .44; and Cooperative English Test, Reading Comprehension section, .60. A number of other linear, partial,
and multiple correlations are reported.

Rosenberg, Seymour and Curties, James. "The Effect of
    Stuttering on the Behavior of the Listener." Journal of
    Abnormal and Social Psychology 49:355-61, July 1954.
                                                        1019
    Listening responses to normal and to stuttering speech
are significantly different in the number of times eye contact
with speakers is broken off, in length of time of such
breaks, and in initiation by listeners of hand and body movements. In terms of learning principles, stuttering may be
considered as a possible negative reinforcer to the listener.
Twenty subjects were used in this experiment.

----, and Cohen, Bertram D. "Speakers' and Listeners'
    Processes in a Word Communication Task." Science
    145:1201-03, September 11, 1964.   1020
    An investigation of the processes by which a speaker

selects verbal clues in order to distinguish one word (referent) from another (nonreferent) and the processes by which
a listener identifies the speaker's referent word. Data from
speakers and listeners were linked to word-association
norms by a stochastic model.

Ross, Ramon. "A Look at Listeners." Elementary School
     Journal 64:369-72, April 1964.   1021
     A battery of tests was administered to 90 fifth-, sixth-,
and seventh-grade pupils who were in the lower third and
upper quarter of their classes in listening as measured by
the STEP test. The following correlations with listening
were reported: intelligence (verbal) .76, (non-verbal) .28,
(total) .51; adjustment (personal) .34, (social) .44; socio-
metric choices (work) .24, (play) .10; reading .74; behavior
.38; and socioeconomic status .48. Good listeners surpassed
poor listeners in all tests except the audiometer test of
hearing.

----. "Teaching the Listener: Old Mistakes and a Fresh
     Beginning." Elementary School Journal 66:239-44, Feb-
     ruary 1966.   1022
     The author suggests that listening skills might be a use-
ful basis for grouping. Teachers should speak less, be economical in their speech, and give a good example of listening. "Listening is an active response to abstract symbols.
A person listens if he thinks listening will provide him with
much or more self-gratification."

Roughton, Ronald Dean. The Study of Sentence Structure as
     a Method of Improving Reading and Listening Compre-
     hension. Master's thesis. Columbus, Ohio: Ohio State
     University, 1959.   1023
     Using as subjects 69 high school English students with
reading difficulties, Roughton reports that intensive discussion and teaching of sentence structure had no appreciable
effect on reading skills, but did have a significantly favorable
effect on listening skills, as measured by the Brown-Carlsen
Test.

Roy, Sister Marie Collette. Multiple Meaning Oral Vocabu-
     lary of Good and Poor Readers. Doctoral dissertation.
     Minneapolis, Minn.: University of Minnesota, 1964.
     Abstract: Dissertation Abstracts 26:910-11, 1965. 1024
     This study using 466 sixth-grade pupils as subjects ex-
amined the skills of deriving meanings of words from context and of recognizing multiple meanings of words. No

significant differences were found between good and poor readers. The author concludes that listening instruction should be an integral part of classroom language arts activities.

Rubenstein, Herbert and Aborn, Murray. "Psycholinguistics." Annual Review of Psychology 11:291-322, 1960.
1025
Lists 155 references.

Ruddell, Robert B. "Oral Language and the Development of Other Language Skills." Elementary English 43:489-98+, May 1966.   1026
A number of research studies on the relationship between listening and reading are reviewed. "An increased awareness of the interrelationships of listening comprehension and reading comprehension skills should be fostered in the classroom... Listening comprehension skills can be taught and would seem to enhance reading comprehension skills."

Ruechelle, Randall C. An Experimental Study of Audience Recognition of Emotional and Intellectual Appeals in Persuasion. Doctoral dissertation. Los Angeles, Calif.: University of Southern California, 1953.   1027
The author reports that untrained audiences were unable to agree significantly on whether two-minute speeches presented on film were based on emotional or on intellectual appeals. Trained speech teachers were able to do only slightly better.

Ruesch, Jurgen and Bateson, Gregory. Communication, The Social Matrix of Psychiatry. New York: Norton, 1951, passim.   1028
Implicit in this excellent discussion of communication from the psychiatric viewpoint is the urgent need for effective listening abilities.

"Rules for Good Listening." Science Digest 38(2):34-35, August 1955.   1029
A resume of an article by Nichols listing a number of poor listening habits.

Rulison, Kathleen Dale. The Analysis and Appraisal of the Listening Course at Los Angeles City College. Master's thesis. Los Angeles, Calif.: University of California at Los Angeles, 1952.   1030
This is a description of a two-credit remedial course

based largely on the writings of Nichols.

Rulon, Philip J. and others.   "A Comparison of Phonograph-
    ic Recordings with Printed Materials in Terms of Knowl-
    edge Gained Through Their Use Alone."   Harvard Edu-
    cation Review 13:63-76, January 1943.   1031
    It was found that on immediate recall of factual and re-
lated knowledge, high school students did better when they
read the material than when they heard it on recordings.
On delayed recall there was little difference.

----.   "A Comparison of Phonographic Recordings with
    Printed Materials in Terms of Motivation to Further
    Study."   Harvard Education Review 13:246-55, May 1943.
                                                             1032
    In terms of motivating high school students to refer to
supplementary reading materials, there was no significant
difference between presentation of printed materials and of
recorded materials.

----.   "A Comparison of Phonographic Recordings with
    Printed Materials in Terms of Knowledge Gained
    Through Their Use in a Teaching Unit."   Harvard Edu-
    cation Review 13:163-75, March 1943.   1033
    The authors found no significant difference in the amount
of learning resulting from a complete high school teaching
unit between presentation of material in textbook form or in
recorded form.

----.   "The Effect of Phonographic Recordings upon Atti-
    tudes."   Harvard Education Review 14:20-37, January
    1944.   1034
    The authors report that material presented in the form
of phonographic recordings had a significantly greater effect
in changing attitudes of high school students than did printed
material.

Russell, David H.   "Auditory Abilities and Achievement in
    Spelling in the Primary Grades."   Journal of Education-
    al Psychology 49:315-19, December 1958.   1035
    A correlation of .33 is reported between listening, as
measured by the Durrell-Sullivan Reading Capacity Test, and
spelling ability of 85 children in grades 1, 2, and 3.
Measures of auditory discrimination showed higher correlations with spelling.   The Durrell-Sullivan's correlation with
all the measures of auditory discrimination was .65.

Russell, David H.   229

----. "A Conspectus of Recent Research on Listening Abili-
    ties." Elementary English 41:262-67, March 1964. Re-
    printed in Listening: Readings. (Edited by Sam Duker.)
    Metuchen, N.J.: Scarecrow Press, 1966. p. 191-200.
                                                      1036
    A review of previous research. The author states that
studies give unequivocal evidence that listening abilities can
be taught. Research is needed to develop materials and devices for teaching listening, and for subtests to measure
particular listening abilities.

----, and Russell, Elizabeth F. Listening Aids Through the
    Grades - One Hundred Ninety Listening Activities. New
    York: Teachers College, Columbia University Bureau of
    Publications, 1959.   1037
    This is a valuable resource for the elementary school
teacher seeking ideas on the teaching of listening.

Russell, R.D. The Relative Effectiveness of Presenting
    Verbal Materials Visually and Orally as Measured by the
    Amount of Recall. Doctoral dissertation. Iowa City,
    Iowa: State University of Iowa, 1923. Summary: "A
    Comparison of Two Methods of Learning." Journal of
    Educational Research 18:235-38, October 1928.   1038
    Russell reports experimental findings to the effect that
at the fifth-grade level materials listened to are learned better than materials read; at the seventh-grade level, the effects of the two types of presentation are equal; and at the
ninth-grade level reading is superior to listening as a means
of learning. Subjects were 1080 pupils.

Rutherford, Lewis Roland. A Survey of Certain Variables
    Related to Speech-Listening. Master's thesis. Morgan-
    town, W. Va.: West Virginia University, 1965.   1039
    Eighty-three sources on listening and speech were ex-
amined and analyzed for speech-listening variables within the
environment.

Ryan, Sister Mary Allan. A Suggested Program of Proced-
    ures and Techniques for Teaching the Art of Listening
    to Upper Elementary Pupils. Master's thesis. Cleve-
    land, Ohio: St. John College, 1962.   1040
    Using 141 eighth-grade pupils as subjects and the STEP
Test as a measure of listening, Ryan reports only a slight
improvement as a result of eight weeks of daily instruction
in listening.

230   Listening Bibliography

Saine, Lynette. "Interrelating Reading and Listening in Corrective and Remedial Classes." Reading and the Language Arts. Proceedings of the Annual Conference on
Reading. Chicago: University of Chicago Press, 1963.
p. 67-71.   1041
Listening is related to reading potential and helps develop word attack skills, vocabulary, and comprehension skills.

"Sample Exercises for Developing Good Listeners." Boston:
Warren English Project, School of Education, Boston
University, no date. Mimeo.   1042
An invaluable list of detailed plans of twelve types of
listening instruction at the high school level.

Sander, Eric K. "Comments on Investigating Listener Reaction to Speech Disfluency." Journal of Speech and
Hearing Disorders 30:159-65, May 1965.   1043
"In the laboratory situation, the reactions of listeners
toward speech disfluency are probably highly contingent upon,
a. whether they are alerted, prior to their listening experience, to the possible presence of stuttering, and b. their assumptions concerning the repetitiousness of the speaker's
behavior."

Sansom, Clive. Speech in the Primary School. London:
A & C Black, 1965.   1044
Children should be taught to listen to each other. The
teacher should be the best listener in the room. Speech is
an act of cooperation between speaker and listener. The use
of games and broadcasts in teaching listening is described.

Sassenrath, Julius Marlin. The Relation Between Auding
and Selected Psychometric Variables. Master's thesis.
Berkeley, Calif.: University of California, 1954. Summary: Sassenrath, Julius M. and Holmes, Jack A.
"Auding and Psycho-Educational Variables." California
Journal of Educational Research 7:99-104, May 1956.
                                                       1045
Through the use of multiple correlation procedures Sassenrath found that the principal components of the variance
in listening were basic social concepts, background in natural science, and "use of sources of information." Tests
used were the California Auding Test and the Heston Personal Adjustment Inventory. Subjects were 97 high school students.

Schaffner, Dorothy W. "The Most Basic Aspect of Counsel-

Schaffner, Dorothy W.   231

ling Is to Be a Good Listener." Instructor 77(1):47,
August/September 1967.   1046
Presents six illustrations showing the listening activities
of a guidance counselor and their importance.

Scheer, Wilbert E. You Can Improve Your Communications.
Swarthmore, Pa.: The Personnel Journal, Inc.; 1962.
                                                         1047
The author deplores the lack of sufficient listening instruction and testing in schools. Listening is hindered by
lack of concentration, by attention to what the listener is going to say, and by hearing only what we want to hear.

Scherer, George A.C. "Reading German With Eye and Ear."
Modern Language Journal 32:179-83, March 1948. 1048
A description is given of a course in German in which
the first year's emphasis was exclusively on reading and listening. The course was given at the University of Colorado.

Schiesser, H. "A Device for Time Expansion Used in Sound
Recording." Translated by Verner Runalds from an article appearing in Funk Und Ton 3:5, 1949. Transac-
tions of the Institute of Radio Engineers, Professional
Group on Audio AU2(1):12-15, January-February, 1954.
                                                         1049
A device which can compress or expand speech without
distortion is described.

Schmidt, Bernardine G. "Auditory Stimuli in the Improvement of Reading." Elementary English Review 18:149-
54, April 1941.   1050
A description is given of an auditory approach to the
teaching of reading.

----. "Teaching the Auditory Learner to Read." Chicago
Schools Journal 19:208-11, May-June 1938.   1051
A more detailed description is given of the program de-
scribed in the previous reference.

----. "Visual and Auditory Associations in Reading Disabil-
ity Cases." Journal of Exceptional Children 10:98-105,
January 1944.   1052
An auditory approach is more effective in remedial reading than a visual one, especially in the case of slow learners.

Schmidt, John W. An Evaluation of Note Taking for Aca-

demic Debate Methods. Master's thesis. Peoria, Ill.:
Bradley University, 1961.   1053
A non-experimental, descriptive study of the merits of
note taking, with a brief discussion of listening.

Schneider, Wallace A. A Review of Some of the Literature
Related to Listening. Master's thesis. Denver, Colo.:
University of Denver, 1950.   1054
A review of some of the then-existing references on lis-
tening, of value only to a beginning student of listening.

Schubert, Delwyn G. "A Comparative Study of the Hearing
and Reading Vocabulary of Retarded College Readers."
Journal of Educational Research 46:555-58, March 1953.
                                                      1055
Using 26 subjects, Schubert found no significant difference between aural and reading vocabularies.

Schultz, Jennye Faye. Potentialities of an Oral Vocabulary
Test. Doctoral dissertation. University Park, Md.:
University of Maryland, 1958. Abstract: Dissertation
Abstracts 20:3667-68, 1960.   1056
Using 224 fifth- and sixth-grade pupils as subjects,
Schultz administered the vocabulary section of the California
Test of Mental Maturity orally one month after the written
administration of the test. The correlation between written
and oral vocabulary was .69. Pupils scoring higher on the
written test were significantly better readers. The group
as a whole performed significantly better on the oral test.
The author suggests that the oral test score may be a good
predictor of reading potential.

Schwanke, Dorothy Marie. The Teaching of Listening: An
Investigation of Methods and Materials. Master's thesis.
St. Cloud, Minn.: St. Cloud Teachers College, 1956.
                                                      1057
A valuable and massive 347-page review of the litera-
ture, consisting principally of lengthy quotations and para-
phrased sections.

Schwartz, Sheila. "What Is Listening?" Elementary English
38:221-24, April 1961.   1058
The key to good listening instruction is the pupil-teacher
relationship, which is more important than direct listening
instruction.

Scott, Louise Binder and Hoops, Eleanor. "Establishing

Better Listening Habits." <u>Instructor</u> 65(6):28+, February 1956.   1059
The authors suggest some aids to listening: development of vocabulary, use by teachers of complete sentences,
and the teaching of phonetic sounds.

Scott, Richard. "Interrelating Reading and Listening in
Grades Nine Through Fourteen." <u>Reading and the Language Arts</u>. Proceedings of the Annual Conference on
Reading. Chicago: University of Chicago Press, 1963.
p. 63-67.   1060
Teachers often ignore the strengths of students who are
poor readers but good listeners. Recordings of dramas and
reading of poetry are recommended as ways of teaching listening.

Scott, Robert J. "Computers for Speech Time Compression."
<u>Proceedings of the Louisville Conference on Time Com-
pressed Speech</u>, October 19-21, 1966. (Edited by Emerson Foulke.) Louisville, Ky.: Center for Rate Controlled Recordings, University of Louisville, 1967. p.
29-35.   1061
Speech compression through a computer simulation of the
Fairbanks method is described. It is possible in this procedure to discard portions of speech in a non-arbitrary way.
    A dichotic presentation is suggested in which the com-
pressed speech is directed to one ear and the material discarded to the other. In a test given to 15 subjects, this
form of presentation was preferred to the presentation of the
compressed speech to both ears.
    Principal disadvantages of computer speech compression
are the lack of availability of suitable facilities to most re-
searchers and the high costs involved.

Scott, Wallace Gene. <u>A Study of the Effects of Voice Characteristics in the Listening Comprehension of Blind
School Children</u>. Master's thesis. Eugene, Ore.: University of Oregon, 1953.   1062
On the basis of an experiment with 28 subjects ranging
from the third to ninth grades, it is reported that male low-
pitched, male high-pitched, female low-pitched, and female
high-pitched voices were preferred, in that order. Comprehension was also significantly better in the case of male low-
pitched voices than otherwise. The author suggests that these
findings have significance for those preparing "talking books."

Seashore, Robert H. "The Importance of Vocabulary in

Learning Language Skills." Elementary English 25:
137-52, March 1948.   1063
There are many fallacies about listening vocabularies.
Young children's vocabularies are much larger than is commonly believed. Vocabulary continues to grow for a longer
period than is suggested by intelligence tests' vocabulary sections.

Sebastian, Virginia Jean. The Development and Evaluation
    of Listening Skills in Grade II. Master's thesis. New
    Haven, Conn.: New Haven State Teachers College,
    1959.   1064
A description of a listening program with emphasis on
analyzing individuals' listening and on making charts containing rules for good listening.

Seegers, J. Conrad. "Needed Emphasis in the Language
    Arts." Education 70:559-64, May 1950.   1065
Studies cited here show that one neglected area which
needs more emphasis in the elementary school language arts
program is listening.

----, and Seashore, R.H. "How Large Are Children's Vo-
    cabularies?" Elementary English 26:181-94, April
    1949.   1066
Auditory recognition of vocabulary is greater than visual
recognition up to the seventh grade, when the two types become about equal.

Selover, Robert B. and Porter, James P. "Prediction of
    the Scholarship of Freshmen Men by Tests of Listening
    and Learning Ability." Journal of Applied Psychology
    21:583-88, October 1937.   1067
A correlation of .53 between an author-made test of listening and scholastic index is reported.

Semrow, Ellen H. "Listen! Don't Detour Ideas." Journal
    of Home Economics 52:721-24, November 1960.   1068
Children learn not to listen when they are constantly
nagged at home and in school.

Sequential Tests of Educational Progress: Listening.
    Princeton, N.J.: Educational Testing Service, 1957.
    Excerpts: Listening: Readings. (Edited by Sam Duker.)
    Metuchen, N.J.: Scarecrow Press, 1966. p. 437-41.
                                                      1069
Two forms at each of four levels are available. Level

four is designed for use in grades 4 through 6; level three
for grades 7 through 9; level two for grades 10 through 12;
and level one for grades 13 and 14.

Sessions, Louise Hale. Developing a Listening Program for
the Intermediate Grades. Master's thesis. San Marcos,
Tex.: Southwest Texas State Teachers College, 1957.
                                                        1070
A description of a listening program for the fourth grade,
which attempts to meet the following needs: identification of
skills involved in general listening ability; a sequential development of these skills; an established procedure for teaching
the skills; and the creation of an awareness of the part of
both pupils and teachers of the values of effective listening.

Seymour, Paul John. A Study of the Relationship Between
the Communication Skills and a Selected Set of Predictors and of the Relationships Among the Communication
Skills. Doctoral dissertation. Minneapolis, Minn.:
University of Minnesota, 1965. Abstract: Dissertation
Abstracts 26:549, 1965.   1071
A description of the listening course given to freshmen
scoring below the 50th percentile on the Brown-Carlsen on
the St. Paul campus of the University of Minnesota. Results
of tests given before and after this course are analyzed in
detail.

Seymour, Ruth. "The Listening Vocabulary." Instructor
73(8):56+, April 1964.   1072
Describes methods for the development of vocabulary,
including the building of one word at a time, keeping a file
of vocabulary deficiencies, and using visual aids. This
article is directed toward the teaching of mentally retarded
children.

Shane, Harold G. "Are You Listening?" Chapter 8 of Research Helps in Teaching the Language Arts. Washington, D.C.: Association for Supervision and Curriculum
Development, 1955, p. 68-72. Summary: NEA Journal
44:402-04, October 1955.   1073
On the basis of an examination of 30 references on listening, the author concludes that the skill of listening can
be taught and evaluated.

Shanker, Sidney. "The Art of Listening Can Be Taught."
New York State Education 49(7):24+, April 1962. 1074
The academic high school pupil can be motivated to im-

prove his listening if he is shown the relationship between success in college and skill in listening. Instruction in the art of note-taking is advocated.

Shepherd, Terry R.   A Study of the Effectiveness of Listen-
    ing Instruction in Grades Five and Six.   Master's thesis.
    Charleston, Ill.:   Eastern Illinois University, 1962.
                                                                1075
    In an uncontrolled experiment using 323 fifth and sixth grade pupils as subjects, Shepherd found that two weeks of intensive instruction in listening, which stressed reasons for listening and principles of listening, resulted in a statistical-ly significant improvement in listening as measured by the STEP Test.

Shibley, John Dahir.   An Investigation of Some Aspects of
    Audience Perception During the Communication Act.
    Doctoral dissertation.   Columbus, Ohio: Ohio State Uni-
    versity, 1964.   Abstract: Dissertation Abstracts 25:
    4866-67, 1965.   1076
    A set of cognition, recognition, relational, and retention scales was developed and experimentally applied to 166 sub-jects who listened to an eight-minute speech.   All scales, except the relational one, were found to be reliable.   The only statistically significant correlation was between recogni-tion and retention.   No significant difference in results was found between two groups who were told to listen to words, and to the speech as a whole, respectively.

"Shifting Attention."   Science Newsletter 68:356, December
    3, 1955.   1077
    Errors in comprehension increase when a continued al-ternation of attention from visual to aural signals is re-quired.

Shurtleff, Wade E.   "Is Management Listening?"   Personnel
    28:101-07, September 1951.   1078
    One of the most overlooked tools of management is the fine art of listening.   When management listens it tends to hear statements of dissatisfaction with its procedures.   This may account for the great lack of listening by management.

Siewert, Eleanor Annable.   The Construction of a Listening
    Test Suitable for Use in the Elementary School.   Mas-
    ter's thesis.   Ithaca, N.Y.:   Cornell University, 1965.
                                                                1079
    The development of a listening test suitable for use in

the second through fifth grade is described.   Text of the test
is included.

Sikkink, Donald Elwyn.   An Experimental Study of the Ef-
    fects on the Listener of Anti-Climax Order and Authority
    in an Argumentative Speech.   Doctoral dissertation.
    Minneapolis, Minn.:   University of Minnesota, 1954. Ab-
    stract: Dissertation Abstracts 14:2157, 1954.   Summary:
    Southern Speech Journal 22:73-78, Winter 1956.   1080
    It is reported that no significant difference in shift of at-
titude was found between groups hearing speeches in regular
or anti-climatic order and groups hearing speeches including
or not including authority quotations.

Silverman, Phyllis.   "Listening--A Pathway to Learning."
    Peabody Journal of Education 42:40-44, July 1964. 1081

Simon, Charles W. and Emmons, William H.   Considera-
    tions for Research in a Sleep-Learning Program. Santa
    Monica, Calif.: Rand Corporation, 1954.   1082
    A thorough analysis of previous studies and various ex-
periments carried out by the authors.   Conclusion: "Of the
ten studies which have been examined, none satisfactorily
controlled the level of sleep and there is reason to suspect
that whatever learning took place did so during a waking interval.   Other methodological inadequacies could be found."
The authors state that the subject of sleep-learning is worthy
of further research, but at present there is no evidence that
this phenomenon exists.

----, and ----.   "Learning During Sleep?" Psychological
    Bulletin 52:328-42, July 1955.   1083
    The Rand Corporation experiments on sleep-learning
are described and evaluated.

----, and ----.   "Responses to Material Presented During
    Various Levels of Sleep." Santa Monica, Calif.: The
    Rand Corporation. 1954. (mimeo.)   1084

----, and ----.   "The Non-Recall of Material Presented
    During Sleep." Santa Monica, Calif.: The Rand Corpo-
    ration, 1954. (mimeo.) Excerpts: Journal of Psychol-
    ogy 69:76-81, March 1956.   Summary: Science 124:1066-
    69, November 30, 1956.   1085
    Using an electroencephelograph to determine the degree
of sleep, Simon and Emmons found that a very carefully de-

signed experiment on 21 subjects failed to reveal any evidence that subjects retained material presented aurally during sleep. In the second study the findings were identical even when the material was repeated many times.

Simons, Herbert William. A Comparison of Communication
    Attributes and Rated Job Performance of Supervisors in
    a Large Commercial Enterprise. Doctoral dissertation.
    Lafayette, Ind.: Purdue University, 1961. Abstract:
    Dissertation Abstracts 22:3378-79, 1962.   1086
    A survey of supervisory employees of a large urban convention hotel revealed that successful supervisors were more willing to listen permissively to employees with reference to complaints, personal problems, and suggestions than were those supervisors rated as less successful.

Sims, V.M. and Knox, L.B. "The Reliability and Validity
    of Multiple Response Tests When Presented Orally."
    Journal of Educational Psychology 23:656-62, December
    1932.   1087
    The authors found that orally presented multiple-response test items were slightly more difficult than the same items presented visually, but that both modes had substantially the same reliability.

Simula, Vernon L. "Broadening Our Perspectives of Listen-
    ing and Speaking Problems." Reading and Inquiry. In-
    ternational Reading Association Conference Proceedings,
    Vol. 10, 1965. (Edited by J. Allen Figurel.) Newark,
    Del.: International Reading Association, 1965. p. 49-
    51.   1088
    These four types of listening problems faced by teachers may well be due to the climate created by the teacher: 1. Failure to follow directions may be an avoidance of ambiguous situations. 2. Inattentiveness may be due to lack of motivation. 3. Forgetting may be a way of avoiding situations that are psychologically threatening. 4. Lack of comprehension may stem from the teacher's lack of organization (no preview; no opportunity for pupils to relate to their own past experience; no purposes defined; teacher's choice of words a possible obstacle to the child).
    "In dealing with the problems of speech and listening let us shift our focus. Instead of wording our objectives in terms of teaching children to listen and to speak effectively, let us focus on teaching elementary boys and girls to think and to communicate effectively. By doing so, many of our listening and speaking problems can be alleviated and others

prevented."

Sincoff, Michael Zolman. The Development and Comprehen-
    sion of Isolates of Meaning-Capacity and Their Applica-
    tion to Upward Directed Listening in Industry. Master's
    thesis. University Park, Md.: University of Maryland,
    1966.   1089
    Nineteen foremen at a Naval Ordinance Laboratory were
subjects. Five judges were trained in identifying meaningful
units in longer passages, which are referred to as isolates
of meaning-capacity.
    A three-minute tape of the War of Ghosts was played
for each subject individually, after which subjects repeated
the story on tape. These tapes were then judged for the
number of isolates of meaning-capacity. Judges' opinions
were very reliable. It is suggested that subjects having the
highest scores were the better listeners.

Singer, Harry. Substrata-Factor Reorganization Accompany-
    ing Development in Speed and Power of Reading at the
    Elementary School Level. Cooperative Research Project
    No. 2011, Office of Education, Department of Health,
    Education, and Welfare. Riverside, Calif.: University
    of California, Riverside, 1965.   1090
    Data obtained by testing 927 pupils in grades three
through six were elaborately factor analyzed. The Durrell-
Sullivan Reading Capacity Test was used as a measure of
listening. Listening was found to be a major factor in children's reading skills.

Skiffington, James Stephen. The Effect of Auding Training
    on the Reading Achievement of Average Eighth-Grade
    Pupils. Doctoral dissertation. Storrs, Conn.: Univer-
    sity of Connecticut, 1965. Abstract: Dissertation Ab-
    stracts 26:3508-09, 1966.   1091
    Twenty-six 25-minute tapes based on EDL and SRA ma-
terials were administered to 74 pupils over a period of nine
weeks. There was a significantly greater gain, in both
reading and listening, by the experimental group than by a
comparable control group. STEP Listening and Iowa Silent
Reading were used as pre- and post-tests. The following
correlations are reported: between reading and listening before the experiment, .52 for the control group and .56 for
the experimental group; after the experiment, .56 and .45
respectively; between listening and intelligence, .46 for both
groups.

Small, Arnold M. Jr. "Audition." Annual Review of Psy-
    chology 14:115-54, 1963.   1092
    Lists 297 references.

Smith, A. Arthur, Malmo, Robert B., and Shagars, Charles.
    "An Electromyographic Study of Listening and Talking."
    Canadian Journal of Psychology 8:219-27, December
    1954. Abstract: American Psychologist 8:437-38,
    August 1953.   1093
    Twenty-two psychiatric patients and 11 normal subjects
acting as controls listened to faulty sound recordings. It
was found that during listening, rising and falling gradients
of tension were observed in speech muscles and in the ex-
tensors of the arms in both groups.

Smith, C.P. "Sins of Contemporary Education." Education-
    al Research Bulletin 33:197-202, November 10, 1954.
                                                          1094
    One of the most serious shortcomings of education at the
primary, secondary, and college levels is the failure to
teach listening properly.

Smith, David Allen. An Experimental Study of the Ability of
    Listeners to Discriminate Between Straight News and
    Personal Opinion in a Radio News Broadcast. Doctoral
    dissertation. Tallahassee, Fla.: Florida State Univer-
    sity, 1957. Abstract: Dissertation Abstracts 17:3127-
    28, 1957.   1095
    In this study of 160 undergraduate students, the only sig-
nificant differences were found in reading ability and the
labeling of opinion statements as such by the newscaster.
An average of 50% correct discriminations were made. Assessing straight news was done better than was assessing
opinion.

Smith, Donald E.P. (Editor.) Michigan Successive Discrimi-
    nation Listening Program. Books I and II and Teacher's
    Script. Ann Arbor, Mich.: Ann Arbor Publishers,
    1964.   1096
    A set of lessons in listening in modified workbook form,
giving pupils practice in many aspects of listening.

Smith, Dora V. "Basic Aims for English Instruction."
    English Journal 31:40-55, January 1942.   1097
    This article includes, among 13 basic aims, the teach-
ing of listening in all social situations and listening to the
radio.

----. "Growth in Language Arts as Related to Child Development." Teaching Language in the Elementary School.
43rd Yearbook, Part II, N.S.S.E. Chicago: University
of Chicago Press, 1944. Chapter 5, p. 52-97.   1098
There is considerable evidence that listening aids recognition of correct English structure.

----. "Learning to Listen--Listening to Learn." NEA
Journal 47:100-01, February 1958. Also in Teaching in
the Elementary School. (Edited by Lester D. Crow,
Alice Crow, and Walter Murray.) New York: Longmans Green, 1961, p. 283-86.   1099
Listening is not something to be taught apart from other
school subjects but should be integrated into all instruction.

Smith, Grace Brinner. Relationship of Listening with Intelligence and Spelling Achievement of Primary Grade
Pupils. Master's thesis. Normal, Ill.: Illinois State
Normal University, 1963.   1100
Using the My Weekly Reader Test as a measure of listening, the author reports a correlation of .29 with spelling
and .32 with intelligence.

Smith, Henry P. and Dechant, Emerald V. Psychology in
Teaching Reading. Englewood Cliffs, N.J.: Prentice-
Hall, 1961, p. 140-46.   1101
A useful summary of a number of articles on listening.

Smith, Jack Ernest. Reading, Listening, and Reading-Lis-
tening Comprehension by Sixth-Grade Children. Doctoral dissertation. New York: Columbia University, 1959.
Abstract: Dissertation Abstracts 20:959-60. 1959. 1102
In an experimental study with 180 subjects, the McCall
Crabbe passages were administered orally, in written form
and in a combination of the two modes. It was found that
reading was the most effective, followed by the combined
oral-visual presentation. Among subjects of low I.Q. there
was no significant difference.

Smith, Leota Eleanor. Auditory Discrimination and First
Grade Reading Achievement. Master's thesis. Normal,
Ill.: Illinois State Normal University, 1957.   1103
Smith reports that a group of 16 first-grade children
given intensive training in auditory discrimination performed
significantly better on a reading readiness test than did an
equivalent group not given such training.

Smith, Mapheus. "Communicative Behavior." Psychological Review 53:294-301, September 1946.   1104
The reciprocity involved in effective communication implies listening.

Smith, Nila B. "Language: A Prerequisite for Meaningful
Reading." Reading and the Language Arts. Proceedings
of the Annual Conference on Reading. Chicago: University of Chicago Press, 1963. p. 3-12.   1105
The skills of listening and oral language are prerequisite
to understanding specific word meanings, not only in the
lower grades but at all educational levels.

Smith, Sister Mary Joan and Sister Mary Nona. Guiding
Growth in Christian Social Living. Washington: Catholic
University of America Press, 1944. I: 124-25, 173-74,
222-23; II: 123-24, 189-90, 265-66; III: 153-54, 257-58.
                                                1106
Objectives and techniques for the teaching of listening
are listed and discussed separately for each school grade
from first to eighth inclusive.

Smith, Thomas Wood. Auding and Reading Skills as Sources
of Cultural Bias in the Davis-Eells Games and California
Test of Mental Maturity. Doctoral dissertation. Los
Angeles: University of Southern California, 1956. Ex-
cerpts: Listening: Readings. (Edited by Sam Duker.)
Metuchen, N.J.: Scarecrow Press, 1966. p. 125-30.
                                                1107
Using 302 fifth-grade pupils in six communities in Los
Angeles County as subjects, Smith administered the California
Mental Maturity Test, the California Achievement Battery,
the Davis Eells Games, and the listening test used by Hall
in his thesis. The last consisted of the oral administration
of the Gates Silent Reading Test and the memory section of
the California Mental Maturity Test. Listening skill was
found to be a significant source of intelligence test bias when
such tests were given to children at varying culture levels
and to be just as important a factor in this respect as reading skill. Among the correlations reported: listening and
occupational rank of parent .33; reading and occupational
rank of parent .31; Davis Eells Games score and listening
.50; Davis-Eells Games score and reading .39; listening and
reading .48; listening and total I.Q. as measured by California Mental Maturity Test .41; and reading and total I.Q.
as measured by California Test of Mental Maturity .75.

Snider, Mary Edna. Effective Listening in Grades K-5.
    Master's thesis. Union, N.J.: Newark State College,
    1962.   1108
    A description of a unit on listening at the first-grade
level. The only evaluation made was by means of an anecdotal record.

Solheim, A.K. "School and Radio Listening Habits." Jour-
    nal of the Association for Education by Radio 5:67-68,
    January 1947.   1109
    The use of radio in schools makes the teaching of listen-
ing an absolute essential.

Solomon, S. "Listen to Understand." Senior Scholastic,
    Teachers' Edition 68(2):18T, February 9, 1956.   1110
    Using audio-visual aids is helpful in the teaching of lis-
tening. The importance of listening is effectively illustrated
when a sound film is run silently.

Sommer, Gerhart R., Mazo, Bernarr, and Lehner, George
    F.J. "An Empirical Investigation of Therapeutic 'Lis-
    tening'." Journal of Clinical Psychology 11:132-36,
    April 1955. Abstract: American Psychologist 7:534,
    September 1952.   1111
    When taped protocols of therapeutic sessions were pre-
sented to nine graduate students in clinical psychology and to
ten psychologists, the experimenters found that the ability to
give content of the protocols was about equal for both groups.
The students, however, tended to be more inclined to make
interpretations. This article includes a splendid discussion
of the role of listening in therapeutic procedures.

Sondel, Bess. Are You Telling Them? New York: Pren-
    tice-Hall, 1947. Excerpt: National Parent-Teacher
    42(6):7-9, February 1958.   1112
    Intelligent listening is associated with a mature mind.
Collaboration is essential to conversation.

----. "Communication As Crucial in Education." School
    and Society 67:443-45, June 12, 1948.   1113
    Purposeful listening requires that the logical structure
of the communication and the motive of the speaker be examined before evaluation takes place.

----. "Everybody's Listening." National Parent-Teacher
    45:14+, January 1951.   1114
    Good listening requires an ability to distinguish between

244 Listening Bibliography

essential points and details, between facts and opinions, and
between information and persuasion.

----. Speak Up! A New Approach to Communication. Chicago: University of Chicago Press, 1952.   1115
Listening is an active process in response to the speaker's desire to be understood and to motivate the listener to
feel and act.

Spache, George. "The Construction and Validation of a
Work-Type Auditory Comprehension Test." Educational
and Psychological Measurement 10:249-53, Summer 1950.
1116
A description of the Auditory Comprehension Section of
the Triggs Diagnostic Reading Test. A reliability coefficient
of .788 is reported.

Spearritt, Donald. A Factorial Analysis of Listening Comprehension. Doctoral dissertation. Cambridge, Mass.: Harvard University, 1961. Also: Listening Comprehension--
A Factorial Analysis. A.C.E.R. Research Series No. 76.
Melbourne, Australia: Australian Council for Educational
Research, 1962.   1117
A factor analysis was performed on data gathered by ad-
ministrating 34 tests to 300 sixth-grade pupils in ten classes.
A factor of "listening comprehension" was isolated. High
correlations between this factor and the factors of verbal
comprehension, inductive reasoning, and span memory are
reported.

Speech Association of America. Interest Group: Speech in
the Secondary School. "Fundamentals of Speech: A
Basic Course for High Schools." Speech Teacher 8:93-
113, March 1959.   1118
The proposed course includes a section on listening.

Spencer, Edward Merritt. The Retention of Orally Presented
Materials. Doctoral dissertation. Iowa City, Iowa:
State University of Iowa, 1940. Summary: Journal of
Educational Psychology 32:641-55, December 1941.
1119
The pupils in 80 sixth-grade classes were used as subjects to determine whether an auditory or a visual presentation of two 600-word articles would lead to better comprehension. Little difference was found. On tests of delayed recall it was found that immediate tests of recall improved

retention.

Spicker, Howard H. Listening Comprehension and Retention
   of Normal and Retarded Children as Functions of Speaking Rate and Passage Difficulty. Doctoral dissertation.
   Nashville, Tenn.: George Peabody College for Teachers,
   1963. Abstract: Dissertation Abstracts 24:1925, 1964.
                                                         1120
   Describes an experimental study performed to determine
the relative listening comprehension and retention of a group
of mentally retarded children with the same mental ages as
the members of a control group of normal children. The material was presented at speeds ranging from 125 wpm to 275
wpm. No significant difference was found in the listening
comprehension of the two groups, but the retention of the
older retarded group was better than that of the younger
normal group. Both groups had better comprehension at the
lower speeds of presentation.

Spitzer, Herbert F. Manual of Directions--Spitzer Study
   Skills Test. New York: Harcourt, Brace and World,
   1956.   1121
   Presents the following correlations between subtests of
the Spitzer Study Skills Test and Brown-Carlsen test results.

	using dictionary	using index	sources of information	graphs, maps, etc.
Grade 10	.60	.52	.25	.58
Grade 11	.61	.56	.25	.63

Spruell, Mary. Listening and Related Variables. Master's
   thesis. East Lansing, Mich.: Michigan State University, 1962.   1122

Stampfl, Thomas G. The Effect of Repetition of Auditory
   Material Presented During Sleep. Master's thesis.
   Chicago, Ill.: Loyola University, 1953.   1123
   Using six subjects, Stampfl reports that he was unable
to establish that learning of nonsense syllables took place
during sleep.

Stanton, Frank M. "Memory for Advertising Copy Presented
   Visually vs. Orally." Journal of Applied Psychology
   18:45-64, February 1934.   1124
   Fictitious advertising copy was presented visually by
means of printed booklets and orally over a public address

system to four groups of college students. Tests for recall
given one, seven, and 21 days later showed that the auditory
approach was more effective.

Stark, Joel.   An Investigation of the Relationship of the Vocal
    and Communicative Aspects of Speech Competency with
    Listening Comprehension.   Doctoral dissertation.   New
    York: New York University, 1956.   Abstract: Disserta-
    tion Abstracts 17:696, 1957; and Speech Monographs 24:
    98-99, June 1957.   1125
    Using 175 college speech students as subjects, Stark re-
ports the following correlations with listening, as measured
by the Brown-Carlsen Test: vocal speech capacity .36;
communicative speech competency .59; and intelligence .68.

Starkweather, John A.   "A Speech Rate Meter for Vocal Be-
    havior Analysis."   Journal of the Experimental Analysis
    of Behavior 3:111-14, April 1960.   1126
    A description of the "Speech Rate Meter," a device
which operates automatically from the recording of a single
voice.   A graph shows that the pulses of speech produced
had a close correspondence to word count, but syllabification
was not detectable.   High reliability is claimed for the device.

Starmer, Garrett L.   "And Shun the Frumious Jabberwock."
    Phi Delta Kappan 34:239-40, March 1953.   1127
    An amusing account of the reading of a completely mean-
ingless speech full of high-sounding phrases to 73 college
freshmen and sophomores.   Only ten students showed an
awareness of the lack of meaning.

Steeg, Jacquelin.   An Exploratory Study of the Relationship
    Between Listening and Scholastic Achievement.   Master's
    thesis.   Athens, Ohio: Ohio University, 1960.   1128
    Using 192 college speech students as subjects, Steeg re-
ports that the correlation between results on the Brown-Carlsen Test and grade point average during the first college
semester was .37.   The correlation between listening test
score and grades in lecture courses was .40.   This compares to a reported correlation of .50 between grades and
the Ohio State Psychological Examination.

Steer, M.D.   "Speech Intelligibility in Naval Aviation."
    Journal of Speech Disorders 10:215-19, September 1945.
                                                         1129
    Very little is known about methods of training for good

listening during flight. It is suggested that such ability may
be increased by familiarity with standard voice procedures;
familiarity with expected messages; concentration on the entire message rather than on isolated and unintelligible words;
attempts to "fill in" or construct a whole for a partial pattern; attention to the message rather than to distracting elements; and active practice in listening to typical communications under simulated or actual flight conditions.

Stein, Lila. Sleep Learning. Master's thesis. New York:
    City College of the City University of New York, 1965.
                                                      1130
    Material was played to four sleeping subjects at times
when there had been a total absence of alpha waves for 30
seconds and during REM (Rapid Eye Movement) periods.
Word association techniques were used to measure learning.
It was found that: 1. There were no alpha waves during
REM periods. 2. Increased motivation, by the offer of a
financial reward for best performance, did not tend to greater
learning. 3. Indirect techniques of testing did not indicate
that material presented during sleep had any effect. It was
concluded that there can be no verbal memory of auditory
stimuli presented during sleep.

Stephenson, Howard. Listen and Win. New York: Good
    Reading Rack Service, 1968.   1131
    Directed to those who have to listen to supervisors, this
booklet describes several techniques for better listening.
Emphasis is laid on repeating a question before replying,
making sure an answer given is understood, taking advantage
of the difference in the speed of one's mind and the speed of
speech, and looking at the speaker to ascertain the real
meaning of the words used.

Sterner, Alice, Sanders, Katherine M., and Kaplan, Milton
    A. Skill in Listening. NCTE Pamphlets on Communica-
    tion, No. 5. Chicago: National Council of Teachers of
    English, 1944.   1132
    True literacy may well include possession of listening
skills. Listening is a more social experience than reading.
Research is needed on listening vocabulary.

Stevens, Walter W. "How Well Do You Listen?" Adult
    Education 12(1):42-47, Autumn 1961.   1133
    The good listener should give full attention; remain
calm and detached; let his response be based on his own
critical reflection rather than on one forced upon him by the

listening group; listen for unity and structure; listen for reasoning and evidence.

----. "Polarization, Social Facilitation, and Listening."
   Western Speech 25:170-74, Summer 1961.   1134
   An audience maneuvered into joint action by a speaker
is said to be polarized. When a listener is polarized, he
relinquishes his own sense of values and adopts the values of
the audience. "The critical listener tries to maintain his intellectual free will. No matter what the audience thinks of
the speaker, no matter how it reacts to his skill and charm,
the reflective auditor attempts to make an individual judgment independent of others in terms of his own criteria, to
make his response truly his and not one subliminally forced
upon him by the group."

Stewart, Nathaniel. "Listen to the Right People." Nation's
   Business 51(1):60-63, January 1963. Reprinted in Lis-
   tening: Readings. (Edited by Sam Duker.) Metuchen,
   N.J.: Scarecrow Press, 1966. p. 382-88.   1135
   A good executive is discriminating in deciding to whom
he will listen. Listening only to confidants is dangerous.
Executives must distinguish between those who come in with
decisions and those who are coming in for decisions.

Still, Dana Swank. The Relationship Between Listening Ability and High School Grades. Doctoral dissertation.
   Pittsburgh, Pa.: University of Pittsburgh, 1955. Abstract: Dissertation Abstracts 15:1761-62, 1955.   1136
   Using 317 ninth- through twelfth-grade pupils as subjects, Still reports the following correlations with listening
as measured by the Brown-Carlsen Test: grade index .66;
I.Q. .54; and reading .44.

Stites, William Harrison. A Study of Some Factors Relating
   to Speaking Effectiveness of the Basic Communications
   Students of the University of Denver. Master's thesis.
   Denver: University of Denver, 1948.   1137
   One hundred seventy-three Basic Communications Course
students were judged as to speech effectiveness by five
trained judges. A battery of tests was administered, including a Listening Attitude and Preference Inventory, drafted by
the author, and the Listening Comprehension Test used by
Harry Goldstein in his thesis. In comparing the 20 most effective speakers to the 20 least effective speakers, a signifi-
can difference was found in performance on the Goldstein
test. Only four of the 55 items on the Inventory showed a

significant difference.

Stodola, Quentin, Schwartz, Donald F. , and Kolstoe, Ralph
    H. Administering a Listening Comprehension Test
    Through Use of Teacher-Readers, Sound Film and Tape
    Recorders. Fargo, N.D.: North Dakota State Univer-
    sity, 1962. Summary: North Dakota Teacher 41(8):
    13+, April 1962.   1138
    The STEP test was administered to all Fargo, N.D.
fourth- through twelfth-grade public school pupils. No significant differences were found between four modes of administration: 1. by classroom teachers untrained in test administration; 2. by classroom teachers specially trained in the
administration of the STEP Listening Test; 3. by a film in
which a trained speaker presented the material; and 4. by a
tape taken from the audio portion of the film.

----. "Listening - Neglected Skill. " Professional Growth
    for Teachers (An Arthur C. Crofts publication.) Janu-
    ary 1958, p. 1-4.   1139
    Listening instruction should be integrated with all sub-
jects. The author discusses the experiences of teachers in,
and techniques for, teaching listening for information, listening critically, and listening for pleasure. Evaluation of listening by use of teacher-made tests and by standardized published tests is described.

Stone, D.R. "A Recorded Auditory Apperception Test as a
    New Projective Technique." Journal of Psychology 29:
    349-53, April 1950.   1140
    A projective test on ten records, consisting of non-verb-
al human sounds, dramatic episodes, animal sounds, sounds
from nature, and mechanical sounds, is described. It is
suggested that norms could be developed for this test.

Story, M.L. "Need for Critical Listening." High School
    Journal 38:297-99, May 1955. Digest: Educational
    Digest 21:40-41, September 1955.   1141
    The greatest deficiency in listening instruction is in the
area of critical listening.

Stratton, Ollie. "Techniques for Literate Listening." Eng-
    lish Journal 37:542-44, December 1948.   1142
    The author advocates making outlines of discourses
heard in high school assemblies and over the radio as a way
of improving listening skills.

Strauss, George and Leonard R. Sayles. Personnel: The
    Human Problems of Management. Englewood Cliffs,
    N.J.: Prentice-Hall, 1960. Chapter 10, "Interviewing:
    The Fine Art of Listening," p. 217-37.   1143
Listening is one of the most important of all management tools. Listening is a method which will win for a superior the confidence of his subordinates. Listening is more
than not talking; it is an active process of understanding oral
communication.

Strickland, Ruth. "The Interrelationship Between Language
    and Reading." Volta Review 60:334-36, September 1958.
                                                        1144
Listening, hearing, and paying attention are three separate skills. What one reads or listens to must be put into
proper perspective.

----. "Language Readiness for Oral Reading." Oral As-
    pects of Reading. Proceedings of the Annual Conference
    on Reading. Chicago: University of Chicago Press,
    1955, p. 11-15.   1145
Listening is the first need of children of all ages.

Stromer, Walter F. An Investigation into Some of the Rela-
    tions Between Reading, Listening, and Intelligence.
    Doctoral dissertation. Denver: University of Denver,
    1952. Abstract: Speech Monographs 21:159-60, August
    1954.   1146
Using 24 college students as subjects, Stromer reports
that a group trained to listen to a recording while reading
a passage performed better on both speed and comprehension
than did groups who read silently or listened without reading.
A test devised to determine listening proficiency is described and the text is given.

----. "Learn How to Listen." This Week Magazine, Feb-
    ruary 21, 1960, p. 13-15.   1147
Some poor listening habits: tuning out one's mind;
thinking we already know what is going to be said; looking
for mannerisms of the speaker instead of listening; doing
other things while "listening;" hearing words instead of
ideas. A short listening test is included.

----. "Listening--How?" English Journal 41:318-19, June
    1952.   1148
This is a description of a listening course given at the
University of Denver which deals with the analysis of poor

listening habits and ways of altering them.

----. "Listening and Personality." Education 75:322-26,
    January 1955.   1149
    Personality factors in listening are generally ignored in
listening tests. Good listeners are usually well enough adjusted so that they can "afford" to listen.

----. "Listening for Learning and Living." New Outlook
    for the Blind 48:171-78, June 1954.   1150
    The rate on talking book records can be increased with-
out loss of comprehension.

----. Strength of Opinion, Memory Span, and the Ability to
    Gather Meanings from Contextual Clues as Factors in
    Listening. Master's thesis. Denver: University of Den-
    ver, 1950.   1151
    Stromer reports that scores on tests he devised on mem-
ory span and on contextual clues correlated only slightly with
instructors' rating of students for general listening ability.
A test on strength of opinion correlated very highly with
these ratings.

Strong, Lydia. "Do You Know How to Listen?" Manage-
    ment Review 44(80):630-35, August 1955. Reprinted:
    Inspection News 45:20-21+, March 1960.   1152
    Four steps in listening: make sense out of sound; under-
stand what is being said; tell fact from fancy; and listen with
imaginative understanding of the other person's point of view.
Barriers to good listening: listening only to the words; bias;
boredom; and pretended listening. A ten-item "Listening
Quiz" is included.

Stump, Noah F. The Experimental Development of an Audi-
    tory Group Test of Intelligence. Doctoral dissertation.
    Ithaca, N.Y.: Cornell University, 1936.   1153
    Description of the development of an oral intelligence
test which yielded results that correlated satisfactorily with
the results of a written group intelligence test.

----. "Listening Versus Reading Method in True-False Ex-
    aminations." Journal of Applied Psychology 15:555-62,
    December 1931.   1154
    Eighty-four percent of students preferred a written to
an oral test, principally because of the control given them
to distribute their time on the written test.

----. "Oral Versus Printed Method in the Presentation of
True-False Examinations." Journal of Educational Research 18:423-24, December 1928.   1155
There was a better correlation between mental ability
and the oral test results than between mental ability and the
written test results.

Sullivan, G.W. "Listening Behavior in the Secondary School."
American Teacher 31:12-13, December 1946.   1156
Listening skills should be taught; they should not be al-
lowed to become a fetish.

Sullivan, Helen Blair. Construction and Evaluation of a
Measure of Auditory Comprehension. Master's thesis.
Boston: Boston University, 1937.   1157
This is a description of a listening test for ages seven
to twelve, composed of picture identification, word lists,
and paragraph comprehension. High reliabilities are reported for the subtests.

----. "A New Method of Determining Capacity for Reading."
Education 59:39-45, September 1938.   1158
The construction, validation, and standardization of the
Durrell-Sullivan Reading Capacity Test are described.

Sur, William Raymond and Schuller, Charles Francis.
Music Education for Teen-Agers. Second edition. New
York: Harper & Row, 1966. p. 233-45.   1159
A successful teacher of listening to music must know
not only music but also the emotional and intellectual reactions of the students in order to succeed in a directed listening experience. Suggestions are made concerning specific
methods of teaching listening.

Surles, Lynn and Stanbury, W.A. "How to Communicate by
Listening." Textile World 111(3):119-20, March 1961.
                                                     1160
Genuine listening is a vital link in communication. Six
rules for listening to help others: 1. Take time to listen.
2. Let angry, impassioned people talk themselves out. 3.
Signal your attention. 4. Let a worried man talk himself
out. 5. Steer the talk in helpful directions. 6. Leave de-
cision-making alone. Four rules for listening to help yourself: 1. Erase your prejudices. 2. Concentrate. 3. Take
it easy. 4. Adopt the talker's orientation.

Swanson, Bessie R. Music in the Education of Children.

San Francisco, Calif.: Wadsworth, 1961. p. 227-28.

1161

In the highest type of analytical listening, the ability to
follow a melody line within the texture of the musical composition is basic.   Understanding rhythm is just as important
to perceptive listening.

Swenson, Helen Booth.   A Study of the Use of the Black-
    board as an Aid to Listening Comprehension in Sixth-
    Grade Classes.   Master's thesis.   Austin, Tex.: Uni-
    versity of Texas, 1956.   1162
Using 253 sixth-grade pupils as subjects, Swenson found
that the visual presentation of key phrases on the blackboard
aided in the comprehension of orally presented passages.

Szucs, Sister Mary Athanasia.   A Proposed Program of
    Teaching Listening Skills in a First Grade Through Lan-
    guage Arts Activities.   Master's thesis.   Cleveland,
    Ohio: St. John College, 1957.   1163
A program is described which includes informal conversations, discussion, telephone conversations, social introduc-
tions, story telling, poetry, and phonics.

Tabor, Doris Dee Hiles.   Differential Effectiveness of Vari-
    ous Instructional Methods Involved in a Listening Com-
    prehension Program.   Doctoral dissertation.   Lincoln,
    Neb.:   University of Nebraska, 1967.   Abstract: Dis-
    sertation Abstracts 28:509A, 1967.   1164
In an education orientation course, four groups of 40
college freshmen were given four sessions on listening; the
sessions covered the importance of listening, listening for information, listening for enjoyment and critical listening.   One
group heard the ten-minute lectures live followed by a practice session.   The second group heard the live lecture without the practice session.   The other two groups heard the
lecture on tape, one with a practice session and one without.
All students showed gains on the post-test as compared to
the pre-test but the gains were not statistically significant.
There was no significant difference between the live lecture
groups and the tape groups.   There was a significant difference in favor of the groups having practice.

Tanner, Doyle Boyd.   A Comparison of the Influence of
    Three Environments Upon Critical Listening in the Fifth
    Grade.   Master's thesis.   Logan, Utah: Utah State Uni-
    versity, 1961.   1165
Using 90 fifth-grade pupils as subjects, Tanner found

254 Listening Bibliography

that listening comprehension was not affected significantly by
either musical background or other background sounds.

Tapp, J.L. "Children Can Understand Rumor." Social Edu-
    cation 17:163-64, April 1953.   1166
    A description of a lesson illustrating the distortion which
occurred when a description of a picture was relayed from
one pupil to another.

Tarkanian, Lois. Teaching Listening in the Primary
    Grades: Comparison of a Program Recommended by
    Language Arts Authorities with Teaching Practices in
    San Bernardino County, California. Master's thesis.
    Fresno, Calif.: Fresno State College, 1964.   1167
    A survey of the literature of listening, designed to de-
termine the practices in teaching listening by 100 elementary
school teachers.

Tatum, George Liston Jr. Communication in the Sales Pro-
    gram of the International Business Machines Corpora-
    tion. Doctoral dissertation. Evanston, Ill.: North-
    western University, 1954.   1168
    The importance to sales personnel of good listening is
stressed.

Taylor, Calvin W. "Listening Creatively." Instructor
    73(6):5+, February 1964.   1169
    Very little is known about children's listening processes,
although much of classroom time is spent in listening.
Classroom exercises in listening should provide for differing
sets of mind and differing thinking processes.

Taylor, Edward. Verbal Listening Skills and Their Con-
    comitants in the Seventh-Grade Population at Hayward.
    Master's thesis. Berkeley: University of California,
    1950.   1170
    Using 293 seventh-grade pupils as subjects and an au-
thor-made test as a measure of listening, Taylor reports
the following correlations with listening: mental age .51;
reading grade placement .46; and aural acuity .19.

Taylor, Hazel Scott. A Study of the Effects of a Planned
    Daily Listening Program on Reading Progress of Third
    Grade Children. Master's thesis. Lubbock, Texas:
    Texas Technological College, 1964.   1171
    A class of 24 was given daily 30-minute lessons based
on the SRA Listening Skill Builders. The reading improvement of this group after 16 weeks was significantly greater

Taylor, Hazel Scott   255

than that of the control group.

Taylor, Josephine L. "Use of Compressed Speech, Tapes
    and Discs and of Variable Frequency Power Supply with
    Selected Children and Adults." Proceedings of the
    Louisville Conference on Time Compressed Speech, Oc-
    tober, 19-21, 1966. (Edited by Emerson Foulke.)
    Louisville, Ky.: Center for Rate Controlled Recordings,
    University of Louisville, 1967. p. 55-70.   1172
    Describes the reactions of 33 visually handicapped sub-
jects to mechanically speeded and to compressed speech.
While generally favorable to both types of rate increase, the
reactions were mixed.

Taylor, Stanford E. Listening. What Research Says to the
    Teacher, No. 29. Washington, D.C.: National Educa-
    tion Association, 1964.   1173
    A review of research findings and a list of suggested
activities for teaching listening. A 29-item bibliography.

----. Studies of the Listening Activity. Huntington, N.Y.:
    Educational Developmental Laboratories, 1963. Re-
    printed: Staiger, Ralph C. and Culbreth, Y. Melton
    (eds.). 12th Yearbook of the National Reading Confer-
    ence. Milwaukee: National Reading Conference, 1963.
    pp. 189-201.   1174
    A number of ways of testing listening skills and the results
of five separate experiments are presented. The author concludes that the tests described are sufficiently discriminating
of listening abilities, if the premise is accepted that academic
achievement and performance on a standardized reading test
characterize the quality of listening.

Tempel, Iola M. Implication for the Teaching of Listening
    in the Elementary Classroom Based on an Analysis of
    the Literature. Master's thesis. De Kalb, Ill.: North-
    ern Illinois University, 1962.   1175
    A review of some of the current literature on listening.

"Ten Aims for Next Ten Years." Phi Delta Kappan 35:364,
    May 1954.   1176
    A group of 76 school administrators ranked as the first
educational aim: "Children should be taught to be critical
observers and listeners."

Terango, Larry. "Are We Teaching Children to Listen and
    Speak Effectively?" Ohio Schools 37(7):10-11, October
    1959.   1177

Tezza, Joseph S. The Effects of Listening Training on Au-
    dio-Lingual Learning. Doctoral dissertation. Pitts-
    burgh, Pa.: University of Pittsburgh, 1962. Abstract:
    Dissertation Abstracts 23:2035, 1962.   1178
    Using 120 high school students as subjects and the Brown-
Carlsen Test as a measure of listening, Tezza reports that
ten weeks of listening training in English did not significantly affect aural comprehension of Russian.

"Think While You Listen." Supervisory Management 10(9):51-
    52, September 1965.   1179
    Failure in listening is a key cause of mistakes. To lis-
ten well: 1. Take advantage of speed of thought by looking
ahead to check points speaker is developing. 2. Read the
thoughts behind the words being spoken. 3. Summarize frequently. 4. Be sure you understand the intended meaning of
the speaker's words. 5. Don't be thrown off base by bias.
6. Don't be too quick to argue.

Thompson, David W. and Fredricks, Virginia. Oral Inter-
    pretation of Fiction. Minneapolis: Burgess Publishing,
    1964.   1180
    The nature of imaginative listening, which is necessary
for the proper interpretation of poetry and drama, is described.

Thompson, Ernest Clifford. An Experimental Investigation
    of the Relative Effectiveness of Organizational Structure
    in Oral Communication. Doctoral dissertation. Minne-
    apolis: University of Minnesota, 1960. Abstract:
    Dissertation Abstracts 21:270, 1960.   1181
    Three groups of college speech students heard passages
which were well organized, passages in which the sentences
within a division of the passage had been randomly ordered,
and passages in which the order of the sentences had been
rearranged. Each group contained students who were in the
upper, middle, and lower third on the Goyer Organization of
Ideas Test.
    Those hearing the well organized speech performed sig-
nificantly better on an immediate and on a delayed test of
comprehension. There was no significant difference in shift
of opinion. The students who had the best scores on the
Goyer test also had the best scores on the comprehension
test.

Thurlow, Willard R. "Audition." Annual Review of Psy-
    chology 16:325-58, 1965.   1182

Lists 273 references.

Tiffany, William Rand, and Bennett, Delmond N. "Intelligi-
    bility of Slow-Played Speech." Journal of Speech and
    Hearing Research 4:248-58, September 1961.   1183
In this experiment it was found that slowing down the
rate at which a tape was played did not affect intelligibility
until the rate was below 61% of the normal rate. This was
true even when no provision was made for controlling distortion. Training (consisting of practice and feedback concerning errors made) was found effective in increasing the rate
of intelligibility.

Tipton, Margaret West. An Analysis of Current Theory,
    Practice, and Experimentation in the Teaching of Listen-
    ing. Master's thesis. Bowling Green, Ohio: Bowling
    Green State University, 1954.   1184
An analysis of the treatment of the subject of listening
in five series of high school English textbooks led to the
author's conclusion that the approaches and practice exercises were unimaginative and did little to arouse the interest
of pupils.

Tireman, L.S. and Woods, Velma. "Aural and Visual Com-
    prehension of English by Spanish-Speaking Children."
    Elementary School Journal 40:204-11, November 1939.
                                                     1185
The authors report that Spanish-speaking pupils did better on the visual than on the auditory part of the Durrell-
Sullivan Reading Capacity Test. They conclude that the
school failed to provide for children who speak Spanish at
home a program for growth in aural and spoken English comparable to the reading program.

Tompkins, Phillip K. and Samovar, Larry A.   "An Experi-
    mental Study of the Effects of Credibility on the Compre-
    hension of Content." Speech Monographs 31:120-23,
    June 1964.   1186
Insofar as amount of learning was concerned, a group
of beginning speech students was not affected by the credibility assigned to the source of a taped speech by the introduction. The group showed significant changes of attitude
toward the subject and toward the speaker's credibility after
hearing the expository speech.

Toussaint, Isabella H. "A Classified Summary of Listen-
    ing--1950-1959." Journal of Communication 10:125-

34, September 1960. Reprinted in Listening: Readings.
(Edited by Sam Duker.) Metuchen, N.J.: Scarecrow
Press, 1966. p. 155-64.   1187
Research is summarized under headings of definition,
importance of listening, factors influencing learning, relationship of reading and listening, and the feasibility of teaching
listening.

----. Interrelationships of Reading, Listening, Arithmetic
   and Intelligence and Their Implications. Doctoral dissertation. Pittsburgh, Pa.: University of Pittsburgh, 1961.
   Abstract: Dissertation Abstracts 22:819, 1961. Summary: Cleland, Donald L. and Toussaint, Isabella H.
   "The Interrelationships of Reading, Listening, Arithmetic Computation and Intelligence." Reading Teacher 15:
   228-31, January 1962.   1188
   Using 172 intermediate-grade pupils as subjects, Toussaint administered a battery of tests. Many linear, partial
and multiple correlations are reported in this study, which
used excellent statistical analysis of the data gathered. It
is reported that the STEP Listening Test scores, arithmetic
test scores, and group intelligence test scores yield the best
prediction of potential reading ability.

Townsend, Agatha. "A Bibliography on Auding." Reading
   Teacher 17:549-51, April 1964.   1189
   Reports on listening research have not been involved as
much as they should have been with hearing and its role in
auditory perception. Annotated 30-item bibliography.

----. "Interrelationships Between Reading and the Language
   Arts Areas." National Conference on Research in English. Interrelationships Among the Language Arts.
   Chicago: National Council of Teachers of English, 1954,
   p. 12-22.   1190
   Questions the close relationship so often claimed to exist between reading and listening skills.

Travers, Robert M.W. "Transmission of Information to Human Receivers." Educational Psychologist 2(1):1-5,
   December 1964.   1191
   Travers questions the statements made in books on
audio-visual materials to the effect that 1. more information is acquired when the same information is transmitted
simultaneously through both the auditory and visual modalities
than when a single modality is employed; and 2. other things
being equal, the more realistic a presentation is, the more

effective will be the transmission. He cites contrary evidence produced by experiments reported in this paper and states that these statements are not in accord with psychological theory.

Travis, Lee Edward. "The Psychotherapeutical Process."
Handbook of Speech Pathology. (Edited by Lee Edward
Travis.) New York: Appleton, 1957. p. 967-68. 1192
The speaker-listener interaction is the matrix of society.
The listener always responds to the speaker; sometimes
more, sometimes less; sometimes painfully, sometimes joy-
fully; sometimes feelingly, sometimes intellectually. In the
response, the speaker sees his own reflection.

Traxler, Arthur E. "Some Data on the Results of the Sequential Tests of Educational Progress (STEP) Level 3,
Form A, for Small Groups of Pupils in Two Independent
Schools for Girls." Educational Records Bulletin 72:69-
73, July 1958.   1193
On the basis of the administration of Level 3 STEP
Tests to 70 seventh- and eighth-grade pupils, various correlations are reported. Most startling are the high correlations
of listening with the other individual tests (e.g., with social
studies, .84) which the author says is due to a large verbal factor in all the tests, including mathematics.

Treanor, John H. "For Every Lesson, Listen!" Elementary English 33:292-94, May 1956.   1194
An emotional appeal for the recognition of the importance
of the aural aspects of life.

----. "Listen Before Writing." Elementary English 30:
207-09, April 1953.   1195
The author advocates using things that have been listened to as topics for compositions in the elementary schools.

Triggs, Frances O. "A Comparison of Auditory and Silent
Presentation of Reading Comprehension Tests." 14th
Yearbook of National Council on Measurements Used in
Education. 1957, p. 1-7.   1196
In general, it may be said that auditory comprehension
gives a basis for predicting reading potential.

Trivette, Sue Eloise. An Investigation of the Effect of
Training in Listening for Specific Purposes. Master's
thesis. Johnson City, Tenn.: East Tennessee State
College, 1959. Summary: Journal of Educational Re-

search 54:276-77, March 1961.   1197
In an uncontrolled experiment the author found that 77
per cent of a class improved scores in listening, as measured by Maurice Lewis' test, after using the Gates-Peardon
Practice Exercises in Reading as listening exercise material.

Trotter, William D.   "Listener Adaptation to Cerebral Pal-
    sied Speech."   Central States Speech Journal 10:23-24,
    Winter 1959.   1198
Speech samples of ten cerebral palsied children were
rated by twelve advanced speech pathology students at one-
week intervals on three occasions.   Although the same tapes
were presented each time, the speech students judged that
eight of the ten children had less severe problems on the
third round than on the first.

Trotzig, E.G.   "Is It Goodbye to Book Learning?" Phi
    Delta Kappan 38:360-64, June 1957.   1199
The author bemoans the "passing" of reading and the
rise of listening.

"The Trouble with Listening."   Supervision 27(7):21, July
    1965.   1200
A summary of an address by Dr. Ralph Nichols on the
subject of listening.

Tucker, Margaret F.   Listening Lessons in Connected Speech
    for Puerto Rican College Students for the Purpose of Im-
    proving Aural Comprehension in English.   Master's thes-
    is.   Albuquerque: University of New Mexico, 1963.
                                                   1201
This thesis, primarily concerned with auditory discrimination rather than with listening, presents exercises which
are useful for the teaching of listening to Puerto Rican college students.

Tucker, Raymond K.   "Review of 'Listening Is Good Busi-
    ness.' "   Speech Teacher 12:172-73, March 1963. 1202
A favorable review of a record containing a speech by
Ralph G. Nichols.

Tucker, W.S.   "Science of Listening."   19th Century 97:
    548-57, April 1925.   1203
In this early article stress is laid on the complexity of
the listening act.

Turchan, Norman R.   "An Evaluation of a Program in Read-

ing and Listening." Reading and the Language Arts.
Proceedings of the Annual Conference on Reading. Chicago: University of Chicago Press, 1963. p. 217-21.

1204

A description of the program used in teaching language
arts in the Gary, Indiana schools, which includes instruction
in listening. The following types of listening are discussed:
social, secondary, aesthetic, critical, concentrative, and
creative.

Tver, Dave. "The Art of Listening." Oklahoma Teacher
47(5):12-14, January 1966. 1205
Listening can be learned. There are four levels of listening: 1. making sense out of sound; 2. understanding
what is being said; 3. telling fact from fancy; and 4. listening with imaginative understanding to the other person's
viewpoint.
Barriers to good listening include: 1. listening only
for verbal content; 2. bias; 3. allowing emotional words or
ideas to increase our prejudices; 4. distorting speaker's
presentation so that only the part we agree with is heard;
5. boredom due to thought speed differential; 6. apathy because the subject is too difficult; and 7. pretending to listen.

Tyler, Tracey F. "Listening--The Neglected Phase of Communication." Journal of the Association for Education
by Radio 6:71, January 1947. 1206
We need to re-examine the proper relation between
reading and listening in the entire English curriculum.

----. "Listening, the Number One Problem." Journal of the
Association for Education by Radio 8:85, April 1949.

1207

Many factors influence listening. Among these are intelligence, reading comprehension, vocabulary, interest,
physical fatigue, concentration, and the ability to look for
main ideas rather than for specific facts.

Uddhayanin, Phayear. The Role of Listening in the Teaching of English as a Second Language. Master's thesis.
Lubbock, Tex.: Texas Technological College, 1964.

1208

Listening can be an important element in learning a
foreign language.

Utigard, Caryl Nereed. A Comparison of the Effectiveness
of Magnetic Tape and the Regular Classroom Teacher

upon Growth in Listening Ability. Master's thesis.
Seattle: University of Washington, 1962.   1209
In an experiment using 39 seventh-grade pupils as subjects, Utigard reports no difference between results of tests
following stories read by the teacher and of tests following
stories pre-recorded on tape by the same teacher.

Utzinger, Vernon Alfred. An Experimental Study of the Ef-
    fects of Verbal Fluency Upon the Listener. Doctoral
    dissertation. Los Angeles: University of Southern Cali-
    fornia, 1952. Abstract: Speech Monographs 20:161,
    August 1953.   1210
Using the passages prepared by Cartier, Harwood and
Goodman-Malamuth, the author found that the comprehension
of 240 high school juniors and 240 college students was not
significantly affected by the degree of fluency with which the
passages were read to them.

Van Garrett, Wouter. "Do You Ever Stop to Listen?"
    American Mercury 83(394):143-44, November 1956.
                                                   1211
    A good listener is usually regarded as a good conversa-
tionalist.

Van Mondfrans, Adrian P. An Investigation of the Interac-
    tion Between the Level of Meaningfulness and Redundancy
    in the Content of the Stimulus Material, and the Mode of
    Presentation of the Stimulus Material. Master's thesis.
    Salt Lake City: University of Utah, n.d.   1212
Auditory presentation of meaningless materials, such as
nonsense syllables, is less effective than a visual presentation. In the case of meaningful materials, there was no significant difference between the two methods.

Van Wingerden, Stewart. A Study of Direct, Planned Lis-
    tening Instruction in the Intermediate Grades in Four
    Counties in the State of Washington. Doctoral disserta-
    tion. Pullman, Wash.: Washington State University,
    1965. Abstract: Dissertation Abstracts 26:5310-11,
    1966.   1213
Results of a questionnaire addressed to a sample of 300
fourth- through sixth-grade teachers. The 266 responses
indicated that a great amount of listening instruction took
place in the classrooms of the respondents.

Vance, Robert S. "Do You Really Know How to Listen?"
    Family Digest 17(7):52-57, April 1962.   1214

Poor listening irritates people. Three rules for good
listening are given: 1. look interested; 2. practice over-
coming a tendency to be distracted; 3. get physically ready
for listening by sitting erect.

Vancurra, Rudolph H. "Flesch Readability Formula Applied
   to Television Programs." Journal of Applied Psychology
   39:47-48, February 1955.   1215
This is a report on the application of the Flesch formula
to daytime television programs. No attempt was made to
validate the use of the formula on aural materials.

Vavra, Catherine. "Barriers to Communication." Journal
   of School Health 27:58-60, February 1957.   1216
Communication is hampered when the listener is not considered. Words that will not be understood must not be
used. The personal-emotional needs of the listener, as well
as of the speaker, must be considered. The listener should
not judge the speaker solely on the basis of his own point of
view. When the listener fears that disagreement will be
penalized, he stops paying attention. Feedback is valuable
in the communicative process.

Verburg, Wallace A. "Children Tell Us If We Listen."
   University of Kansas Bulletin of Education 6:67-69,
   May 1952.   1217
Teachers often continue to talk even when they are not
being listened to. Teachers should take time to listen to
children.

Veronese, J. Paul. Effect of Practice in Listening upon
   Reading Comprehension on Secondary School Level.
   Master's thesis. Milwaukee: Cardinal Stritch College,
   1960.   1218
Using 44 ninth-grade pupils as subjects, Veronese found
no significantly different improvement in reading between two
groups, one of which had been given listening lessons twice
a week for eight weeks.

Villarreal, Jesse J. A Test of the Aural Comprehension of
   English for Native Speakers of Spanish. Doctoral dissertation. Evanston, Ill.: Northwestern University,
   1947.   1219
The development of a recorded listening test is described in detail. The text of two forms of the test is included. High reliability and validity are reported.
Specifications for such a test are given as follows:

1. The ability of a person to understand a second language lies in the ability to use the symbols of the second language as if they were the symbols of his own language, not necessarily with comparable fluency but in comparable living situations.

2. It is practical and desirable to present to the subject a representative sampling of the oral communication situations that occur within the speech community where the foreigner desires to use English.

3. Aural comprehension must be measured through the aural modality.

Vilscek, Elaine. "Lessons for Moonbound Listeners." The
    Packet 17(2):3-11, Winter 1962-63.   1220
"In the sequential development of the language arts, listening occurs as the infant begins to associate sounds meaningfully. It is the foundation for speech patterns, vocabulary development, comprehension in reading, and written communication skills."

To teach listening effectively in the primary grades:
1. determine the listening levels and needs of the pupils;
2. set definite purposes for listening; and 3. integrate listening experiences with other curricular areas. The need for a listening test suitable at the primary level is stressed. Twenty-five specific techniques for teaching listening are listed.

Vineyard, Edwin E. and Bailey, Robert B. "Interrelationships of Reading Ability, Listening Skill, Intelligence and Scholastic Achievement." Journal of Developmental
    Reading 3:174-78, Spring 1960.   1221
On the basis of a statistical study of scores on the STEP Listening Test, the reading section of the Cooperative English test, the ACE test and of grade point averages, the authors report a number of linear, partial, and second-order partial correlations. The relationship between listening and academic achievement is marked.

Voelker, Francis H. A Study of the Effectiveness of Teaching Listening to Eleventh-Grade Students at Foley High
    School. Master's thesis. St. Cloud, Minn.: St.
    Cloud State College, 1959.   1222
Ninety-nine English students served as subjects in an experiment in which one group was given no specific training in listening, one was given a unit on listening consisting of 14 daily lessons, and the third was given follow-up work after experiencing the same unit as the second group. All

Voelker, Francis H.   265

three groups improved in listening, as measured by the
Brown-Carlsen Test, but there was no significant difference
between the groups.

Vohs, John L.   Delivery and Attention: An Experimental
    Investigation. Master's thesis. Bozeman, Mont.:
    Montana State University, 1961.   1223
    The results of an experiment using 141 college speech
students show that good delivery results in the retention of
more information than poor delivery. When listeners engage
in a distracting task while listening, their retention is ad-
versely affected in direct proportion to the complexity of the
task.

Voor, John B.   The Effects of Practice upon Comprehension
    of Time-Compressed Speech. Master's thesis. Louis-
    ville, Ky.:   University of Louisville, 1962.   1224
    Using 50 college psychology students as subjects, Voor
conducted an experiment in which the students listened to
five taped stories, the rate of which had been doubled to 380
wpm by the use of a Tempo Regulator. It was found that
optimum levels of listening comprehension were reached only
after the subjects had listened to several passages. There
was a statistically significant improvement in comprehension
scores over the five trials.

Voorhees, Harold E.   "Methods of Gaining Concentration in
    Listening."   Projects of the Fourth Workshop in Basic
    Communications: University of Denver 1946. (Edited
    by Edwin L. Levy.) Denver: University of Denver
    Press, 1946, p. 71-73.   1225
    The emphasis to date has been on gaining the audience's
attention by speech techniques, but finding ways to help the
audience to acquire skills of attending would be more fruit-
ful.

Wachner, Clarence.   "Listening in an Integrated Language
    Arts Program."   Elementary English 33:491-96, Decem-
    ber 1956.   1226
    Successful listening depends on a listener's background
of information and experience and is closely linked to good
human relations. Openmindedness, which is essential, does
not mean a lack of one's own opinions.

Wade, Irene.   "The Possibilities of Teaching Listening in
    Basic Communications."   Projects of the Fourth Work-
    shop in Basic Communications, University of Denver

1946. (Edited by Edwin L. Levy.) Denver: University
of Denver Press, 1946, p. 41-45.   1227
Merely providing a listening situation is not teaching listening. It may not be possible to lengthen the span of attention, but proper training can result in bringing the listener's
mind back to the subject at hand more quickly.

Wagner, Guy, Alexander, Mildred, and Hosier, Max.
"Building Listening Power with Instructional Games."
Midland Schools 73(6):12-13+, February 1959.   1228
The following ideas for teaching listening are advanced:
1. The teacher should let the children know that he places
a high value on good listening. 2. The teacher might talk
less. 3. Normally, things should be said only once. 4.
Children should be allowed to discuss the importance of listening. 5. Oral and written summaries of material that has
been listened to should be requested. 6. Listening courtesy
should be stressed. 7. Listening should be discussed with
parents. 8. Children should make a chart of good listener
characteristics. 9. Listening games should be played at appropriate times.
Examples of games designed for instruction in listening
are given.

----, Hosier, Max, and Blackman, Mildred. Listening
Games--Building Listening Skills with Instructional
Games. Darien, Conn.: Teachers' Publishing Corpo-
ration, 1962.   1229
Games may be utilized to teach the skills of listening.
Detailed descriptions are given of 37 "easy-to-play" games;
40 games "requiring more skill;" and 34 games which "chal-
lenge top intellects."

----, and Gjerde, W.C. "Listening Too Is Important."
Midland Schools 66:18-19, March 1952.   1230
A good listener has an interest in people, hears people
out, respects the other person's right to express an opinion,
has an interest in conveying points of view, and is interested
in broadening his viewpoint rather than in merely defending
a position.

----, and Hosier, Max. "Providing Practice in Developing
Listening Power." Midland Schools 74(2):16-17, October 1959.   1231
A comprehensive list of suggestions of ways of teaching
listening is presented.

Wagner, Guy, Alexander, Mildred, and Hosier, Max   267

----, Alexander, Mildred, and Hosier, Max. Strengthening
   Fundamental Skills with Instructional Games. Cedar
   Falls, Iowa: J.S. Latta and Son, 1959.   1232
   Twenty-one games suitable for the teaching of listening
are described. A grade level from kindergarten to sixth
is suggested for each game.

----.   "What Schools Are Doing in Developing Listening Power." Education 78:247-52, December 1957.
                                                      1233
   A description of the material on the teaching of listening
found in curriculum bulletins of Tampa, New York, St. Paul,
Brentwood, Mo., Akron, and Rockville, Md.

Walker, Lalla A. "Is Anybody Listening?" Tennessee
   Teacher 21(5):6-7+, December 1953.   1234
   The lag in the teaching of listening is due to the lag in
research, but in the meantime there is much that can be
done by the classroom teacher to improve children's listening. A comprehensive and valuable list of activities is presented.

----. "Nashville Teachers Attack the Problem of Listening."
   Education 75:345-48, January 1955.   1235
   Walker reports that a taped test she devised showed
that listening skills of Nashville pupils were low at both the
elementary and the secondary levels, although there were
marked individual differences.

Wallace, Sarah L. "Who Is Listening?" Wilson Library
   Bulletin 42:295-300, November 1967.   1236
   Willingness and preparation are essential to good listening. A listener must be willing not only to hear but to
credit the speaker's integrity. Suspicion means that, in advance, the listener does not believe what the speaker will
say. Preparation for listening is based on education and
previous knowledge. Without reliable listeners, communication is fruitless.

Wallerstein, Harvey. "Electromyographic Study of Attentive
   Listening." Canadian Journal of Psychology 8:228-38,
   December 1954.   1237
   In an experiment designed to investigate muscular activity during sustained attention, two groups of subjects were
requested to listen to three successive presentations of a recorded detective story and a philosophical essay. Results
showed rising gradients of tension from forehead to chin

throughout the course of listening. Listening to the story
tended to produce increases of greater magnitude than did
listening to the essay. Forearm muscles failed to show any
clear variations during listening. The author suggests that
the rising gradients of muscle tension may be associated
with increased comprehension or organization of incoming
verbal material which may take place during listening.

Wance, William W. "Supervisors Must Know How to Lis-
    ten." Journal of the American Society of Training Di-
    rectors 9(2):19-21+, March-April 1955.   1238
    The author describes an eleven-session course for first-
line supervisors and management personnel on the importance
of listening in interview situations.

Warland, Steven Guy. An Experimental Study of the Effect
    of Visual Delivery Upon Listener Response to the Oral
    Interpretation of Literature. Master's thesis. Lincoln,
    Neb.: University of Nebraska, 1966.   1239
    An oral presentation of poetry and prose by two readers,
in person and on tape, was listened to by 98 interpretive
speech students, divided into four groups. It was found that
visual delivery was superior in aesthetic response, degree
of interest, and quality of technique.

Washington State Speech Association. A Guidebook for Teach-
    ing Speaking and Listening in the Senior High School.
    Seattle: University of Washington Press, 1960.   1240
    An outline of procedures, methods, and specific tech-
niques for teaching listening skills at the high school level is
given on pages 11-15.

Watkins, Merle Catherine. Factors in the Relationships of
    Listening, Reading, and Intelligence of 250 Second-
    Grade Students of Des Moines, Iowa. Master's thesis.
    Des Moines, Iowa: Drake University, 1960.   1241
    Watkins reports correlations of .46 between listening and
reading and .43 between listening and Otis Intelligence Test
score.

Watts, Marjorie S. "Do You Listen?" Senior Scholastic
    Teacher's Edition 48:17-18, April 8, 1947.   1242
    Listening implies participation, while hearing alone does
not.

Waugh, Evelyn. "The Amenities in America." Atlantic
    Monthly 183:79-80, January 1949.   1243

A humorous criticism of Americans' failure to listen.

Waugh, Rosalind. Listening, A Key to Third-Grade.
  Master's thesis. Newark, N.J.: New Jersey State
  Teachers College at Newark, 1955.   1244

Weatherhead, Arliene LaVerne. A Survey of Significant
  Publications in the Area of Listening and an Evaluation
  of Their Significance in Understanding the Listening
  Process. Master's thesis. Sacramento, Calif.: Sacramento State College, 1962.   1245
  A bibliography of 149 items on listening published since
1955, including 57 items in books on speech and other subjects. A useful summary of the content is made under the
headings of psychological, philosophical, and "semantologi-
cal" factors. An analysis of the art of listening, based on
the contents of the reviewed literature, discusses the essential elements of listening, the poor listener, the speaker's
responsibility, the good listener, and the teaching of listening.

Weaver, Wendell William. An Examination of Some Differences in Oral and Written Language Using the Cloze
  Procedure. Doctoral dissertation. Athens, Ga.: University of Georgia, 1961. Abstract: Dissertation Abstracts 22:2702, 1962.   1246
  Selections from the Davis Reading Test and the STEP
Listening Test were presented orally and in writing. Cloze
testing was used. It is reported that there was a significant difference in test performance between passages read
and passages listened to, in favor of the former. There
was no difference in the test results between passages taken
from the Davis test, which were assumed to have been prepared for reading, and those taken from the STEP test,
which were assumed to have been prepared for listening.
  The author summarizes his findings as follows: "When
the subject reads, the sequence is under his control. If he
listens, its sequence is under the control of the speaker.
The reader can determine rate, repetition, redundancy, and
the nature of the sequence to examine and re-examine. He
has certain clues in the graphology (e.g. to, two, too)
which are not present in the aural presentation. In the aural situation the listener must conform to the rate, repetition, redundancy and sequence of the speaker. Unless he is
able to review the input from the speaker internally, he has
no control in a formal situation. Memory, then would seem
to be an important factor in listening. Miller theorizes that

meaningful material is "clumped" for storage; and thus while
delayed recall does not produce exact duplicates of large
amount of input information, it reproduces an equivalent coding. The equivalent coding is noisier (that is, it contains
more idiosyncracies) than the written form of the original
message; and this noise seems to lower the predictability of
long segments when transmitted aurally."

----. "The Predictability of Omissions in Reading and Lis-
    tening." Problems, Programs, and Projects in College-
    Adult Reading. Eleventh Yearbook of the National Read-
    ing Conference. Milwaukee: National Reading Confer-
    ence Inc., 1962. p. 148-53.   1247
    It is estimated that the maximum informational trans-
mission of impromptu speech is about 26 bits of information
per second. Silent reading's maximum capacity is between
44 and 50 bits of information per second. The reader has
the advantage of spatial and sequential clues. A discussion
of types of redundancy in both reading and listening is also
found here.

Webb, Wilse B. and Wallon, Edward J. "Comprehension by
    Reading Versus Hearing." Journal of Applied Psychol-
    ogy 40:237-40, August 1956.   1248
    For a group of male college students, reading unfamiliar
story material was more effective than listening. Comprehension and retention were measured by a true-false test.

Webber, Guylene Blair. A Study of the Changes of Auditory
    Word Recognition Scores of First Grade Children Follow-
    ing Training in Focused Listening Comprehension.
    Master's thesis. Denton, Tex.: Texas Women's Uni-
    versity, 1964.   1249
    Twenty-five children received listening instruction, which
is described in detail. The gain of this group in word recognition skills and in other respects was greater than that of
the control group.

Wehr, Olive. "Why Johnny Doesn't Listen." Montana Edu-
    cation 34(3):7, November 1957.   1250

Weinland, James D. and Gross, Margaret V. Personnel
    Interviewing. New York: Ronald Press, 1952, passim.
                                                        1251
    Most ineffective interviewing occurs when an interviewer
only pretends to listen and responds automatically with
cliches. When the interviewer listens intelligently and pa-

tiently, the interviewee will often solve his own problems by talking them out.

Weir, Sister Mary Edith. Development of the Listening Skills in the English Program of the Primary Grades. Master's thesis. Cleveland, Ohio: St. John College, 1957.   1252
A content analysis of a set of language textbooks shows that ample material exists for the teaching of conversational, appreciative, exploratory, and critical listening.

Weir, Thomas A. A Study of the Listening Vocabulary of Children in the First, Fourth, and Sixth Grades in the Elementary School. Doctoral dissertation. Columbus, Ohio: Ohio State University, 1951.   1253
This is an extensive and carefully performed survey of the listening vocabulary of 900 St. Louis elementary school children. Using various word lists (Buckingham-Dolch, Dale, and Thorndike Lorge), Weir examined the vocabulary ranges in grades one through eight and their relationships to the word lists. He also examined the relationships between an established written vocabulary word list (Rinsland) and the relationship of vocabulary to amount of radio and television listening experiences. The findings are very extensive and tend to show a lower level of vocabulary than is generally considered likely. Weir advances a number of reasons for this discrepancy. In his conclusions he emphasizes the great individual differences found, the varying relationship between reading and listening vocabularies found at different grade levels, and the formulation of a desirable criterion for amount of vocabulary needed for various school purposes.

Weisberger, Robert A. and Rasmussen, Warren. "A Teaching System for Music Listening." Audiovisual Instruction 11:106-09, February 1966.   1254
A programmed instructional device known as the "Edex Teaching System" is described in detail. It is reported to produce good results in terms of improved listening abilities.

Weiss, Debrah. "Listening Comprehension." Reading Teacher 20:639-47, April 1967.   1255
A review of research on the relationship between reading and listening, on conditions affecting listening comprehension, and on ways to improve listening. 31-item bibliography.

Weissman, Stuart L. and Crockett, Walter H. "Intersensory
Transfer of Verbal Material." American Journal of
Psychology 70:283-85, June 1957.   1256
Auditory training in nonsense syllables increased visual
recognition of these syllables. Thirty subjects were used.

Weitzman, Elliot D., Fishbein, William, and Graziani,
Leonard. "Auditory Evoked Responses Obtained from the
Scalp Electroencephalogram of the Full-Term Human
Neonate During Sleep." Pediatrics 35:458-62, March
1965.   1257
Sleeping neonates showed electrical responses to auditory
stimuli on the encephalograph. The subjects ranged in age from
1.5 hours to 15 days.

Welch, Isom Lin. An Investigation of the Listening Proficiency of Stutterers. Doctoral dissertation. Columbia,
Mo.: University of Missouri, 1960. Abstract: Dissertation Abstracts 21:270-71, 1960.   1258
Using as subjects 20 college students who were stutterers and 20 who were not, and the STEP Test as a measure
of listening, Welch found, in a carefully performed experiment, that there was no evidence to support the frequent
statements of speech pathologists that stutterers are less
efficient listeners than non-stutterers.

Wells, Charlotte. "The Child's Equipment for Language
Growth." National Conference on Research in English.
Factors That Influence Language Growth. Chicago:
National Council of Teachers of English, 1953, p. 1-8.
                                                    1259
This is a good discussion of children's early develop-
ment in the use of language and of the vital role listening
plays in that development.

Welsh, George B. An Investigation of Some Predictive Factors in Auding Ability. Doctoral dissertation. Pittsburgh, Pa.: University of Pittsburgh, 1954. Abstract:
Dissertation Abstracts 14:2407-08, 1954 and Speech
Monographs 22:153, June 1955.   1260
Sixty first- through third-grade children were tested in
various areas. The auditory subtests of the Monroe Reading
Aptitude Test and the Durrell-Sullivan Reading Capacity Test
were used as measures of listening. Ratings by parents,
teachers and classmates were obtained on each child's listening and speaking skills. As the result of a factor analysis, the author concludes that listening ability is a central

factor with no direct relation to reading ability and that it is
adequately measured by the tests used.

Wesley, Peggy Hearst. A Study of the Relationship Between
    Listening Performance and Aspects of the Personality
    Structure. Master's thesis. Columbus, Ohio: Ohio
    State University, 1964.   1261
    Administration of the STEP Listening Test and the Ros-
enzweig Picture-Frustration Study to 251 fourth- and fifth-
grade pupils showed a significant difference between grades
on the STEP but not on the Rosenzweig.

West, Dorothy Ardythe. Report of Progress Toward the Ex-
    perimental Development of an Elementary Evaluative
    Listening Test. Master's thesis. Brookings, S.D.:
    South Dakota State College, 1958.   1262
    This is a description of a carefully developed test of
critical listening based on taped passages followed by questions on theme, suggested action, ideas and supporting material. Text of test is given.

Westover, Frederick L. "A Comparison of Listening and
    Reading as a Means of Testing." Journal of Educational
    Research 52:23-26, September 1958.   1263
    Using 198 college psychology students as subjects, West-
over reports no group differences in oral or written administration of tests during a semester, although differences between students were consistent. Students tended to prefer
the written form.

Wever, Ernest Glen. "Hearing." Annual Review of Psychol-
    ogy 2:65-78, 1951.   1264
    Lists 94 references.

----. "Hearing." Annual Review of Psychology 13:225-50,
    1962   1265
    Lists 201 references.

Whan, Forest L. "Training in Listening and in Voice and
    Diction for the Airplane Pilot." Quarterly Journal of
    Speech 30:262-65, October 1944.   1266
    Whan advocates repeated practice under simulated flight
conditions as the best way to teach listening to pilots.

Wheeler, Lester R. and Wheeler, Viola D. "Some Charac-
    teristic Differences and Similarities Among the Language
    Arts." Journal of Education 138(1):2-8, October 1955.

1267
The natural skills of speaking and listening are more important than reading and writing. Listening ability can be
used as a measure of reading potential.

Whitfield, George W. Listening Instruction a Factor in Im-
    proving Listening Comprehension. Doctoral dissertation.
    Fayetteville, Ark.: University of Arkansas, 1964. Ab-
    stract: Dissertation Abstracts 25:1796, 1964.   1268
Using the Brown-Carlsen as a measure of listening, the
author found that an experimental group given daily listening
lessons for six weeks scored significantly better than a control group. The subjects were 130 basic speech course students. No pre-test was given.

Whittaker, Margie E. A Comparison of an Auditory Projec-
    tive Technique and a Paper-Pencil Questionnaire with
    Respect to Hostility. Master's thesis. Seattle: Uni-
    versity of Washington, 1964.   1269
An auditory projective test was constructed, consisting
of ten sounds presented on tape. Eighty-four subjects were
asked to respond to these sounds by writing stories about
each. Subjects had been selected on the basis of their performance on the Sarason Hostility Scale. The projective test
appeared to distinguish with high reliability between those
scoring high and low on the Sarason scale.

Whyte, William H. Is Anybody Listening? New York:
    Simon and Schuster, 1952.   1270
This book is about communication in business. Much of
what is said is relevant to the listening phase of communication but the book is not, as the title indicates, primarily
concerned with listening.
The sheer act of listening may in itself at times be far
more effective than anything said. The fine art of listening
remains one of the most overlooked tools of management.

Widener, Ralph W. A Preliminary Study of the Effects of
    Training in Listening. Master's thesis. Norman, Okla.:
    University of Oklahoma, 1950.   1271
This is a description of a manual for teaching listening
which consists largely of exhortatory passages.

Wiksell, Wesley A. "Problems of Listening." Quarterly
    Journal of Speech 32:505-08, December 1946.   1272
A very good summary of the nature of listening, the different kinds of listening, and the relationship between listen-

ing and reading.

Wikstrom, Walter S. "Lessons in Listening." Conference
    Board Record 2(4):17-20, April 1965.   1273
    Training in listening is discussed both in general terms
and with specific reference to the Basic Systems' taped
course, which is said to be extremely satisfactory. The listening improvement due to this course still was in effect
several months later as verified by testing at Pfizer Co.

Wilkie, LeRoy and Vervalin, Charles. "The Elusive Art of
    Listening: Part 1. Listen Your Way to Supervisory
    Success." Hydrocarbon Processing and Petroleum Re-
    finer 41(8):146-50, August 1962.   1274
    In listening to a speech, listen for content and ignore a
speaker's delivery. Seek something in the talk that is meaningful to you. Look for key ideas and avoid getting emotionally involved with the topic. Avoid taking too many notes
and make a conscious effort to develop good listening habits.
The good listener does not shy away from difficult subjects.
Just as in psychoanalysis, the listener should not lead, but
he should allow the speaker to find his own solutions.

----, and   ----.   "The Elusive Art of Listen-
    ing: Part 2. You Can Breach the 'Semantic Barrier!'."
    Hydrocarbon Processing and Petroleum Refiner 41(9):
    268-72, September 1962.   1275
    To improve your comprehension of a speaker's message,
improve your vocabulary, look for hidden meanings, do not
let mispronunciations by the speaker affect your getting
meaning, look for illogical comparisons. An important factor in good listening is memory. Review immediately after
listening is helpful.

----, and ----. "The Elusive Art of Listening: Part 3.
    How Humble Oil Taught Good Listening." Hydrocarbon
    Processing and Petroleum Refiner 41(11):250-55, Novem-
    ber 1962.   1276
    This is a description of a 14-month listening course
consisting of a two-hour session every other week. The
Brown-Carlsen Listening Test was used as a pre- and post-
test. An improvement of 15 per cent was noted. A list of
the recorded material used for exercises is included.

Williams, Catherine Walker. A Study of the Relationships
    Between Language Achievement and Listening Abilities
    of Sixth Grade Pupils of West Savannah School, Savannah,

Georgia. Master's thesis. Atlanta: Atlanta University,
1956.   1277

Williams, Frederick Dowell. An Experimental Application
of the Semantic Differential and "Cloze" Procedure as
Measurement Techniques in Listening Comprehension.
Doctoral dissertation. Los Angeles: University of
Southern California, 1962. Abstract: Speech Monographs
30:191, August 1963 and Dissertation Abstracts 23:2628-
29, 1963. Summary: Dickens, Milton and Williams,
Frederick. "An Experimental Application of 'Cloze'
Procedures and Attitude Measures to Listening Comprehension." Speech Monographs 31:103-08, June 1964.
                                                         1278
Using as subjects 253 college speech students, Williams
found that attitudes toward the subject matter of two expository speeches had little effect on comprehension or retention. On one selection the results of a multiple choice test
and a test requiring replacement of deleted words correlated
very highly, but on the other selection there was no significant relationship.

Williams, Maurice Mitchell. Improvement of Listening
Through Special Methods and Techniques. Master's thesis. Atlanta: Atlanta University, 1958.   1279
Using 32 fourth-grade pupils as subjects and the STEP
Test as a measure of listening, Williams reports that the
group given six weeks of listening instruction showed a significantly greater improvement in listening than did the control group.

Williams, S.G. "You Hear with Your Mind." Textile
World 109(10):103+, October 1959.   1280
To check on the effectiveness of a listener ask him to
repeat what has been said or to answer questions about it.
If one is going to listen at all, one should do so entirely.
Practice in repeating what one listens to will develop one's
listening skills.

Willis, La Wanda. Development of Listening Skills as an
Element of the Elementary Language Arts Program.
Master's thesis. Brownsville, Tex.: Howard Payne University, 1963.   1281
On the basis of a thorough examination of some of the
literature on listening, including textbooks on elementary
school teaching methods, the author presents a comprehensive plan for the teaching of listening in the elementary school.

Wilmer, Harry A. "An Auditory Sound Association Technique." Science 114:621-22, December 7, 1951. 1282
An auditory projective test, made up of 21 different kinds
of sounds and combinations of sounds, is described. No results of administering the test are given.

----, and Husni, May. "The Use of Sounds in a Projective
Test." Journal of Consulting Psychology 17:377-83, October 1953.   1283
A recorded projective test is described. Sample protocols are included.

Wilson, Alan R. Construction and Evaluation of a Test of Lis-
ening Abilities for the Third Through Sixth Grades. Master's thesis. Berkeley: University of California, 1955.
1284
The construction and validation of a listening test are described. Text of the test is not included.

Wilson, Wm. Charles. Some Interrelationships of Verbal and
Musical Abilities in Elementary School Children. Doctoral
dissertation. Berkeley: University of California, 1960.
Excerpts: Listening: Readings. (Edited by Sam Duker.)
Metuchen, N.J.: Scarecrow Press, 1966. p. 442-48. 1285
Using 369 sixth-grade pupils as subjects, Wilson administered the STEP Listening Test and several tests of music. The
correlations between listening and the various items in the
music tests were low but positive. The author concludes
that while the factor analysis showed separate factors of listening and musicality, there must be a common factor of a
general nature which contributes to skill in both.

Wilt, Miriam E. "Let's Teach Listening." Creative Ways
of Teaching the Language Arts. Leaflet 4. Champaign,
Ill.: National Council of Teachers of English, 1957.
1286
The first step in teaching listening is for the teacher to
examine her own listening habits. "Children learn best those
things they live and do; they learn from each other. They
cannot learn how to speak by listening entirely to the teacher
speak, nor can they learn to listen to their peers when they
seldom have the opportunity to listen to their peers." A
number of activities useful in teaching listening are listed.

----. "Listening Skills Can Be Improved." Instructor
72(5):6+, January 1963.   1287
Although children listen when they first come to school,

they do not do so objectively, appreciatively, or critically.
To teach them to do so is the task of the school. What the
child is asked to listen to in school should be worthy of
time and thought. Without pre- and post-discussion, listening skills will not improve by the mere act of listening.

----. "Speaking and Listening in the Elementary School."
Pennsylvania University Schoolmen's Week Proceedings,
1951:132-38.   1288
A particularly harmful classroom practice is that of having children listen to material being read aloud that they
have already read silently.

----. A Study of Teacher Awareness of Listening as a Fac-
tor in Elementary Education. Doctoral dissertation.
State College, Pa.: Pennsylvania State College, 1949.
Abstract: Abstracts of Doctoral Dissertations, Pennsylvania State College 12:229-33, 1949. Summary: Journal
of Educational Research 43:626-36, April 1950, and The
Teaching of Listening and Why. Monograph on Language
Arts, No. 66. New York: Row-Peterson, 1951. Excerpts: Listening: Readings. (Edited by Sam Duker.)
Metuchen, N.J.: Scarecrow Press, 1966. p. 63-80.
                                                           1289
In answer to a questionnaire, teachers estimated that
elementary pupils spent 77 minutes per day in listening. Observations in 18 classrooms showed that children were expected to listen an average of 158 minutes a day. Of this
time 54 per cent was spent in listening to the teacher.
Sixty-one per cent of the teachers rated reading as the most
important language art skill; 16 per cent ranked listening as
the most important.

----. "Teach Listening?" Grade Teacher 81(8):51+, April
1964.   1290
Merely hearing words does not assure perception. Definite teaching techniques are required to teach skills of selective, accurate, critical, and appreciative listening. Teaching is necessary to prevent deterioration of listening skills.
A busy, active classroom is best for learning to listen.
Teachers need to know more about children's listening than
tests will reveal. Anecdotal records are valuable for this
purpose.

----. "Teaching of Listening and Why." Educational
Screen 31:144-46+, April 1952.   1291
Shared listening experiences are the best activities for

the teaching of listening.

----. "What Is the Listening Ratio in Your Classroom?"
    Elementary English 26:259-64, May 1949.   1292
    A plea to teachers to analyze the listening situation in
their classrooms. Listening is not a cure-all but it can
help learning if properly employed.

Winges, Sara A. The Intelligibility of Interrupted Speech.
    Bachelor's thesis. Louisville, Ky.: University of Louis-
    ville, 1963.   1293
    An experiment is described in which speech was inter-
rupted once every 50 milliseconds. It was found that intelligibility declined rapidly from the point where over 60 per
cent of the original material was deleted.

Winkler, Pauline A. "Psychology of Listening." Education
    on the Air, Fifth Yearbook. Columbus, Ohio: Institute
    for Education by Radio, 1937, p. 347-49.   1294
    Winkler deplores the lack of information available about
listening in 1937.

Winkles, Blanche. The Development of a Listening Test for
    Grades Two Through Six. Master's thesis. Glassboro,
    N.J.: Glassboro State College, 1963.   1295
    The construction and validation of the Vidal Listening
Test are described. Text of the test is included.   •

Winter, Clotilda. "Listening and Learning." Elementary
    English 43:569-72, October 1966.   1296
    The STEP Listening Test was administered to 563 pupils
in 26 fourth, fifth, and sixth-grade classes. No significant
difference was found between the scores of the fourth and
fifth grades, but significant differences were found between
the scores of the fourth and sixth grades and between the
fifth and sixth grades. A number of correlations are reported.

Winters, Alice Swaggerty. Research in Four Areas of Lan-
    guage Arts: Oral Composition, Written Composition,
    Listening, and Usage Completed from 1950 Through
    1961. Master's thesis. Lawrence, Kansas: University
    of Kansas, 1962.   1297
    Full abstracts are given of eleven research studies in
listening.

Wirth, Myrtle. A Review of Research in Listening Develop-

ment in Intermediate Grades. Master's thesis. Man-
hattan, Kan.: Kansas State University, 1962.   1298
  On the basis of an examination of 43 references on listening, which are discussed and analyzed, the author presents a plan for teaching listening in the elementary school
intermediate grades.

Wiseman, Gordon and Barker, Larry. Speech--Interperson-
  al Communication. San Francisco: Chandler, 1967.
  p. 234-54.   1299
  A 49-frame program for the teaching of listening skills.

Withrow, Eleanor M. The Effect of Training in Listening
  upon Achievement in Reading. Master's thesis. Greeley, Colo.: Colorado State College of Education, 1950.
                                                    1300
  Sixty-four junior high school remedial reading pupils
served as subjects in an experiment in which one group was
given regular reading instruction and one was given listening
instruction instead. There were 30 lessons for each group
over a period of six months. At the end of the period the
groups were equal in reading for general significance, reading to predict outcomes, and reading to follow directions,
but the group that had had the listening instruction was significantly better than the other group in reading to note details.

Wittich, W.A. Why Won't Willie Listen? Randolph, Wisc.:
  Educators Progress Service, n.d.   1301
  The author states that the schools devote adequate time
to perfecting reading skills, but there is an almost complete
disregard of methodological approaches to the perfection of
listening. This is ironical since so much learning takes
place through listening. Some techniques useful in teaching
listening: 1. Alerting pupils to their responsibility to be
good listeners. 2. Acquainting learners with listening re-
sponsibilities to be assumed for certain types of classroom
activities. 3. Teaching note-taking and outlining skills.
4. Advising listeners that there is a difference between listening for important and for unimportant information.

Witty, Paul A. and Sizemore, Robert A. "Studies in Listening." Elementary English 35:538-52, December 1958;
  36:59-70, January 1959; 36:130-40, February 1959;
  36:297-301, May 1959. Excerpts: Listening: Readings
  (Edited by Sam Duker.) Metuchen, N.J.: Scarecrow
  Press, 1966. p. 406-12.   1302

An excellent review of research on listening as compared to reading as a medium for learning.

Woliung, Dorothy Cole. Listening: Its Relationship with Intelligence. Master's thesis. Normal, Ill.: Illinois State Normal University, 1962.   1303
A correlation of .61 between listening, as measured by the STEP Test, and intelligence, as measured by the Kuhlmann-Finch Intelligence Test, is reported. The subjects were 54 intermediate-grade elementary school pupils.

Wood, C. David. Comprehension of Compressed Speech by Elementary School Children. Report on Title VII, Project Number 1300, Grant No. 7-24-0210-263. Bloomington, Ind.: Indiana University, 1965. Also Doctoral dissertation. Bloomington, Ind.: Indiana University, 1965. Abstract: Dissertation Abstracts 27:336A-37A, 1966.   1304
Ninety elementary pupils, divided equally among the first, third, and fifth grades, served as subjects. Fifty short imperative sentences, at a variety of compressed rates varying from 175 to 400 wpm, served as stimuli. The child's compliance with the command was used as a measure of comprehension. As the rate of presentation increased, comprehension decreased. At no presentation rate was the level of comprehension below 75%. Average comprehension was 94% for the fifth grade, 92% for the third grade, and 84% for the first grade. The effect of intelligence test scores on comprehension was not statistically significant.

Wood, Marion. "Methods That Open Doors for the Professional Secretary: 2. Do You Help Build the Professional Secretary's Listening Quotient?" Business Education World 43(5):27-29, January 1963.   1305
Listening is an essential characteristic of the professional secretary. There is no best way to build listening skills. A number of suggestions, including giving instructions on tape, practice in typing to dictation, oral tests, and giving instruction in note taking, are given.

Woods, L.E. "On the Art of Listening." Personnel Journal 36:303-04, January 1958.   1306
In listening it is necessary to look beyond the sounds and words for the facts and the realistic meaning of the words used. It is necessary to distinguish between the description and the interpretation of an event.

Worcester, D.A. "The Ability to Follow Oral and Written
    Directions." Educational Research Bulletin 4:250-51,
    September 9, 1925.   1307
    In an experiment in the administration of the Army Alpha
examination involving 220 subjects, Worcester found a significant difference in favor of oral over written directions.

----. "Memory by Visual and Auditory Presentation."
    Journal of Educational Psychology 16:18-27, January
    1925.   1308
    A good review of previous studies on the relative merits
of learning by visual means as compared to aural means.
An experiment involving 13 subjects is reported which shows
no significant difference between the two modes.

Wright, C.W. "Lively Listening Training." Newsletter
    Business and Professional Speaking Interest Group SAA.
    November 1962, p. 3-4.   1309
    In a reply to an article by Petrie, Wright states that
businessmen do improve their listening as a result of instruction. He decries efforts to require statistically sup-
ported proof of every such improvement.

Wright, Evan Leonard. The Construction of a Test of Lis-
    tening Comprehension for the Second, Third and Fourth
    Grades. Doctoral dissertation. St. Louis, Mo.: Wash-
    ington University, 1957. Abstract: Dissertation Ab-
    stracts 17:2226-27, 1957.   1310
    This is a thorough and carefully done account of the
preparation of a listening test for the early elementary
grades. Wright reports a reliability of .84 and bases his
claim to validity on satisfactory correlations with teacher
ratings, pupil ratings, the Durrell-Sullivan Reading Capacity
Test, and the Nashville test. The population to which the
test was given consisted of 152 second-graders, 163 third-
graders, and 173 fourth-graders.

Wright, Milton. The Art of Conversation. New York: Mc-
    Graw-Hill, 1936, p. 293-318.   1311
    An attentive, sympathetic, and alert listener is an asset
to a conversation.

Wygand, Leonora. The Relationship of Reading Comprehen-
    sion to Listening Comprehension. Master's thesis.
    New York: Queens College, 1966.   1312
    A third-grade class was given thirty 15-minute lessons
on listening, which consisted of reading aloud the McCall-

Crabbe Standard Test Lessons and asking the children to
check correct answers. No significant difference was found
in the performance of this group on the Durrell-Sullivan
Reading Test and a control group.

Wynn, Dale Richard. "Children Should Be Seen and Not
    Heard." New York State Education 41:353-56, February
    1954.   1313
    When teachers listen to children they learn about them,
and they also give children a sense of security and acceptance.

----. "A Good Listener." NEA Journal 42:502, November
    1953.   1314
    A school superintendent, to be a good listener, should
listen to an entire problem before reacting, take time to listen to people, refrain from arguing, listen for what is not
said, relax, express appreciation for the bringing of a problem to him, and make himself available.

Yaeger, Sister Miriam. Listening: Its Measurement and
    Relation to Intelligence of Primary Children. Master's
    thesis. Milwaukee: Cardinal Stritch College, 1958.
                                                       1315
    Yaeger formulated a listening test, the text of which is
given, for primary children. She administered it to 2,000
parochial school children. She reports a correlation with
the Lorge Thorndike Intelligence Test of .57.

Yates, Paul S. The Relation between Reading Recognition
    Vocabulary and Hearing Recognition Vocabulary and
    Their Respective Correlations with Intelligence. Master's
    thesis. St. Louis: Washington University, 1937. 1316
    Yates reports that intelligence is more highly correlated
with reading than with oral vocabulary. The reading vocabulary is less than the hearing vocabulary up to the fifth
grade, about equal in the fifth grade and larger thereafter.
These findings are based on the administration of the Word
Meaning section of the Stanford Reading Test to 25 pupils in
each grade from three to six.

Yoakam, Richard E. The Effect of Vocabulary Difficulty up-
    on the Comprehension of Radio News. Master's thesis.
    Iowa City, Iowa: State University of Iowa, 1947. 1317
    Tests involving three versions of a radio news story
were administered to 578 high school pupils. Comprehension
was in direct proportion to the difficulty level of the vocabu-

lary used.

"You CAN Remember What You Hear." Modern Materials
    Handling 18(2):81, February 1963.   1318
    Listening involves self discipline, an alert mind, and
practice. A good way to improve listening effectiveness is
to analyze speeches on radio and television. Evaluate the
arguments given and isolate the propaganda techniques used.

Young, James D. An Experimental Comparison of Vocabu-
    lary Growth by Means of Oral Reading, Silent Reading,
    and Listening. Doctoral dissertation. Los Angeles:
    University of Southern California, 1951. Excerpts:
    Speech Monographs 20:273-76, November 1953.   1319
    Using 150 college students as subjects, Young reports
that students required to read passages aloud showed a significantly greater improvement in vocabulary than did a
group who read the passages silently. Both groups performed better than a group to whom the passages were read.

Young, William E. The Relation of Reading Comprehension
    and Retention to Hearing Comprehension and Retention.
    Doctoral dissertation. Iowa City, Iowa: State Univer-
    sity of Iowa, 1930. Summary: Journal of Experimental
    Education 5:30-39, September 1936.   1320
    Using 24 classes of fourth, fifth, and sixth grades in six
school systems as subjects, Young found that better comprehension of passages resulted when the passages were read
to the pupils than when they read them themselves.

Zeligs, Rose. Glimpses into Child Life. New York: Wil-
    liam Morrow, 1942. Chapter 11, "Learning to Listen,"
    p. 97-104.   1321

Zelko, Harold P. Are You a Good Listener? New London,
    Conn.: National Foremen's Institute, 1955.   1322
    A good listener refrains from interruptions, premature
comments, probing questions, and direct advice. Barriers
to good listening include: daydreaming; disregard of speaker's background; letting personal feelings govern reaction;
dislike of speaker; listening in order to reply rather than in
order to understand; resisting change; and letting one's mind
wander. Ten basic rules for good listening are given:
1. Realize the values of listening. 2. Analyze your faults--
and correct them. 3. Eliminate the barriers. 4. Develop
a listening attitude. 5. Dispel your prejudices while listening. 6. Listen for understanding. 7. Listen alertly.

8. Listen for purpose and ideas. 9. Evaluate facts and
opinion. 10. Reply pleasantly--and apply what you've heard.

----. "Art of Listening." Rotarian 87:27, December 1955.
                                                        1323
    A popularized account of the importance of listening.

----. "Ask Them What They Think--Then Listen." Super-
    visory Management 1(4):37-41, March 1956.   1324
The best tool available to management for obtaining
ideas of subordinates is listening. Eight barriers to good
listening are listed: status of speaker and listener; attitudes
and prejudices; "I" versus "You" feelings; desire to contra-
dict rather than to understand; desire to keep things as they
are; physical conditions; language; and rate of speaking and
listening.

----. "Guide to Good Listening." The County Agent and
    Vocational Agriculture Teacher 15:41-43, October 1959.
                                                        1325
    Six guides to better listening are discussed: 1. Develop
a positive attitude about listening. 2. Regard listening as
an active skill. 3. Concentrate on the message. 4. Sift
facts from inference and opinion. 5. Try to be open-minded.
6. Ask questions.

----. How To Be a Better Listener. New York: A Help
    Yourself Booklet, 1958.   1326
    An excellent summary of information about listening,
which includes a discussion of why we don't listen, reasons
for listening, attitude, and physical and mental tools for listening.

----. "An Outline of the Role of Listening in Communica-
    tion." Journal of Communication 4:71-75, Fall 1954.
                                                        1327
    An excellent summary of the role of listening.

----. "You Can Be a Good Listener." Parade, September
    22, 1957. p. 12-13.   1328
    Good listening is necessary in both personal and busi-
ness life. To become a good listener: 1. Stop being preoccupied with yourself. 2. Don't let your dislike for a person keep you from getting his message. 3. Don't be eager
to talk. 4. Cultivate the art of positive rather than passive
listening. 5. Ask questions. A 10-question quiz is included.

Zemlin, W.R. "The Use of Bandwidth and Time Compression for the Hearing Handicapped." Proceedings of the Louisville Conference on Time Compressed Speech, October 19-21, 1966. (Edited by Emerson Foulke.) Louisville, Ky.: Center for Rate Controlled Recordings; University of Louisville, 1967, p. 95-97.   1329

After extensive experimentation with slow-played speech combined with a proportional amount of time compression, the author concludes that "recognition of speech material is dependent upon frequency patterns rather than frequency distribution per se; that restoration of time on band-width compressed speech at least partly overcomes the distortion effects; and, finally, frequency shifts beyond a certain amount, regardless of time restoration, seems to transcend a listener's realistic and previous language experience, and the listener's common experience of human speech. When this realm is transcended, intelligibility suffers."

Ziemann, Norman Carl. A Study of the Communication Courses in Selected Colleges and Universities in the United States. Doctoral dissertation. Evanston, Ill.: Northwestern University, 1960.   1330

A survey of communication courses given at 80 colleges revealed that there was almost universal inclusion of listening improvement as one of the principal goals, but only lip service to this goal was given in most cases.

Zimmerman, George H. "Listen." Music Educators Journal 47(6):29-31, June-July 1961.   1331

Listening to music and listening to the spoken word require exactly the same mental processes. The teacher must be a good listener and make children's listening experiences stimulating in both cases.

Zinkin, Vivian. "An Experiment in Listening." Clearing House 31:482-86, April 1957.   1332

A fairly long passage on John Dryden was read to 67 students. Only 33 were able to state the central idea. This way of learning was approved by 32 students and disapproved by 28.

Author Index to Entries

Aborn, Murray 1025
Abrams, Arnold Gerald 1
Abrahamson, Leonard S. 2
Achtenhagen, Olga 3
Adams, Harlen M. 4, 5, 6, 7, 8
Adams, John 9
Adkins, Leslie Gene 10
Adler, Mortimer J. 11
Ainslee, Douglas 12
Ainsworth, Stanley 13, 14
Alcott, Myra H. 15
Alexander, Mildred 1228, 1232
Allen, Hugh S. Jr. 16
Allison, James M. 17
Alston, Fannie C. 18
Altshuler, Morton W. 19
Amato, Anthony J. 92
Anderson, Harold A. 20, 21, 22
Anderson, Irving H. 23
Anderson, Jack Charles 24
Anderson, Lorena 25
Anderson, Rhea 26
Andrade, Manuel 27
Anilla, Sister Mary 28
Anunson, Duane Harley 29
Appell, Clara 30
Appell, Morey 30
Applegate, Mauree 31, 32
Armacost, George H. 111
Armentrout, W. D. 35
Armstrong, Hubert Coslet 36
Armstrong, Martin 37
Arndt, C. O. 38
Arnold, Margaret 39
Arnold, Robert Lloyd 40

Artley, A. S. 42
Asher, James John 43
Asher, James J. 44
Atkinson, Chester J. 45
Austin, Martha Lou 46
Auston, John T. 47

Bailey, Robert B. 1221
Bakan, Paul 48
Baker, Howard S. 49
Baker, William D. 50
Baldauf, Robert John 51
Ball, Thomas S. 52
Ballenger, Marcus Taylor 53
Bang, Read 54
Bar, Asher 55
Barbara, Dominick A. 56, 57, 58, 59
Barbe, Walter 60
Barker, Larry L. 62, 1299
Bateman, David 63
Bateman, Dorothy 716
Bates, Gregory 1028
Beach, Barbara R. 275
Beardsley, Paul W. 64
Beattie, Willieam Edward 65
Beery, Althea 66, 67, 68
Beighley, Kenneth C. 69, 70
Bennett, Delmond N. 1183
Berkowitz, Alan 589, 591
Bernardoni, Louis C. 52
Bellamy, Martha J. L. 71
Bennett, Clayton L. 72
Benoit, Robert W. 73
Berarducci, Joanne 74
Berg, Paul C. 75
Berry, David R. 76
Bixler, Ray H. 421, 424
Biggins, Mildred E. 77

287

Biggs, Bernice Prince 78
(also see Bernice Prince)
Bird, Donald E. 79, 80, 81,
82, 83, 84, 107, 816
Bischoff, Robert W. 85
Bixler, Ray H. 86
Black, James Menzies 87
Black, John W. 88
Blackman, Mildred 1229
Blain, Beryl Bruce 89
Blair, Herbert 90
Blake, Howard E. 91, 92
Blake, Marie Frances 93
Bland, Merton Lois 94
Blewett, Thomas T. 95
Bliesmer, Emery P. 96
Bloom, Anna K. 97
Blount, Sam 98
Blubaugh, Jon A. 99
Bohan, Ruth 100
Bohn, Thomas W. 101
Bois, J. S. A. 102
Boltwood, Robert M. 103
Bonner, Myrtle C. S. 104
Bopp, Sister John Mary 105
Bossard, James H. S. 106
Breiter, Lila R. 107
Brennen, Frances Robinson
108
Brewster, Lawrence Walter
109
Brigance, William Norwood
110
Briggs, Thomas H. 111
Bright, Catherine May 112
Brilhart, Barbara Lieb 113
(also see Barbara Lieb)
Broadbent, Donald E. 114,
115, 116, 117, 118, 119,
120, 121, 173, 622
Broadway, JoAnn Chamber-
lin 122
Brodie, Tom 123
Brodinsky, B. P. 124
Brooks, Keith 125
Brown, Charles T. 126, 127,
128, 129

Brown, Donald Pardee 130,
131, 132, 133, 134
Brown, James I. 135, 136,
137, 138, 139, 140, 141,
142, 143, 144, 145, 146,
147, 148, 891
Brown, Kenneth Lee 149
Bruce, Grant 281
Bruce, Roslyn Sherman 706
Brunson, F. Ward 150
Buck, Myrtess Crawford 151
Buehler, E. C. 1007
Bull, Storm 152
Buntley, Arline 250
Burk, Kenneth W. 291
Burnes, John Walter 154
Burns, Paul C. 155
Burton, Mary 156
Bushby, Martha J. 157
Butler, Samuel 158

Caarewe, Glendoris 159
Cantrell, Clara 159
Caffrey, John 160, 161, 162,
163, 164
Calearo, C. 165
Callahan, Gertrude M. 166
Calway, Marion Fladstol 167
Campanella, S. Joseph 168
Campbell, Howard Josef 169
Campbell, Paul Newell 170
Caughran, A. M. 197
Canfield, George Robert 171,
172
Cantor, Nathaniel 174
Cantril, Hadley 175
Canute, Russell J. 176
Cardozo, Robert 178
Carlson, Evelyn F. 179
Carlson, Raymond P. 180
Carlton, Robert L. 181
Carnegie, Dale 182
Carpenter, Edith Caryl 183
Carpenter, Helen M. 184
Carr, Jack A. 61
Carroll, John B. 185

Carter, Burnham 186
Carter, Raymond E. 187
Cartier, Francis A. Jr. 188, 189, 482, 526, 529, 1210
Caruthers, Helen Post 190
Carver, Merton E. 191
Casambre, Alejandro Jiminez 192
Cashman, Mildred Berwick 193
Cashman, Paul H. 194, 195
Caskey, Clark Charles 196
Cathcart, Robert 795
Cecile, Sister Marie 198
Chafe, Warren J. 199
Chall, Jeanne S. 200
Chapman, J. Crosby 201
Chapman, W. D. 202
Chase, Stuart 203
Cheatham, Paul J. 204
Chenette, Louis F. 205
Childers, Dorothy Bell 206
Chisholm, Francis P. 207
Christensen, Gordon V. 208
Chrobak, Jean Frew 209
Clark, Genevieve 210
Clark, Kathryn B. 211
Clymer, Theodore 212
Cochran, John Rodney 213
Codey, Mother M. Irene 214
Coffey, Sister M. Sylvester 215
Coffman, William E. 216
Cohen, Bertram D. 1020
Cohen, John 217, 218
Cohen, Rose G. 219
Coladarci, A. P. 221, 367
Cole, Sister Mary Ethel 220
Collins, Beverly Nann 222
Collins, Helene I. 223
Comfort, Iris Tracy 26, 224
Commins, W. D. 225
Conboy, William Andrew 230, 1007
Condon, Edwyna Forsyth 231
Conlon, Sister Therese Ellen 232

Cook, Joseph W. 233
Coomaraswamy, Ananda K. 234
Cooper, J. Louis 235
Corey, Stephen M. 236, 237, 238
Corson, John J. 239
Cortright, Rupert L. 240
Cotton, Jack C. 241
Coulter, V. C. 242
Cox, Marion Monroe 243 (see also Marion Monroe)
Coyne, John Martin 244
Cramer, H. Leslie 245
Crane, Forrest F. 246
Crawford, C. C. 247
Crawford, C. DeLisle 248
Crawford, Sallilu H. 98
Crink, Cedric L. 250
Crockett, Walter H. 1256
Crook, Frances E. 251
Crosby, Muriel 252
Cross, M. A. 253
Cullen, Stanley R. 254
Curties, James 1019
Curtis, Alberta 255
Cypreanson, Lucile 256

Dahle, Thomas L. 257, 258
Dale, Carol 259
Dale, Edgar 260, 261, 262, 263
Dance, Frank E. X. 264
Daniels, J. T. 265
Darley, Frederic L. 266
Davis, Carl J. 267
Davis, H. 268
Davis, P. A. 268
Dawson, Mildred 269, 270, 271, 272, 273
Day, Phyllis Winifred 274
Day, Willard F. 275
De Boer John J. 276, 277
Dechant, Emerald V. 1101
Dedmon, Donald 63
de Hoop, Wietse 278, 279, 280

Demos, George 281
Denny, Terry 282
de Souza, Albert M. 283
Deutschman, B. 284
Devine, Thomas G. 285, 286, 287
De Wick, Henry N. 288
Dial, Harold E. 200
Diamond, Rose 289
Dias, Earl J. 290
Dickson, W.J. 1013
Diehl, Charles F. 291
Dietze, Hildegard 292
Dills, Eva L. 293
Dixon, Carmen 72
Dixon, Norman R. 294
Doden, Sheila M. 296
Dolcini, Mary Ellen 297
Donald, Brother 298
Doob, Leonard W. 299
Dorval, Bertha Mae 300
Dover, C.J. 301
Dow, Clyde Walton 302, 303, 304, 305, 306, 307, 308, 963
Doyle, Loretta 309
Drake, Elizabeth 310
Drake, Francis E. 311
Dreher, John J. 847
Drieman, G.H.J. 312, 313
Drucker, Peter F. 314
Duker, Sam 315, 316, 317, 318, 319, 320, 321, 322, 323, 324, 325, 326, 327, 328, 329, 330, 331, 332, 333, 334, 335
Dumdie, Milton Frederick 336
Duncan, Charles Howard 337
Dunlap, Vivian H. 338
Dunn, Joseph 339
Durrell, Donald B. 340
Dvores, Florence 341
Dwyer, Ethel T. 342
Dwyer, William Michael 343
Dyer, Frederick C. 344
Dyer, Henry S. 345

Early, Margaret J. 346, 347, 348, 349, 902
Eastman, Milton 350
Edelberg, Ann Rita 351
Edgar, Kenneth Frank 352
Edinger, Lois Virginia 353
Edith, Sister M. 354
Edman, Irwin 355
Egan, J.P. 357
Ehart, Violette Hunt 358
Ehrmann, Eliezer L. 359
Eisenstadt, Arthur 360
Eiserer, Paul E. 361
Ekwald, Eldon E. 362
Elfering, Sister Mary Michelle 363
Elliff, Gertrude 364
Elliott, Charles Ray 365
Elliott, Donald N. 366
Elson, E.F. 367
Emanuel, Eleanor 368
Emmerich, David S. 369
Emmons, William H. 1082, 1083, 1084, 1085
Emslie, Elizabeth A. 370
Enc, Mitat Ahmet 371
Enevodsen, Jessie V. 310
Engel, Emily 372
England, Don W. 373
Enochs, James B. 374
Erickson, Allen G. 375
Erickson, C.I. 376
Erway, Ella Anderson 377
Ethel, Sister M. 378
Evans, Annette Vista 379
Evans, Bertrand 766
Everitt, William Littell 382, 386
Evertts, Eldonna L. 380
Ewing, H.W. 381

Fairbanks, Grant 23, 382, 383, 384, 385, 386, 387, 487, 751
Fang, Irving 388
Farrar, Larston D. 389
Farrell, Edmund J. 390

292

295

Miller, G. A. 828, 829
Miller, James Nathan 830
Miller, Julie F. 831
Miller, Nathan 832
Miller, Helen Rand 277
Mills, Barriss 833
Mills, Donna M. 834
Mingoia, Edwin 835
Minshall, Lucille 26
Miron, Murray S. 383
Mirrielis, Lucia B. 836
Meyers, Robert M. 60
Mobray, G. H. 837
Moe, Ivar L. 838
Moldstad, John Alton 839
Molitoris, Anna 840
Moll, Karl R. 862
Monroe Marion 841, 842 (see
  also Cox, Marion Monroe)
Moore, Eva A. 843
Moore, Sid F. 816
Morkovin, Boris V. 844
Morris, June 845
Morrison, James H. 846
Moser, Henry M. 847
Moushegian, George 619
Murphy, George 848
Murphy, Mary Ellen 849
Murphy, Sister Miriam Melda
  850
Murphy, William Carl 851
Murray, Elwood 852
Muth, Cecelia 853
Myers, Ruth L. 854

Nafziger, Vivian Beulah 855
Napier, Grace D. 856
Nathan, Ernest D. 859
Needham, Arnold E. 860
Needham, Arthur 861
Nelson, Harold E. 862, 863
Neville, Mark A. 864, 865
Neville, Mary H. 866
Newman, E. B. 868
Newman, John B. 590
Nichols, Lois K. 869
Nichols, Ralph G. 34, 264,

575, 728, 742, 870, 871,
872, 873, 874, 875, 876,
877, 878, 879, 880, 881,
882, 883, 884, 885, 886,
887, 888, 889, 890, 891,
892, 893, 894, 895, 896,
897, 898, 1029, 1200,
1202
Nicholson, Harold 899
Niles, Doris 900
Niles, Lyndrey Arnand 901
Niles, O. S. 902
Nilsen, Thomas Robert 903
Noel, Elizabeth 904
Nolan, Carlson Y. 267, 905,
  906, 907
Noll, Gary A. 796
Nona, Sister Mary 1106
Norris, Cynthia M. 437 (see
  also Graae, Cynthia Mor-
  ris)
North, Robert D. 908
Nye, Irene 910

Oberembt, Sister M. Doris
  911
O'Connor, Olwyn 912
Odom, Charles L. 913
O'Donnell, Robert J. 914
Olsen, James 915
O'Neill, John Joseph 916
Ongman, Edward Earl 917
O'Reilly, Francis J. 918
Ormsby, Bill 919
Orr, David B. 436, 438, 920,
  921, 922, 923
Overstreet, Bonaro H. 924
Owen, Jason Camillous 925
Oyster, Mary Mercedes 926

Packer, Frederick C. Jr.
  927
Page, Paul R. 928
Palacios, John R. 601
Palmer, Brother Michael 929
Parke, Margaret B. 930
Paton, Wenda Carter 931

Roughton, Ronald Dean 1023
Roy, Sister Marie Collette 1024
Rozensweig, Mark R. 962
Rubenstein, Herbert 1025
Ruddell, Robert B. 1026
Ruechelle, Randall C. 1027
Ruesch, Jurgen 1028
Rulison, Kathleen Dale 1030
Rulon, Phillip J. 1031, 1032, 1033, 1034
Russell, David H. 700, 1035, 1036, 1037
Russell, Elizabeth 1037
Russell, R.D. 1038
Rutherford, Lewis Roland 1039
Ryan, Sister Mary Allan 1040

Saine, Lynette 1041
Samovar, Larry A. 1186
Sander, Eric K. 1043
Sanders, Katherine M. 1132
Sansom, Clive 1044
Sassenrath, Julius Marlin 1045
Sayles, Leonard R. 1143
Schaffner, Dorothy W. 1046
Scheer, Wilbert E. 1047
Scherer, George A.C. 1048
Schiesser, H. 1049
Schmidt, Bernardine G. 1050, 1051, 1052
Schmidt, John W. 1053
Schneider, Wallace A. 1054
Schubert, Delwyn G. 1055
Schuller, Charles Francis 1159
Schultz, Jennye Faye 1056
Schwanke, Dorothy Marie 1057
Schwartz, Donald F. 1138
Schwartz, Sheila 1058
Scott, Carol Thacker 695
Scott, Louise Binder 1059
Scott, Richard 1060
Scott, Robert J. 1061
Scott, Wallace Gene 1062

Seashore, Robert H. 1063, 1066
Sebastian, Virginia Jean 1064
Seegers, J. 1065, 1066
Selover, Robert B. 1067
Semrow, Ellen H. 1068
Sessions, Louise Hale 1070
Seymour, Paul John 1071
Seymour, Ruth 1072
Shagars, Charles 1093
Shane, Harold G. 1073
Shanker, Sidney 1074
Shepherd, Terry R. 1075
Shibley, John Dahir 1076
Shurtleff, Wade E. 1078
Siewert, Eleanor Annable 1079
Sikkink, Donald Elwyn 474, 1080
Silverman, Phyllis 1081
Simon, Charles W. 1082, 1083, 1084, 1085
Simons, Herbert Williams 1086
Sims, V.M. 1087
Simula, Vernon L. 1088
Sincoff, Michael Zolman 1089
Singer, Harry 580, 1090
Sizemore, Robert A. 1302
Skiffington, James Stephen 1091
Small, Arnold M. Jr. 1092
Smith, A. Arthur 1093
Smith, C.P. 1094
Smith, David Allen 1095
Smith, Donald E.P. 1096
Smith, Dora V. 1097, 1098, 1099
Smith, Grace Brinner 1100
Smith, Henry P. 1101
Smith, Jack Ernest 1102
Smith, Leota Eleanor 1103
Smith, Mapheus 1104
Smith, Nila B. 1105
Smith, Sister Mary Joan 1106
Smith, Thomas Wood 1107
Snider, Mary Edna 1108
Solberg, Rona 199

299

Wilson, Alan R. 1284
Wilson, William Charles 1285
Wilt, Miriam E. 1286, 1287, 1288, 1289, 1290, 1291, 1292
Winges, Sara A. 1293
Winkler, Pauline A. 433, 1294
Winkles, Blanche 1295
Winter, Clotilda 1296
Winters, Alice Swaggerty 1297
Wirth, Myrtle 1298
Wiseman, Gordon 62, 1299
Withrow, Eleanor M. 1300
Wittich, W.A. 1301
Witty, Paul A. 1302
Wolftgange, Sister L. Marie 125
Woliung, Dorothy Cole 1303
Wood, C. David 1304
Wood, Marion 1305
Woods, L.E. 1306
Woods, Velma 1185

Worcester, D.A. 1307, 1308
Wright, C.W. 1309
Wright, Evan Leonard 1310
Wright, Milton 1311
Wygand, Leonora 1312
Wynn, Dale Richard 1313, 1314

Yaeger, Sister Miriam 1315
Yates, Paul S. 1316
Yoakam, Richard E. 1317
Young, James D. 1319
Young, William E. 1320

Zeligs, Rose 1321
Zelko, Harold P. 1322, 1323, 1324, 1325, 1326, 1327, 1328
Zemlin, W.R. 1329
Ziebarth, E.W. 560
Ziemann, Norman Carl 1330
Zimmerman, George H. 1331
Zinkin, Vivian 1332
Zollinger, Marian 269

Subject Index

303

480, 482, 517, 751, 826, 996
Intelligence, effect on 1304
Measures of 423
Method of compression, effect of, on 417
Reaction time, effect of, on 420
Pitch variance, effect of, on 421
Reader's voice quality, effect of, on 417
Reading rate, effect of, on 423
Retention 417
Sex, and 478
Teaching 371, 417, 423, 920, 1224
    As new language 418, 420
    Effect of 665, 923
    Practice, effect of 1224
    Prolonged exposure 418
Conference on 421
Description of 424
Distortion, in 418
Dichotic presentation of discard 768, 1061
Expanded speech 382, 1049, 1183
Filtering, selective 418
Information processing capacity 622, 872, 883, 922
Intelligibility 384, 387, 418, 422, 423, 482, 515, 558,
    622, 668, 672
    Discard interval, effect of, on 245, 387
    Distortion, effect of, on 683
    Frequency patterns, effect of, on 943, 1329
    Interrupted speech, effect of, on 1293
    Measures of 423
    Sampling interval, effect of, on 245
Interrupted speech 828
Language Master, use of, in 558
Listenability of 388, 478, 527
Listening to 387, 395, 826, 863, 966
Mentally retarded, and 279, 287, 1120
Methods of compression 416, 420, 423, 782, 1224
    Chop-splice 463, 464, 465, 554, 555, 672
    Compression described 382, 383, 385, 386, 417, 463,
        464, 465, 484, 487, 672, 751, 768, 1049, 1224
    Computer 202, 1061
    Mechanical 1172
    Rapid play-back 289
    Rapid speech 480
    Selective 202
    Tape loop 202
Needed research 418, 425
Pause time 291, 711

Details, listening for 352, 373, 687, 791
Diagrams, 243, 459
Dichotic hearing 369
Difficulty, effect of, 478, 839, 998
Directions, listening to and for 3, 97, 211, 272, 352, 378,
545, 587, 723, 724, 861, 964, 1088, 1307
Disabilities 452
Disadvantaged children 483, 596, 1107
Discipline 812
Discussion, listening in 174, 432, 1163
Distraction 1214
Doctoral dissertations, discussion of 317
Doctoral dissertations, listing of 19, 36, 40, 51, 69, 78,
89, 94, 95, 96, 104, 109, 113, 131, 137, 149, 154, 161,
167, 169, 170, 171, 172, 176, 180, 181, 188, 191, 192,
197, 213, 214, 230, 231, 240, 244, 248, 258, 278, 283,
285, 297, 302, 337, 352, 353, 371, 375, 377, 380, 388,
391, 392, 395, 406, 412, 443, 464, 468, 472, 479, 480,
482, 486, 489, 499, 503, 508, 510, 511, 512, 514, 526,
533, 541, 545, 547, 558, 562, 566, 567, 577, 578, 602,
607, 612, 613, 622, 636, 641, 642, 644, 646, 653, 654,
658, 659, 661, 662, 667, 672, 678, 680, 681, 683, 689,
691, 696, 697, 709, 711, 719, 720, 721, 725, 738, 739,
751, 752, 764, 770, 771, 778, 785, 789, 794, 797, 798,
800, 801, 803, 811, 819, 826, 838, 839, 851, 863, 873,
903, 916, 925, 934, 936, 943, 945, 951, 958, 961, 970,
983, 987, 989, 993, 1005, 1015, 1016, 1018, 1024, 1027,
1038, 1056, 1071, 1076, 1080, 1086, 1091, 1095, 1102,
1107, 1117, 1119, 1120, 1125, 1136, 1146, 1153, 1164,
1168, 1178, 1181, 1188, 1210, 1213, 1219, 1246, 1253,
1258, 1260, 1268, 1278, 1285, 1289, 1304, 1310, 1319,
1320, 1330
Dramatizations 300
Durrell-Sullivan Reading Capacity Test 348, 524, 640, 708,
825, 835, 925, 1035, 1090, 1185, 1260, 1310, 1312

Educability and listening 543
Elements of listening 656, 1272, 1133
Emotions and listening 11, 60, 822, 1216
Empathy 253, 538, 1230
English as second language 1208
English courses, teaching of listening in 3, 6, 50, 132, 233,
531, 594, 792, 803, 1023, 1097, 1098, 1184, 1195, 1206,
1252
Environment and listening 249
Evaluation of listening 138, 271, 339, 676, 796, 1139 (See
also Tests for listening.)

Evaluation as part of listening 411
Expanded speech (See Compressed speech.)

Factor analysis 213, 512, 580, 641, 1015, 1090, 1117, 1260, 1285
Fallacies 587
Feedback 811, 1216
Foreign language teaching 345, 359, 364, 472, 649, 1003, 1048, 1178, 1185, 1208
Foreign students 494, 635

Gates Silent Reading Test 1107
General semantics and listening 265, 627, 1017
Gestures 468
Guides to good listening 1325, 1326, 1327, 1328

Habits, listening 547, 702
Hearing 110, 115, 116, 117, 118, 120, 357, 366, 401, 519, 570, 617, 619, 698, 729, 868, 959, 1025, 1092, 1182, 1264, 1265
    And listening 14, 58, 59, 131, 263, 401, 447, 542, 563, 620, 641, 730, 873, 975, 1021, 1144, 1170, 1242
    Loss, effect of, on listening 620, 975
Heston Personal Adjustment Inventory 1045
Home life, listening in 106, 224, 457, 581, 583, 596, 612, 675, 712, 718, 769, 831, 895, 1068
Human relations and listening 124, 852, 1226

Ideas, listening to and for 822, 843
Importance of listening 298, 320, 523, 605, 735, 784, 895, 904
Individual differences 411
Industrial communication, list of sources 694
Inferences 352, 378
Informational capacity of ear and eye 401, 616, 617
Integrity 557
Intelligibility 208, 245, 525, 554, 555
International communication 537
Interest and listening 138, 458, 642, 685, 803, 1214
Interruptions 117, 739, 808, 828, 917, 1165
Interscholastic contests 875
Interviewing 97, 408, 1238, 1251
Iowa Basic Skills Test 767, 819
Iowa Silent Reading Test 396, 503, 968, 1091
Isolates of meaning 1089

Kindergarten 212, 516, 1259

Kinds of listening 6, 9, 11, 38, 58, 72, 81, 90, 179, 203,
    209, 250, 253, 271, 295, 301, 318, 374, 400, 407, 414,
    442, 451, 454, 458, 462, 474, 476, 502, 538, 539, 543,
    563, 582, 593, 613, 627, 632, 645, 674, 685, 734, 772,
    788, 801, 822, 845, 859, 872, 880, 883, 890a, 894, 935,
    954, 956, 997, 1014, 1095, 1114, 1133, 1152, 1180, 1204,
    1207, 1236, 1242, 1252, 1272, 1311
  Accurate listening 5, 28, 59, 349, 734, 848, 902, 914
  Active listening 6, 58, 126, 534, 686, 924, 1115
  Appreciative listening 250, 300, 349, 451, 615, 674, 697,
    902, 1252
  Attentive listening 120, 218, 253, 271, 300, 318, 354,
    391, 410, 414, 451, 502, 707, 730, 788, 864, 997,
    1008, 1088, 1144, 1225, 1311
  Concentrative listening 186, 209, 250, 300, 451, 495,
    632, 674, 752, 895, 1047, 1204, 1207
  Conversational listening 5, 6, 12, 25, 39, 81, 109, 147,
    179, 250, 271, 432, 451, 546, 598, 674, 951, 1112,
    1163, 1211, 1252, 1311
  Creative listening 247, 534, 550, 674, 1169, 1204
  Critical listening 5, 39, 203, 209, 221, 242, 243, 248,
    250, 260, 269, 285, 299, 316, 318, 405, 411, 451,
    477, 507, 547, 587, 664, 674, 686, 697, 761, 762,
    763, 764, 818, 848, 902, 904, 914, 932, 950, 981,
    995, 1114, 1134, 1140, 1141, 1165, 1166, 1176, 1204,
    1252, 1262
  Purposeful listening 5, 205, 300, 349, 405, 686, 752,
    848, 1113
  Responsive listening 309, 848, 1115
Knowledge about listening questioned 48, 123, 505, 656,
    945, 946, 947, 948, 949, 1199
Kuder Preference Scale 543, 642
Kuhlmann-Anderson Intelligence Tests 396, 767

Language ability 225, 456
Language arts 28, 42, 67, 243, 249, 251, 252, 270, 380,
    565, 842, 982, 1024, 1190, 1267
  Listening instruction as part of 60, 781, 926, 982, 1011,
    1065, 1226, 1252
Language development, role of listening in 1259
Leadership 707
Lectures 99, 598, 700, 965, 1015
Levels of listening 228, 290, 344, 400, 410, 501, 1205
Listenability 63, 89, 188, 189, 200, 482, 525, 526, 527,
    528, 529, 535, 558, 630, 714, 783, 789, 826, 837, 839,
    1016, 1215, 1253
Literacy 234, 1132

Longitudinal study of listening 748
Lorge Thorndike Intelligence test 925, 1315

Main idea, listening for 378, 381, 547, 587, 687, 1207, 1332
Masking of speech 829
Master's theses, discussion of 327
Master's theses, listing of 1, 10, 15, 17, 24, 29, 43, 53,
55, 64, 65, 71, 73, 74, 77, 93, 99, 100, 101, 105, 107,
108, 112, 122, 151, 156, 157, 187, 190, 199, 206, 208,
209, 219, 220, 222, 223, 232, 233, 259, 265, 274, 292,
293, 296, 300, 309, 336, 338, 341, 342, 343, 358, 363,
365, 368, 370, 372, 373, 379, 396, 403, 415, 430, 439,
440, 441, 455, 463, 469, 477, 478, 484, 490, 513, 515,
516, 518, 520, 521, 524, 530, 535, 536, 542, 543, 544,
563, 568, 572, 579, 584, 588a, 596, 599, 600, 620, 624,
626, 630, 633, 634, 637, 640, 643, 645, 652, 664, 665,
666, 674, 679, 682, 688, 695, 699, 703, 705, 708, 724,
725, 731, 732, 740, 759, 767, 773, 774, 777, 779, 783,
787, 790, 792, 793, 799, 802, 807, 808, 809, 823, 825,
827, 840, 849, 850, 855, 866, 901, 911, 914, 917, 926,
929, 931, 932, 933, 942, 944, 960, 968, 973, 975, 976,
981, 984, 985, 990, 994, 998, 999, 1001, 1002, 1004,
1017, 1023, 1030, 1039, 1040, 1045, 1053, 1054, 1057,
1062, 1064, 1070, 1075, 1079, 1089, 1100, 1103, 1108,
1122, 1123, 1128, 1130, 1137, 1151, 1157, 1162, 1163,
1165, 1167, 1170, 1171, 1175, 1184, 1197, 1201, 1208,
1209, 1212, 1218, 1222, 1223, 1224, 1239, 1241, 1244,
1245, 1249, 1251, 1252, 1261, 1262, 1269, 1271, 1277,
1279, 1281, 1284, 1295, 1297, 1298, 1300, 1303, 1312,
1315, 1316, 1317, 1318
Maturity and listening 1112
Memory span 120
Mental hygiene 361
Metropolitan Reading Readiness Test 518, 773
Mildred Templin Speech Sound Discrimination Test 563
Minnesota, University of, teaching of listening at 893, 1071
Mood and listening 247
Motivation and listening 609, 859, 864, 1088
Multi-channel listening 933
Music, listening to 205, 296, 486, 695, 743, 928, 931, 949,
953, 957, 1159, 1161, 1254, 1285, 1331
Music in listening tests 342, 695

Nature of listening 28, 79, 81, 82, 87, 228, 229, 348, 873,
874, 895, 898, 902, 1203, 1272
Nelson Denny Reading Test 923

Neonates, auditory responses of 1257
Non-verbal communication 596
Note-taking 7, 9, 138, 186, 196, 211, 214, 236, 247, 295,
    587, 686, 730, 740, 771, 849, 864, 874, 932, 1053, 1074
Nurses 393

Openmindedness 867, 1113, 1151, 1226
Oral administration of tests 111, 136, 142, 146, 267, 333,
    508, 573, 621, 625, 710, 913, 1056, 1087, 1107, 1117,
    1152, 1153, 1154, 1155, 1263
Oral language and listening 380, 746
Oral reading and listening 713, 1289
Organizational skills and listening 552, 587
Otis Intelligence Test 929, 1241
Otis Quick-Scoring Mental Ability Tests 522
Outlining and listening 901, 1142

Personality and listening 59, 708, 1149
Physical comfort 730, 822, 834, 1214
Physicians 550, 734
Physiological aspects of listening 13, 126, 639, 717, 1093,
    1237
Pilots 1266
Pintner-Cunningham Primary Mental Test 653
Poetry 105, 479, 1060, 1163
Practice 246, 1164
Preparation for listening 229, 1236
Problem solving 551
Professional listener 631
Projective tests, oral 601, 700, 706, 1140, 1269, 1282,
    1283
Propaganda 299, 832, 950
Psychiatric view of listening 56, 58, 59, 669, 810, 1028,
    1111, 1192
Psycholinguistics 1025

Questions in classroom and listening 238, 412

Radio 4, 8, 97, 175, 215, 227, 240, 255, 560, 615, 817,
    844, 1109, 1318
Rapid listening (See Compressed speech.)
Rate-controlled speech (See Compressed speech.)
Readers, retarded, listening instruction of 232, 701
Reading and listening compared 77, 104, 136, 164, 170, 191,
    237, 243, 251, 273, 287, 303, 304, 325, 348, 370, 373,
    375, 390, 396, 405, 406, 489, 491, 492, 503, 508, 510,
    513, 514, 526, 532, 533, 541, 626, 636, 637, 642, 647,

Reading and listening compared (cont.)
652, 663, 693, 701, 720, 721, 738, 760, 778, 790, 802,
825, 834, 840, 841, 866, 873, 944, 958, 983, 1018,
1050, 1060, 1102, 1136, 1146, 1170, 1188, 1190, 1193,
1206, 1207, 1221, 1241, 1246, 1249, 1260, 1272, 1302,
1312
Reading and listening to change attitudes 533
Reading Braille and listening compared 756, 845, 905, 906,
907
Reading, effect on, of instruction in listening 206, 220, 232,
235, 336, 448, 567, 648, 659, 774, 779, 783, 785, 797,
807, 819, 968, 984, 993, 1023, 1026, 1090, 1091, 1218,
1300
Reading, effect of training in, on listening 231, 336, 567,
647, 648, 714, 785
Reading improvement course 725
Reading potential 61, 448, 696, 712, 838, 925, 969, 1041,
1188, 1196, 1267
Reading, remedial, auditory approach in 282, 1052
Reading, teaching of, auditory approach in 1050, 1051
Reading, training in compared to training in listening 567, 592
Recall 230, 300
Receptivity to ideas 217
Religious basis for teaching listening 604
Research on listening needed 20, 162, 485, 548, 714, 715,
733, 734, 883, 884, 886, 946, 947, 948, 949, 991, 1036,
1132
Review of listening literature 222, 270, 335, 634, 681,
703, 814, 889, 1039, 1054, 1057, 1073, 1101, 1175,
1245, 1281
Review of listening research 75, 195, 275, 286, 322, 323,
347, 485, 508, 574, 651, 670, 727, 734, 755, 884, 886,
888, 949, 991, 1026, 1036, 1132, 1173, 1187, 1255, 1297,
1298, 1302
Review of research on comparisons of auditory and visual
presentation 191, 204, 275, 510, 681, 1308
Retention, aids to 229
Rosenzweig Picture-Frustration Study 1261
Rumors 1166

Seashore Measures of Musical Ability 563
School administrators 1314
Science teaching 334
Scolding 997, 1068
Sentence structure 1023
Sequence 300, 378
Set and listening 128, 642, 873, 949, 990

Teaching of listening (cont.)
    Aims of 318; 405, 834, 842, 880, 976, 1106, 1118
    Basic Systems' "Effective Listening" 744, 854, 909, 1273
    British viewpoint 1044
    Classroom listening centers 483, 561, 571, 593, 603,
      673
    College 83, 135, 138, 176, 194, 257, 263, 305, 306, 308,
      311, 375, 377, 397, 441, 446, 455, 473, 488, 547,
      606, 607, 608, 610, 682, 726, 752, 784, 794, 795,
      833, 860, 885, 893, 896, 945, 973, 1011, 1030, 1071,
      1148, 1164, 1268, 1271, 1330
    Elementary school 25, 26, 28, 30, 32, 38, 66, 67, 68,
      91, 100, 155, 166, 193, 206, 220, 222, 223, 228,
      232, 235, 250, 269, 271, 272, 274, 283, 293, 300,
      309, 318, 319, 332, 336, 346, 350, 352, 354, 363,
      378, 392, 394, 410, 411, 412, 432, 481, 493, 499,
      500, 508, 511, 518, 521, 546, 568, 569, 571, 572,
      576, 577, 578, 612, 623, 640, 643, 653, 658, 659,
      664, 674, 677, 680, 697, 705, 721, 722, 723, 732,
      745, 764, 767, 774, 779, 780, 781, 783, 785, 790,
      794, 797, 798, 799, 803, 807, 816, 819, 821, 834,
      836, 840, 842, 844, 848, 853, 857, 858, 869, 889,
      902, 915, 930, 935, 942, 964, 968, 970, 971, 974,
      982, 984, 993, 999, 1000, 1001, 1006, 1010, 1037,
      1040, 1044, 1058, 1059, 1064, 1070, 1075, 1091, 1106,
      1108, 1120, 1162, 1163, 1167, 1171, 1197, 1234, 1249,
      1252, 1279, 1286, 1287, 1289, 1292, 1298,
    Games 32, 643, 675, 821, 822, 1228, 1229, 1232
    Materials 4, 8, 26, 74, 167, 215, 274, 284, 310, 377,
      397, 398, 445, 728, 791, 817, 879, 902, 912, 914,
      927, 930, 964, 974, 1096, 1110, 1162, 1163, 1209,
      1271, 1299
    Procedures 21, 22, 215, 226, 227, 228, 235, 260, 269,
      274, 277, 284, 285, 300, 310, 315, 320, 324, 350,
      352, 353, 364, 375, 378, 411, 447, 457, 575, 576,
      577, 610, 615, 660, 664, 680, 690, 724, 744, 752,
      756, 780, 791, 804, 817, 818, 824, 836, 844, 853,
      861, 869, 872, 891, 894, 902, 910, 912, 930, 932,
      935, 964, 989, 997, 1000, 1007, 1042, 1060, 1091,
      1099, 1101, 1110, 1142, 1171, 1176, 1207, 1227, 1231,
      1233, 1252, 1286, 1287, 1289, 1291
    Secondary school 3, 38, 97, 227, 233, 259, 277, 290,
      316, 397, 431, 444, 506, 585, 586, 587, 594, 724,
      777, 791, 792, 814, 815, 816, 817, 818, 823, 849,
      865, 879, 902, 914, 927, 961, 976, 995, 1002, 1023,
      1042, 1074, 1118, 1156, 1218, 1222, 1240, 1300
    Surveys of 794, 932, 1167, 1213